A

Domestic Violence
and Health Care

Sherri L. Schornstein

Domestic Violence and Health Care

What Every Professional Needs to Know

SAGE Publications
International Educational and Professional Publisher
Thousand Oaks   London   New Delhi

For information address:

SAGE Publications, Inc.
2455 Teller Road
Thousand Oaks, California 91320
E-mail: order@sagepub.com

SAGE Publications Ltd.
6 Bonhill Street
London EC2A 4PU
United Kingdom

SAGE Publications India Pvt. Ltd.
M-32 Market
Greater Kailash I
New Delhi 110 048 India

Printed in the United States of America

Library of Congress Cataloging-in-Publication Data

Schornstein, Sherry L.
   Domestic violence : a primer for healthcare professionals /
author, Sherry L. Schornstein.
      p.   cm.
   Includes bibliographical references.
   ISBN 0-8039-5958-3 (cloth : alk. paper). — ISBN 0-8039-5959-1
(pbk. : alk. paper)
   1. Family violence. 2. Victims of family violence—Medical care.
3. Medical personnel.   I. Title.
RA1122.S36 1997
362.82'92—dc20   96-35629

97 98 99 00 01 02 03 10 9 8 7 6 5 4 3 2 1

Acquiring Editor:	Terry Hendrix
Editorial Assistant:	Dale Grenfell
Production Editor:	Sherrise M. Purdum
Production Assistant:	Denise Santoyo
Typesetter/Designer:	Danielle Dillahunt
Indexer:	Teri Greenberg
Cover Designer:	Candice Harman
Print Buyer:	Anna Chin

CONTENTS

Introduction   vii

Acknowledgments   ix

Reprint Authorizations   xi

1. What Is Domestic Violence?   1

2. Societal Perspectives on Domestic Violence   14

3. The Dynamics of Abuse   46

4. The Medical Response   70

5. Ascertaining the True Cause of Injury and
   Compliance With Injury-Reporting Requirements   98

6. Safety Issues   117

7. Prosecution of Domestic Violence Crimes   136

References   167

Index   177

About the Author   186

This book is dedicated to the staffs of the Term Nursery and of the Neo Natal Intensive Care Unit of Alexandria Hospital, to the staff of the Neo Natal Intensive Care Unit of Children's National Medical Center, and to surgeons Kurt Newman, M.D., and John Bleacher, M.D., who saved my daughter's life.

INTRODUCTION

My objective in writing this book is to raise the awareness of health care professionals and enable them to intervene appropriately when a patient presents signs of being a victim of domestic violence. Domestic violence battering episodes are recurrent (U.S. Dept. of Justice, 1986) and become more frequent and severe over time (Walker, 1984). As an advocate for victims and as a career prosecutor having worked for years in the field of domestic violence, my goal is for this intervention to prevent subsequent battering and domestic homicides.

This book provides practical tools or "how to's," including suggested questions and forms, regarding each step in the examination process. Also provided is vital information concerning the physical safety of medical staff, patients, and others who could be at risk when treatment for a domestic violence victim is provided. Viewing the overall process from my perspective, that of a career prosecutor, will hopefully enhance health care professionals' understanding of the criminal justice process and allay any fears or misconceptions about their potential role in conjunction with such proceedings.

The medical community can be a front-line intervener in the aftermath of a domestic violence episode. For a variety of reasons, not every victim will call 911 for police assistance following a battering attack. However, many victims will seek medical treatment in an emergency department, public clinic, or private doctor's office. Fifteen years ago, Hilberman (1980) described the health care response to domestic violence as characterized by inattention, blame, and disbelief. Unfortunately, to a large degree, that description still remains true today.

It is a recent phenomenon of the last 10 years that organizations and institutions have become involved in responding to violence against women (Commonwealth Fund, 1995). The medical community has been at the forefront of such efforts. In 1989, the American Medical Association launched a campaign to combat family violence. During the same year, the American College of Obstetricians and Gynecologists developed a campaign to aid in the detection and treatment of such victims. In 1991, the Joint Commission on the Accreditation of Healthcare Organizations voted to mandate all hospitals to develop and implement protocols to treat suspected victims of such abuse.

Medical professionals have a unique opportunity to intervene, but many lack the training to recognize the abuse, the tools to intervene when they do recognize it, and information regarding where to refer such victims for additional assistance. Various individuals, particularly in the medical, psychological, and nursing fields, have written articles addressing parts of the intervention issue. However, there is no single, compact but thorough source of information for the health care professional who needs to learn what to do when treating patients. At the other end of the spectrum, the few health care provider manuals that have been written are so lengthy that the reader might feel totally overwhelmed.

It was my intention in creating this book to provide a comprehensive, concise tool for health care professionals currently in the field and for students who will deal with such patients in the future. One could easily read, digest, and begin to apply the information presented here within a matter of days. It is my sincere hope that this book will serve that purpose.

ACKNOWLEDGMENTS

I would like to thank the many friends and colleagues who have inspired and encouraged me over the years as I have endeavored to help victims of domestic violence. Working in this field has given me the opportunity to meet some of the most intelligent, dedicated, and caring individuals I have ever known. Special thanks to Mary Ann Dutton, Ph.D., Clinical and Forensic Psychologist, Bethesda, Maryland, for her friendship, advice, encouragement, and assistance.

I also owe a debt of gratitude to the numerous individuals in the Washington, D.C., area who have been my teachers over the years. I have learned from them tremendously. My sincere thanks to the wonderful members of the D.C. Coalition Against Domestic Violence.

My deep gratitude to my parents, Arlene and Stuart Schornstein, for their compassion, understanding, and encouragement; to my sister Heidi Schandler for her unending support and assistance in the editing process; to my brother-in-law David Schandler for his computer expertise and willingness to help; to my brother and sister-in-law Louis Schornstein and Julianne Graziano for their support; to Dale Grenfell, Senior Editorial Assistant, Sage Publications, for her good sense of humor, encouragement, and guidance; and to my friend Meryl Waxman Ben-Levy for her friendship and support.

I am forever indebted to my friend and colleague Carol Skiles, Federal Bureau of Investigation, for her selfless assistance in editing the many revisions of this book and particularly for her comments regarding the information on hospital security.

I am also indebted to the many individuals and organizations that assisted me in obtaining the vast collection of research materials that went into the creation of this book. I wish to express special thanks to Larry S. Goldman, M.D., Director, Department of Mental Health, American Medical Association; Larry Gallagher and Laura Shedore of the Joint Commission on Accreditation of Healthcare Organizations; Deborah L. Horan, Manager of Special Issues, Division of Women's Health, The American College of Obstetricians and Gynecologists; The Family Violence Prevention Fund's Health Technical Assistance Staff; The Pennsylvania Coalition Against Domestic Violence and the National Resource Center on Domestic Violence; and my wonderful research assistants Robin Jacoby O'Neill, Lisa Mahoney, and Dawn Browning.

My sincere gratitude is owed to all of the wonderful people who took time out of their very busy lives and hectic schedules to read and edit this book and to provide comments: Wayne D. Blackmon, M.D., Psychiatrist, President of the Medical Society of the District of Columbia; Joal Bennett-Blackmon, L.I.C.S.W., Washington, D.C.; Stefan Pasternack, M.D., F.A.P.A., Clinical Professor of Psychiatry and Co-Director, Program in Post-Graduate Studies and Continuing Education in Psychiatry, Georgetown University School of Medicine; Kim Bullock, M.D., F.A.A.F.P., Assistant Chairperson, Emergency Department, Providence Hospital, and Assistant Clinical Professor, Department of Family Medicine, Georgetown University School of Medicine, Washington, D.C.; Marcia Robinson Wolf, Ph.D., Licensed Clinical Psychologist, Bethesda, Maryland; April Rubin, M.D., Washington, D.C.; Michele Grant Ervin, M.D., Chair and Program Director, Department of Emergency Medicine, Howard University Hospital, Washington, D.C.; and Dorothy A. Drago, M.A., M.P.H., Gaithersburg, Maryland.

My deepest gratitude to Robert E. McAfee, M.D., Past President of the American Medical Association, whose comments at the 1994 National Conference on Family Violence: Health and Justice inspired me to write this book.

REPRINT
AUTHORIZATIONS

I gratefully acknowledge permission to reprint from other works as follows:

American Medical Association. (1992). *Diagnostic and treatment guidelines on domestic violence* (p. 12). Chicago: Author. Copyright 1992 by the American Medical Association. Adapted with permission.

American Psychiatric Association. (1994). *Diagnostic and statistical manual of mental disorders* (4th ed., pp. 425, 427-429, 431-432). Copyright 1994 by the American Psychiatric Association. Reprinted with permission.

Battered wives: Help for the secret victim next door. (1976, August). *Ms. Magazine.* Reprinted by permission of *Ms. Magazine,* © 1976.

Boyd, V. D., & Klingbeil, K. S. (1993). *Family violence: Behavioral characteristics in spouse/partner abuse* (revised; chart). Copyright 1993 by Vicki D. Boyd and Karil S. Klingbeil. Adapted with permission.

Campbell, J. C. (1985). *Danger assessment.* Jacquelyn C. Campbell, Ph.D., RN, FAAN, Johns Hopkins University School of Nursing. Reprinted with permission. Please correspond with the author before using for research purposes.

Colburn, D. (1994, June 28). Domestic violence: AMA president decries "a major public health problem." *The Washington Post,* Health Section, p. 10. © 1994, The Washington Post. Reprinted with permission.

Cosgrove, A. (1992). *Medical Power and Control Wheel* and *Advocacy Wheel.* Kenosha, WI: Domestic Violence Project, Inc. Copyright 1992 by the Domestic Violence Project, Inc. Reprinted with permission.

Davis, P. (1994, February 9). Woman pleads guilty in death of son, 2. *The Washington Post,* p. B-1. Copyright 1994 by The Washington Post. Adapted with permission.

District of Columbia Coalition Against Domestic Violence. (1994). *Safety/exit plan.* © 1994, District of Columbia Coalition Against Domestic Violence. Reprinted with permission.

Dotterer, C. S. (1992, June 30). Breaking the cycle of domestic abuse. *The Washington Post,* p. Z-9. Reprinted with permission.

Gaines, J. (1995, March 12). Domestic violence victims are routinely rejected by major insurers. *The Boston Globe,* p. 1. Copyright 1995 by The Boston Globe. Reprinted courtesy of The Boston Globe.

Gentry, C. (1991, August, 18). Women, abusers bond. *St. Petersburg Times,* p. 1-A. Reprinted by permission of St. Petersburg Times, copyright 1991.

Helton, A. S. (1987). *A Protocol of Care for the Battered Woman* ["Cycle of Violence" illustration and "Injury Location Chart"]. White Plains, NY: March of Dimes Birth Defects Foundation. Reproduced with permission of the copyright holder.

Joint Commission on Accreditation of Healthcare Organizations. (1995). *1996 comprehensive accreditation manual for hospitals* (pp. 115-116, 345-347, and 359). Oakbrook Terrace, IL: Author. Copyright 1995 by the Joint Commission on Accreditation of Healthcare Organizations. Reprinted with permission.

Kiernan, L. A. (1993, June 5). Victim "stunned" by N.H. judge; comments, sentence in domestic violence assault prompt outrage. *The Boston Globe,* p. 1. Copyright 1993 by The Boston Globe. Reprinted courtesy of The Boston Globe.

Kosova, W. (1991, December). Knife assailant, healthcare provider. *Washington City Paper,* p. 8. Copyright 1991 by Washington City Paper. Adapted with permission.

National Council of Juvenile and Family Court Judges. (1994). *Family violence: A model state code* (pp. 42-43). Reno, NV: Author. Copyright by the National Council of Juvenile and Family Court Judges. Reprinted with permission.

Pacenti, J. (1995, March 15). Domestic violence victims testify they were denied insurance. *The San Diego Union-Tribune,* p. A-26. Copyright 1995 by the Associated Press. Adapted with permission.

Pence, E., & Paymar, M. (1986). *Power and Control Wheel* and *Equality Wheel.* In *Power and control: Tactics of men who batter.* Copyright 1986 by Minnesota Program Development, Inc. Reprinted with permission.

Pitt, D. (1989, March 27). Hospital police: No guns, no respect, lots of trouble. *The New York Times,* p. B-1. Copyright © 1989 by The New York Times Company. Reprinted by permission.

Powers, R. (1994, May 13). Insurers admit denying policies to battered women. *The Patriot News,* p. A-5. Copyright 1994 by the Associated Press. Adapted with permission.

1

WHAT IS DOMESTIC VIOLENCE?

◈ DOMESTIC VIOLENCE: A WORKING DEFINITION

"Domestic violence" as discussed here is defined as a systematic pattern of abusive behaviors, occurring over a period of time, that may become more frequent and severe and are done for the purpose of control, domination, and/or coercion. Such behaviors may include verbal abuse and threats; physical, psychological, and sexual abuse; and destruction of property and pets. The batterer frequently accomplishes the abuses in an environment of his own creation that ultimately traps the victim in a state of fear, isolation, deprivation, and confusion. (Domestic violence episodes are *not* random acts of violence or incidents of mere loss of temper. Rather, such episodes are part of a complex, continuing pattern of behavior, of which the violence is but one dynamic.)

The perpetrator of such abuses is one who currently is or has been involved with the victim in an intimate relationship (American Medical Association [AMA], 1992a). Such relationships would include current or former spouses; current or former intimate partners who have not been married, including gay and lesbian partners (Island & Letellier, 1991; Lobel, 1986; Renzetti, 1992); and blood relatives or others related by law who reside or have resided together, such as a parent and child.

The focus of this book is adult partner abuse. However, practitioners should note that victims can include children, the elderly (Quinn & Tomita, 1986), and individuals currently engaged to be married or involved in dating relationships (Levy, 1991). Even teen dating partners can be victims of such abuse.

Women are nearly 10 times more likely than men to be the victims of violence by intimates. Family-related violence accounts for only 5% of all violent victimizations against men (U.S. Dept. of Justice, 1994). Due to the overwhelming prevalence of domestic violence against women, this book focuses on the situation of female victim and male batterer. However, medical service providers should not overlook that men also can be the victims of domestic violence.

◙ PREVALENCE

Recent accounts have documented that domestic violence occurs across all of America and around the world (Heise, Pitanguy, & Germain, 1994; MacFarquhar, 1994; Robinson & Epstein, 1994). It occurs in all ethnic, racial, economic, religious, gender, age, and class groups (Massachusetts Coalition of Battered Women Service Groups, 1990). Perpetrators and their victims may be young or old, able-bodied or disabled, rich or poor, educated or illiterate, blue-collar workers, professionals (Adams, 1989), celebrities, superstar athletes, or unemployed. Domestic violence may coincide with the use and abuse of alcohol or drugs. It may be associated with emotional problems or mental disorders, childhood experiences of family violence and abuses, or none of these factors. It occurs in cities, the suburbs, and rural areas. It exists in every dimension of life.

Domestic violence, though traditionally viewed as a private family matter, is in fact a public health problem. Dr. Robert McAfee, past president of the AMA, has referred to domestic violence as "a major public health problem as much as tobacco, AIDS, drug abuse or alcoholism."[1] Former Surgeon General C. Everett Koop identified violence against women by their partners as the most serious health risk for women in the United States. He noted that domestic violence causes more injuries to women than car accidents, muggings, and rapes combined (Stark & Flitcraft, 1985).

Some people describe an "epidemic" of domestic violence—a term that may cause one to envision domestic violence as rapidly spreading or increasing in occurrence. This description, however, more accurately reflects the recent recognition of the shocking magnitude of this problem. *Shocking* is a good word to describe the National Crime Victimization Survey figures released by the National Institute of Justice in January 1994 (U.S. Dept. of Justice, 1994). The data, based on a nationally representative sample survey of women and approximately 400,000 individual interviews, suggested that

- More than 2.5 million women experience violent crime victimization annually.
- Women are about equally likely to experience violent crime perpetrated by a relative, an intimate, an acquaintance, or a stranger.
- About one in four attacks on females involves the use of a weapon by the offender.
- About one in three attacks on females involves a firearm.
- About one third of female victims of violent crime are injured as a result of the crime.

Perpetrators of domestic violence sometimes kill their victims. According to the 1992 Uniform Crime Reports of the Federal Bureau of Investigation [FBI], four women in the United States are killed every day by their male partners. One third of all women who are murdered die at the hands of a husband or boyfriend (U.S. Dept. of Justice, 1992a). Although most people readily imagine personal danger in the form of a stranger on a darkened city street, the truth is that a woman is more likely to be seriously injured by someone she knows inside the perceived safety of her own home.

According to Donna Shalala, Secretary of Health and Human Services, during her presentation to the AMA's 1994 National Conference in Washington, D.C., one out of four women will be assaulted by a household partner in her lifetime, and 20% to 30% of the injuries that send women to hospital emergency rooms result from physical abuse inflicted by husbands or boyfriends. Sixty percent of female homicide victims are killed by someone they know. In the United States, domestic violence is as common as giving birth: about 4 million instances per year.

Abbott, Johnson, Koziol-McLain, and Lowenstein (1995), in a study of 648 female patients in Denver, Colorado, found that one in nine women with a current male partner who sought care in an emergency department was there because of acute domestic violence. They determined that in the emergency department setting, 54.2% of all women had been victims of domestic violence during their lifetimes.

◨ ASSOCIATED COSTS

The dollar costs of domestic violence to society are enormous. Estimates are that between 2 and 4 million women are severely physically abused each year by partners (AMA, 1992a; U.S. Dept. of Justice, 1986) and that 1 million women seek medical treatment each year for such injuries (Congressional Caucus for Women's Issues, 1992). According to a National Crime Survey (1981), it is estimated that medical expenses arising from domestic violence assaults cost more than $44 million per year and result in 21,000 hospitalizations with 99,800 patient days of hospitalization, 28,700 emergency department visits, and 39,900 visits to physicians each year. Our country spends $5 to $10 billion per year on health care, criminal justice, and other social service costs of domestic violence (Harris, 1992). Businesses lose $100 million annually in lost wages, sick leave, absenteeism, and nonproductivity (Colorado Dept. of Health and Colorado Domestic Violence Coalition, 1992).

There are no studies that document the number of domestic violence victims per year who seek mental health care as a result of chronic victimization. Therefore, associated costs cannot be measured.

What about future costs for which society will ultimately bear the burden? Consider what will become of children who have been brutalized or neglected, have been injured in the cross fire, or are the secondary victims as witnesses to the violence. It is known that men who batter their intimate partners are more likely to abuse their children as well (American Psychological Association, 1996). The effects of such violence on children should not be underestimated and should be of concern to all members of society. According to the AMA (1995a), witnessing domestic violence during childhood may cause children to have a variety of physical and emotional problems that can include headaches, abdominal pain, stuttering, enuresis, and insomnia. Such children may also experience separation anxiety, inability to concentrate and stay focused on their schoolwork, aggressive behavior, and guilt about their inability to stop the violence. Children who are abused and who witness the abuse of a parent suffer even more severe problems.

Children also suffer long-term effects from being abused or from witnessing violence. For example, research sponsored by the National Institute of Justice found that childhood abuse increased the odds of future delinquency and adult criminality overall by 40% (U.S. Dept. of Justice, 1992b). In addition, according to the American Psychological Association (1996), boys who witness or experience violence in their homes are at major risk for becoming batterers.

It is hard to imagine the profound effect on children who see their father beating their mother. As those children grow up, their perceptions about how to deal with conflict and control may become skewed. They may equate love with violence. The violence may become a learned behavior. On a more basic level, they may think that it is acceptable for a man to beat a woman. They may grow up believing that violence is the norm and is an appropriate way to solve personal problems or to get what one wants (Dutton & Painter, 1981). Violence in the home thus is perpetuated from generation to generation.

◙ IMPACT ON THE HEALTH CARE COMMUNITY

Many people view the police as the sole first-line response to domestic violence. I believe, however, on the basis of countless interviews with victims of such abuses, that more victims in fact turn to the medical community for help than to the police. Further, most victims seek medical help earlier in the abusive relationship than they seek law enforcement assistance. For various reasons, not every victim will dial 911. Even when victims do dial 911, some will go no further than receiving treatment on the scene by ambulance personnel or fire department emergency medical technicians. However, many victims will seek medical attention, whether in a hospital emergency department, a public clinic, or a private physician's office (Randall, 1991).

A National Crime Survey spanning 1973 to 1987, in which more than 100,000 individuals were interviewed, revealed that in approximately 25% of the violent incidents perpetrated by intimate partners, the victim received medical care: 10% were treated in a hospital or emergency room, 5% in a doctor's office, and 10% in other places (U.S. Dept. of Justice, 1991). It is estimated that at least one in five women seen in emergency departments has symptoms relating to abuse (Browne, 1992).

McLeer and Anwar (1987) referred to chronic victimization as battered women's most serious health problem. They noted that the emergency department is a point of entry into the health care system for severely abused women who may be at the greatest risk for serious physical injury or death. However, Stark et al. (1981) noted that most medical visits of battered women are in nonemergency settings for nontrauma complaints.

The June 17, 1992, issue of the *Journal of the American Medical Association* (AMA, 1992b) identified a high incidence of violence against women by their partners. AMA (1992a) guidelines issued the same day recognized domestic violence as so widespread that doctors were instructed to ask female patients routinely, as part of the medical history, whether they had been abused. Although the AMA guidelines are nonbinding recommendations for physicians, they were the first national attempt by the AMA to address the problem.

In a similar vein, the Joint Commission on the Accreditation of Healthcare Organizations (JCAHO), which accredits U.S. hospitals and hospital-related ambulatory care facilities, voted in 1992 to order all accredited hospitals to develop and follow protocols to provide an effective means of evaluating and treating adults who are suspected victims of abuse (Pike, 1992). As a further refinement to their policies, the 1996 JCAHO standards (JCAHO, 1995) require that hospitals have objective criteria for the identification and assessment of domestic violence victims, that staff members be trained in the use of the criteria, and that appropriate referrals be made to private and public community agencies from a list maintained by the hospital. Hospital policy is required to address a history of abuse as part of assessment, and such information must be included in the patient's medical records.[2]

Recognizing that medical illness and physical injury can result from domestic violence and that proper medical intervention can prevent further violence and its consequences, the American College of Physicians (1986) has taken the position that (a) physicians should become more sensitive to the possibility of domestic violence as a causal factor in illness and injury, and (b) hospitals and organized medical staffs should develop protocols for the identification and treatment of domestic violence victims. In March 1995, the American College of Emergency Physicians (ACEP; 1995) announced as part of its policy that domestic violence identification and assessment are important parts of emergency patient evaluation.

Inasmuch as domestic violence is recurrent (Straus, Gelles, & Steinmetz, 1980), the medical community is in a unique position to provide positive intervention to keep the victim from being subjected to further violence. Consider the following illustration.

Ann sits at the courthouse and waits to be called to testify against the man she believes ultimately would have killed her. Over the course of the past 6 months, she has spent a lot of time sitting and waiting: at the hospital emergency room; with the police, while trying to explain what happened; at the prosecutor's office, to make sure that criminal charges would be filed; and when she went to court to get a civil protection order. As she waits, she reflects on the past few years of her life. Ed once promised to love, honor, and cherish her. Instead, he abused, tormented, and nearly killed her. When she met Ed, he seemed like the man of her dreams: caring, good looking, hardworking, and extremely attentive. She was initially flattered by his jealousies about with whom she spent her time. She was swept off her feet, and they married within 6 months. Ed insisted that Ann quit her job because "no wife of mine should have to work." Ann willingly complied. It was a dream come true, or so it seemed.

But soon her Dr. Jekyll turned into Mr. Hyde. He constantly degraded and humiliated her, often in public. He used the intimacies she had confided to him as material for the jokes he told to others. People would look disgusted or turn their faces away when he did these things, but no one ever told him it was wrong. Friends she had known for years simply stopped inviting them out.

His degradations in private were worse. Although she was 5 feet, 5 inches tall and weighed 125 pounds, Ed constantly told Ann that she was fat. He criticized her every move: the way she ate, how loudly she laughed, and the way she breathed when she slept. He always reminded her how lucky she was to have him because, according to him, no one else would want her. Ed became insanely jealous. He accused Ann of having an affair or fantasizing about having one with any man who smiled at her in his presence. He insisted on knowing where she was at all times. If she was 5 minutes late, he went berserk for hours on end. He made life unbearable if she spoke on the telephone with a friend or wanted to visit her mother or sister. Soon she had cut herself off from all supportive persons in her life. She did not even see it happening.

Then the violence began. Almost anything could and did set off Ed. It could be something Ann said or failed to say, did or did not do, did not do right, or did not do to his satisfaction. She felt as if she were suffocating, walking around constantly holding her breath. Once she had been full of hopes, dreams, and ambitions. Suddenly, her life had narrowed to what to do to keep Ed happy. She prayed to find help and prayed that she would be a better wife so Ed would stop his violence. Ed always blamed Ann for his violence, and she, in turn, blamed herself. He would say things such as "See what you made me do" or "If you would only stop [*whatever*], I wouldn't have to hit you."

Over the years, the violence became more frequent and more severe. She suffered black eyes and split lips from punches to her face; bruises from punches to her abdomen, back, and breasts; a cracked rib; lacerations; bites; a broken tooth; and clumps of her hair ripped out at the roots.

At first, after he beat her, Ed would cry, promise that it would never happen again, and beg her forgiveness. He could be extremely loving when he wanted to be. Sometimes she would see a glimmer of the man with whom she had fallen in love. Sometimes, for a while, it would seem that things had gotten better and that Ed was making an effort to change. She always gave him "one more chance."

Ann's mother suddenly became severely ill. Her mother lived alone and needed help until she got back on her feet again. Ann decided to go to her mother's home for a few days and care for her. Ed supported her decision. When she returned home, however, Ed went wild and beat her brutally. He told her she cared more about her mother than her husband. When she pointed out that her mother had needed her, Ed responded that something could have happened to him while she was off "babying her mother."

At that moment, Ann began to realize that Ed would never change. Suddenly, his promises did not mean anything to her anymore. She knew that she could not go on like this. That is when the threats began. Ed threatened that if she ever tried to leave him, he would hunt her down. Once when she reached for the telephone to call the police, he told her that if he ever spent a night in jail because of her, he would kill her. As she saw the coldness in Ed's gaze as he spoke those words, she knew he would carry out his threat.

Three times she had received medical care. She probably should have seen a doctor after other beatings as well, but Ed would not let her go. Each of the times she went to the hospital, Ed insisted on accompanying her. She would hold her breath as she lied, telling nurses and doctors that she fell or how she bruised easily and was careless. They never pushed her or challenged her explanations. Once a doctor glanced at her over the top of his reading glasses and said dismissively, "That's quite a shiner. You should be more careful in the future." She sensed that he did not want to know what really happened. She volunteered nothing.

Over time, Ann developed other problems too. She did not sleep well and frequently had terrifying nightmares. She had severe migraine headaches and a constant knot in her stomach. She was constantly depressed, felt that she had nothing to look forward to in life, and thought about suicide as a means of escape from Ed. When Ed beat her and she did not get medical care, she drank wine to numb her pain.

Four years into the marriage, Ann became pregnant. Overjoyed, she thought Ed would be happy too. Surely, she thought, he would stop his violence now. Instead, when she told Ed the news, he became enraged, lunged at her, and with all his might punched her repeatedly in the stomach. Stunned and dazed, she managed to escape, run to a neighbor's house, and dial 911. The police arrived, arrested Ed, and charged him with criminal assault. Ann was transported via ambulance to the hospital.

Her prior injuries for which she had received treatment were documented in the medical records. However, the records contained no mention as to the true cause of those injuries. Over the years, Ann had become a makeup artist, covering up her facial injuries. No one but medical staff had seen the numerous injuries her clothing had covered.

The prosecutor filed charges not just for the present crime but for all of the assaults Ed had committed within the statute of limitations. It would basically be Ann's word against his, and Ed was an upstanding member of the community. The prosecutor explained to Ann that although the medical records would help to document the fact of her injuries, her false statements in those records as to the cause of her injuries would be used against her. She would have to explain why she had lied to the doctors. The jury might decide that if she had lied before, they could not believe her now. Ann wished she had told someone the truth about what was happening.

◙ BEING ON THE ALERT FOR VICTIMS

All medical facilities and personnel within the health care system who deal with patients, regardless of the setting, should be on the alert for domestic violence victims. Such settings include all emergency and nonemergency sites, ambulatory and primary care facilities, and mental health and substance abuse programs (Flitcraft, 1992). The fact that all staff within those settings must deal with the aftermath of domestic violence highlights the need to train all concerned. Those involved include doctors, psychiatric staff, residents, nurses, paramedics, emergency medical technicians, social workers, dieticians, receptionists, clerks, support, security, housekeeping staff, and volunteers.

Although more than 1 million women seek medical treatment each year for injuries caused by partners and ex-partners (Congressional Caucus for Women's Issues, 1992), doctors correctly identify the injuries as the result of battering in less than 6% of the cases (McLeer & Anwar, 1989; Stark et al., 1981). Why are so many domestic violence victims not identified by health care providers?

Identifying a domestic violence victim presenting herself for treatment should not be particularly difficult. A health care professional is likely to encounter a domestic violence victim in one of three ways (Rath & Jarratt, 1990).

First, a victim may seek care for traumatic injuries following an assault. If the injuries are serious, the victim may seek care at a hospital emergency department. She may also use the emergency department for less serious injuries if she was beaten during the night with no other immediate 24-hour health care option available or if she is financially limited or lacks insurance. A patient with monetary means may seek nonemergency care from her private internist or specialist. Injuries of the mouth may lead a victim to seek dental treatment.

Second, a victim may seek medical care for somatic problems and/or chronic pain. Although there may not be any obvious physical injuries indicative of physical abuse, such abuse may be the actual cause of the patient's ailment. In 1985, a study was conducted of 151 women ages 19 to 68 at the University of Alabama-Birmingham Pain Center. The women had been referred to the center by their primary physicians for chronic pain that had lasted at least 6 months. The study revealed that 53% of the women had been physically and/or sexually abused and that 71% of the abuse was committed by spouses. For 16% of the women, the abuse was sexual; for 43%, it was physical; and for 41%, it was both sexual and physical. In all of the cases, the abuse began prior to the onset of the chronic pain. Haber and Ross (1985) found that the abused women were twice as likely as nonabused women to have pain that was not related to an injury and to have spontaneous pain (pain that could not be traced to an antecedent). Aside from a hospital emergency department, a battered woman may seek care from a clinic, her family or general practitioner, an internist, or a gynecologist. Again, monetary limitations or the lack of insurance may cause some victims to go to an emergency department.

Third, a victim may seek medical care for psychosocial problems that have arisen secondary to abuse. Such problems include alcohol and drug abuse, as well as attempted suicide. Statistics show that approximately 25% of all women who attempt to take their own lives do so because of the psychological trauma caused by battering (AMA, 1992a). Victims may seek help not only from a hospital or private practitioner but also from a mental health professional, an outpatient clinic, or a substance abuse program.

Common red-flag traumatic injuries and complaints tend to suggest that one is dealing with an abused victim. For example, according to the AMA (1992a), common injuries characteristic of domestic violence assaults include contusions, abrasions, and minor lacerations, as well as fractures or sprains; injuries to the head, neck, chest, breasts, and abdomen; injuries during pregnancy; and repeated or chronic injuries. Physical abuse should be suspected whenever the injuries involve the periphery of the body and there are multiple injuries present. Such a pattern, particularly if in combination with old injuries, suggests abuse. Similarly, Kurz (1990) noted that when evaluating a patient as a possible abuse victim, of particular significance are the type of injury, the location of the injury, and a pattern of new and old or healing injuries.

There are also somatic complaint indicators. The American College of Obstetricians and Gynecologists (ACOG; 1995) stated that somatic complaints in abused women include headaches, insomnia, a choking sensation, hyperventilation, gastrointestinal symptoms, and chest, back, and pelvic pain. Other signs and symptoms include shyness, fright, embarrassment, evasiveness, jumpiness, passivity, frequent crying, being accompanied by one's male partner, drug or alcohol abuse or overuse, and other injuries.

Providers of prenatal care should be on particular alert for domestic violence victims because a woman who lives in an ongoing abusive relationship is more likely to be battered once she becomes pregnant (Straus & Gelles, 1986). The beating of a pregnant woman endangers her life as well as that of her unborn child. This type of abuse has been referred to as child abuse in the womb. Studies have shown that 40% to 60% of domestic violence victims are abused while pregnant (Parker & McFarlane, 1991). In my own experience in talking with victims, a woman's announcement of pregnancy to her partner often resulted in her being beaten by him.

The reasons a man would batter his pregnant partner are complex and varied. They may include jealousy of the unborn child for receiving the love and attention he feels the woman would otherwise show him; anger regarding the additional responsibilities the child will present; feeling less control over the woman; anger that her condition makes her less attractive to him (Helton, 1987); the desire to cause an abortion (Gelles, 1975); anger that the woman is not as energetic or able to care for him as she may have been before the pregnancy; jealousy regarding attention given to the woman and to the unborn child from friends and relatives; denial that the child she is carrying is actually his own; and anger regarding the woman's inherent creative power to bring life into the world.

Battering can kill the unborn fetus. Women who are battered are four times more likely to have miscarriages than those who are not (Bullock, 1989; Helton, 1987). Domestic violence has been identified as one of the risk factors for fetal death in the context of blunt-force trauma on the pregnant woman (Ribe, Teggatz, & Harvey, 1993). The focal point of assaults during pregnancy is frequently the abdomen (Hilberman, 1980). Blunt-force trauma to the abdomen, such as being punched or kicked, may cause fetal death by placental abruption. Such assaults can also cause, among other injuries, antepartum hemorrhage; fetal fractures; rupture of the uterus, liver, or spleen; and premature labor (Saltzman, 1990). Even if a baby survives being battered in the womb, battering can negatively affect the baby's health. For example, battered women are four times more likely to have low-birth-weight babies (Bullock, 1989; Helton, 1987). Birth weight is the most significant predictor of infant wellness and future development.

Pregnancy may provide a key opportunity for battering recognition and intervention because the pregnancy causes a woman to come into frequent contact with her health care provider (McFarlane, Parker, Soeken, & Bullock, 1992). Medical staff should be alert for any patient who misses her appointments, has vague complaints, is injured, or mentions that her partner is possessive (Helton, 1986). Dr. Robert McAfee added that if a woman calls and makes an appointment and a man later calls to cancel it, the patient's chart should be flagged (Colburn, 1994).

The high incidence of domestic violence battering during pregnancy dictates that hospitals should also screen mothers of all newborn babies. This may be a key opportunity for intervention because the mother will be staying overnight in the hospital, but ordinarily the batterer will not. This situation presents a rare occasion during which a knowledgeable person can talk to the victim without the abuser's being able to interfere. Aside from screening for domestic violence, health care providers can provide information concerning the effects of domestic violence on children and other general resource information.

I do not suggest, however, screening or routinely providing domestic violence information to fathers of newborns. If the mother/patient is being battered, providing such information to her abusive partner may cause him to suspect that she is also receiving the same information. If the purpose of providing this information is to give her the tools to use when she is ready and able to take some sort of action, that purpose will have been defeated. In addition, providing such information to the batterer may cause him to suspect that his partner has made statements to the medical staff indicating that he abuses her. A batterer may see this as a challenge to his control over her. She may thereafter be subjected to his retaliatory violence. This may put the woman in extreme danger at a time when she is in a greatly weakened physical condition and is unable and unprepared to leave her abusive partner.

◉ PATIENT EXPECTATIONS

Recognizing that domestic violence victims will seek medical care, it is important to know what such a patient expects from her health care provider. When a person has a broken arm and comes to the emergency department, it is reasonable to assume that the patient wants her arm set. But what if the cause of the broken arm was an abusive, violent partner? Does the patient really want to discuss her "relationship problems" with the physician? Is the violence in her life a "personal problem" that the health care professional should not seek to explore?

Rath and Jarratt (1990) conducted a small-group study of clinic patient volunteers who were asked what they expected from their family doctors regarding spouse abuse. The study found that the women expected the physician to bring up the subject of domestic violence, to take extra time to listen, to give advice, and to offer referrals for counseling and other appropriate services.

Health care providers should not underestimate the positive value of broaching the subject of domestic violence with patients. Burge (1989) suggested that by initiating a discussion about the violence in their lives, physicians send a variety of messages to their patients. These messages include that the problem is not too shameful, deviant, or insignificant to discuss; that the patient's discomfort is understandable; that her reactions to the abuse are rational; and that there is hope that the situation can be changed. Other messages that may be conveyed to the patient include that she is not alone; that no matter what she may have done, the abuse is wrong; that she did not deserve to be battered; and that battering is against the law.

A visit to an emergency department or a doctor's office is an attempt to get help. However, it is extremely important for health care providers to recognize that when intervention occurs through resource options, it should be the patient's decision to seek counseling, pursue civil or criminal legal action, or leave her abusive partner. She is the only person who must face the prospect of divorce, the loss of her home, a child custody battle, the likelihood of retaliatory violence from her partner, and a myriad of other issues. Providers of health care will best assist domestic violence victims by seeking to empower them to help themselves.

◙ Notes

1. From "Domestic violence: AMA President Decries 'a Major Public Health Problem,' " by D. Colburn, June 28, 1994, *The Washington Post,* Health Section, p. 10. © 1994, The Washington Post. Reprinted with permission.

2. From *1996 Comprehensive Accreditation Manual for Hospitals* (pp. 115-116) by the Joint Commission on Accreditation of Healthcare Organizations, 1995, Oakbrook Terrace, IL: Author. Copyright 1995 by the Joint Commission on Accreditation of Healthcare Organizations. Adapted with permission.

2

SOCIETAL PERSPECTIVES ON DOMESTIC VIOLENCE

HISTORICAL PERSPECTIVE

It is difficult to understand the source of present-day domestic violence without looking at the history that has shaped current laws regarding, and perceptions about, women's rights in society. Domestic violence in our society is but one outcome of laws that historically have discriminated against women and of societal views of women as a lesser class. Gender-based violence is the ultimate extension of gender discrimination and the belief that women are innately subordinate to men. It is, after all, the primitive way to "keep a woman in her place." The following is by no means an exhaustive litany. It is intended merely to provide a background for the context of modern-day violence against women.

Ancient History

The Bible is the foundation of all Judeo-Christian ideology. The Bible's first story about mankind, the story of Adam and Eve, portrays woman as the temptress who leads Adam into wrongdoing. It was woman who listened to the serpent, took a bite of the fruit of the tree of knowledge in disobedience to God's mandate, and convinced Adam to do the same. With that bite came the knowledge of good and evil and the Almighty's wrath (Genesis 2:15-22; 3:2-20). In

14

powerful biblical stories, women have been cast in the roles of the seductress, the virgin, the holy mother, and the whore. These images serve as the basis for the most common expectations of what women are and are not supposed to be in our society.

Ancient history reveals that violence against one's wife was not only condoned but expected. For example, in ancient Egypt, it is said that no self-respecting man would have allowed his wife to speak out against him without bashing her teeth in with a brick (Patton, 1994). The right of members of the clergy to beat their wives was affirmed in the Council of Toledo in A.D. 400. The right evolved from ecclesiastical law to common law as men were given the authority to punish their wives physically (Mann, 1994). Through the *Rules of Marriage,* written by Friar Cherubino of Siena between 1450 and 1481, the church encouraged men to beat their wives, instructing:

> When you see your wife commit an offense, don't rush at her with insults and violent blows.... Scold her sharply, bully and terrify her. And if this still doesn't work, ... take up a stick and beat her soundly, for it is better to punish the body and correct the soul than to damage the soul and spare the body.... Then readily beat her, not in rage but out of charity and concern for her soul, so that the beating will redound to your merit and her good. (as quoted in Davidson, 1978, p. 99)

Family matters were originally adjudicated by church courts. When the courts separated from the church, wife beating remained sanctioned under the law on religious grounds (McDonald, 1990). Legal justification for such abuse in present times still finds its basis in religious principle. Simone de Beauvoir (1949/1974) succinctly described the inherent conflict between Christianity, feminism, and the law: "Man enjoys the great advantage of having a god endorse the code he writes; and since man exercises a sovereign authority over women, it is especially fortunate that this authority has been vested in him by the Supreme Being" (p. 691).

Common Law and the "Rule of Thumb"

> A woman, a dog, and a walnut tree, the more you beat 'em, the better they be. (Old English proverb; "Developments," 1993, p. 1498)

> A wife is like an egg; the more she is beaten, the better she is. (Victorian proverb; Pleck, 1979, p. 63)

The laws in the United States come from two primary sources: statute and common law. Statutory laws are enacted by the legislature. Common law is judge-made law. It derives from judicial opinions on legal issues presented for review, usually through cases that are decided in a trial court, then heard in higher courts through the appeals process. American common law is based on English common law. Laws generally reflect societal values and norms.

Women have traditionally been viewed as chattel: the property first of their fathers and then of their husbands. At a wedding, a father *gives* his daughter away to her husband. The classic wedding vow of bride to groom, "to love, honor and obey . . . till death do us part," conveys the expected lifetime subjugation of wife to husband. In addition, men have historically been viewed as the head of the household and master of the castle. As such, men are the supreme authority within the realm of family life.

According to English common law, marriage made husband and wife into one person in the eyes of the law—the husband. The very being or legal existence of the woman was suspended, or incorporated and consolidated into that of the husband. She was considered under her husband's protection and influence, and her "condition" was known as *coverture* (2 William Blackstone, Commentaries * 442). Under this union of person, the wife could not sue or be sued, could not testify for or against her husband, and could not inherit property.

Inheritance laws provided for the real family wealth to benefit only the male children. Personal property was divided equally between males and females, but a son, to the exclusion of his sisters, was heir to all of the real property. When she married, a woman's personal property became absolutely that of the husband. On his death, the husband could bequeath all of the property to someone else.

The use of physical violence against one's wife was legal under the common law. According to Judge William Blackstone,

> The husband also by the old law might give his wife moderate correction. For as he is to answer for her misbehavior, the law thought it reasonable to entrust him with this power of restraining her, by domestic chastisement, in the same moderation that a man is allowed to correct his apprentices or children, for whom the master or parent is also liable in some cases to answer. (2 William Blackstone, Commentaries * 445)

Women who bucked the traditional female role sometimes paid a heavy price for their nonconformity. Documented reports in the mid-19th century reflect that women were legally and involuntarily committed to insane asylums for expression of opinion, their religious beliefs, actions outside the scope of acceptable ladylike behavior of the day, or "hysteria" determined to be caused inherently by their female bodily organs. These commitments were accomplished by fathers, husbands, and brothers. Battering husbands psychiatrically committed their wives as another means of abuse and control. Women who persistently reported being attacked by their husbands with knives, guns, and fists were regarded as delusional. These reports, however, may have been the first documentation of the psychological sequelae of battering (Geller & Harris, 1994). Women who fled abusive husbands were dubbed "runaway wives" (Pleck, 1979).

A review of judicial opinions rendered during the 19th century demonstrates the courts' callous indifference to female victims of battering. The language used in various cases reveals judges' adherence to one of the most deeply ingrained myths about domestic violence: that it is a private matter, not a criminal offense. The various courts often expressed dismay at even having to entertain such unpleasantness in their courtrooms. There is some question in modern times about whether the "Rule of Thumb" actually existed. The case law of this country indicates that it did.

Although judges superficially condemned the right of a husband to beat his wife, courts of the mid-19th century found ways to throw out convictions or to condone battering tacitly in decisions they let stand. For example, in 1824, the Supreme Court of Mississippi held in *Bradley v. State* that a husband could be convicted of an assault and battery on his wife even though at common law a husband had the right to chastise his wife. In reaching its decision, however, the court stated that if the defendant had shown that he had confined himself within "reasonable bounds" when he had thought it proper to "chastise" his wife, the court would have had a more difficult time reaching its decision affirming the trial court verdict of guilty. The court quoted Judge Blackstone in reference to the Rule of Thumb, stating:

> I believe it was in a case before Mr. Justice Raymond, where the same doctrine was recognized, with proper limitations and restrictions well suited to the condition and feelings of those who might think proper to use a whip or rattan, no bigger than my thumb, in order to enforce the salutary restraints of domestic discipline. (Id. at 20)

This court's primary purpose for establishment of the rule that a man may not commit an assault on his wife was not to protect women from abuse but rather "to prevent the deplorable spectacle of the exhibition of similar cases in our courts of justice" (Id. at 22). Further, despite its ruling, the court reiterated the rule of moderate chastisement by husband against wife, noting:

> Family broils and dissensions cannot be investigated before the tribunals of the country, without casting a shade over the character of those who are unfortunately engaged in the controversy. To screen from public reproach those who may be thus unhappily situated, let the husband be permitted to exercise the right of moderate chastisement, in cases of great emergency, and use salutary restraints in every case of misbehavior, *without being subjected to vexatious prosecutions, resulting in the mutual discredit and shame of all parties concerned* [italics added]. (Id.)

In 1864, the Supreme Court of North Carolina held in *State v. Black* that a husband could not be convicted of battery on his wife unless he inflicted a permanent injury or used excessive violence or a degree of cruelty that indicated malignity or vindictiveness. Otherwise, according to the court, "The law will not invade the domestic forum, or go behind the curtain" (Id. at 163). The court further held that it made no difference that the husband and wife were living separate at the time of the assault. The court reasoned that because a husband was responsible for the acts of his wife and was required to govern his household, the law permitted him to use toward his wife "such a degree of force as is necessary to control an unruly temper and *make her behave herself* [italics added]" (Id. at 163). Public sentiment toward domestic violence and the role of public interventions in family matters in 1864 is amply illustrated by the words of the court:

> Certainly, the exposure of a scene like that set out in this case can do no good. In respect to the parties, a public exhibition in the courthouse of such quarrels and fights between man and wife widens the breach, makes a reconciliation almost impossible, *and encourages insubordination* [italics added]; and in respect to the public, it has a pernicious tendency; so *pro bono publico* [for the public good, such matters are excluded from the courts], unless there is a permanent injury or excessive violence or cruelty indicating malignity and vindictiveness. (Id. at 163)

In 1868, the Supreme Court of North Carolina in *State v. Rhodes* refused to hold a husband criminally responsible for having beaten his wife with a stick smaller than the diameter of his thumb because the court did not want to interfere with the sanctity of marriage. The trial judge had thrown the case out, concluding that the defendant had a right to whip his wife with a switch no bigger than his thumb.

The appellate court noted that there was no question that the violence would have constituted an assault and battery "if the subject had not been the defendant's wife" (Id. at 445). Although the court concluded that it was the effect produced, not the manner or the instrument used that counted, the court nonetheless affirmed the lower court's decision. Its opinion, given in what was surely thought to be the most eloquent language of the day, shows the great deference "family matters" were accorded and the great indifference with which violence within the family was handled in the mid-1800s:

> However great are the evils of ill temper, quarrels, and even personal conflicts inflicting only temporary pain, they are not comparable with the evils which would result from raising the curtain and exposing to public curiosity and criticism the nursery and the bed chamber. Every household has and must have a government of its own, modelled to suit the temper, disposition and condition of its inmates. Mere ebullitions of passion, impulsive violence, and temporary pain, affection will soon forget and forgive; and each member will find excuse for the other in his own frailties. But when trifles are taken hold of by the public, and the parties are exposed and disgraced, and each endeavors to justify himself or herself by criminating the other, that which ought to be forgotten in a day will be remembered for life. (Id. at 448)

By 1870, laws forbidding wife abuse appeared in most states. However, police were unlikely to make arrests, and district attorneys were unlikely to prosecute cases (Pleck, 1979). The combined traditional notions of marital privacy and the husband's historical privilege to "discipline" his wife formed a basis for the unwillingness of law enforcement and the rest of the justice system to intervene and treat domestic violence as a crime (Willoughby, 1989).

In 1871, the Supreme Court of Alabama, in *Fulgram v. State,* affirmed a conviction arising from a husband's excessive assault on his wife. The court noted that "moderate correction" to enforce a wife's obedience to a husband's just commands was permissible (Id. at 145-146). In an apparent reference to the Rule of Thumb, the court stated:

> Therefore, a rod which may be drawn through the wedding ring is not now deemed necessary to teach the wife her duty and subjection to the husband. The husband is therefore not justified or allowed by law to use such a weapon, or any other, for her moderate correction. The wife is not to be considered as the husband's slave. And the privilege, ancient though it be, to beat her with a stick, to pull her hair, choke her, spit in her face, or to inflict upon her like indignities, is not now acknowledged by our law. (Id. at 146)

In 1874, in *State v. Oliver,* the Supreme Court of North Carolina put an end to the Rule of Thumb, holding that the old doctrine no longer governed the decisions of that state. According to the court, present civilization dictated that a husband had no legal right to chastise his wife under any circumstances (Id. at 60).

In affirming the defendant's conviction for assault, the court held that under the facts of the case, both malice and cruelty were established. The court noted that the common-law "barbaric" rule was no longer the law. However, due to motives of public policy, to preserve the sanctity of the domestic circle, the court ruled that it would not listen to "trivial complaints." In other words, the court did not want to hear such cases. According to the court, "If no permanent injury has been inflicted, nor malice, cruelty nor dangerous violence shown by the husband, *it is better to draw the curtain, shut out the public gaze, and leave the parties to forget and forgive* [italics added]" (Id. at 61-62).

In 1882, the state of Maryland passed a law that outlawed wife beating and provided a punishment of 40 lashes or a year in jail (Davidson, 1977). It is said that a Baltimore district attorney remarked that after the first man was punished under this new law, "the crime ceased as if by magic" (Davidson, 1977, p. 16). However, one commentator has opined that it is more likely that police simply declined to make arrests when penalties became severe (Pleck, 1979).

In 1891, the case of *Reg v. Jackson* abolished the right of marital chastisement in England.

Efforts to Change the Status Quo

In 1848, the Seneca Falls Convention was held. This gathering of women in upstate New York was the beginning of the feminist movement in the United States. It is noteworthy that this movement began in the era of coverture, when women had no independent rights. Women at the convention produced the Declaration of Sentiments, a statement of women's rights to own property; divorce; speak freely; control their own wages; make contracts; sue and be sued; testify; share in political offices; have equal opportunity in commerce, education, and the professions; and vote (Geller & Harris, 1994).

Women received the right to vote by constitutional amendment in 1920. Over the years, women have also received the other rights advocated at Seneca Falls. The efforts of the Seneca Falls Convention participants may be viewed as the beginning of women's attempts to redress many wrongs to women, including domestic violence.

In 1971, Chiswick Center, the first shelter for battered women, was opened in London (Martin, 1983). During the 1970s, grassroots activists started the battered women's movement in the United States (Martin, 1983). Barely more than 20 years ago, the first U.S. shelter for battered women was opened. In August 1976, *Ms. Magazine* called public attention to domestic violence. The magazine ran on its cover a photograph of an attractive young blonde woman with a huge black eye. The cover read, "Battered Wives: Help for the Secret Victim Next Door."[1]

In 1982, the U.S. Commission on Civil Rights took testimony and prepared a report entitled *Under the Rule of Thumb: Battered Women and the Administration of Justice.* The report provided an evaluation of the treatment of adult female domestic violence victims by the civil and criminal justice systems and by various social service agencies. The report concluded that at every stage of the criminal justice system, significant numbers of such victims were turned away, so that few ever obtained relief. The report also concluded that police officers, prosecutors, and judges often failed to take appropriate action and treated spouse abuse as a private family matter rather than a crime against society. In other words, nothing had changed much in more than 100 years.

In 1990, the National Council of Churches, with 42 million members representing 32 Protestant, Orthodox, and Anglican denominations, urged clergy to respond with greater compassion to domestic violence (Koss et al., 1994). In 1992, "The U.S. Roman Catholic bishops thrust the issue into the open . . . in a statement condemning all domestic violence—physical, psychological and verbal—as 'sinful.' "[2]

One might hope that the treatment of domestic violence victims would change for magnanimous reasons. However, it is often the case that legal action resulting in liability is necessary to motivate change. In response to lawsuits by domestic violence victims, some jurisdictions have enacted "mandatory arrest" laws. Such laws dictate that a law enforcement officer must make an arrest when there is probable cause (i.e., when it is more likely than not) that a specified offense has occurred and when the relationship between the parties falls within the statutory definition. In general, crimes such as assault and battery, threats to do bodily harm, and more serious assaultive conduct fall within the realm of the required conduct for mandatory arrest. In terms of relationships, all mandatory arrest jurisdictions cover current or former husband and wife, and most cover heterosexual couples who reside or have previously resided together and those who have children in common. Some laws cover other blood relatives, as well as persons related by marriage or custody. A few jurisdictions cover homosexual couples who reside or have resided together. A person who is a mere dating partner is often left without protection under mandatory arrest laws. In such a situation, the police may arrest for whatever crime has been committed but are not required to do so.

Pursuant to mandatory arrest, the law enforcement officer has no discretion; if arrest is appropriate, the officer *must* make the arrest. Other jurisdictions have "proarrest" laws or policies, which encourage but do not mandate arrest as the preferred response to domestic violence crimes. At present, an increasing number of jurisdictions have mandatory arrest laws, some have proarrest laws, while others have neither mandatory nor proarrest laws.

In August 1994, Congress passed the Violent Crime Control and Law Enforcement Act of 1994, which includes the Violence Against Women Act of 1994 (VAWA). For the first time in the history of this country, Federal law states that domestic violence is a crime. The Federal approach reflects a recognition that domestic violence is a national problem (Klein, 1995). The act has a host of provisions, including new Federal criminal statutes for interstate domestic violence, a civil rights cause of action, full faith and credit for civil protection orders issued in other jurisdictions, and funding for a wide assortment of programs. The act also mandates that various studies be performed. One of the studies is to be conducted by the Center for Disease Control, Injury Control Division. The purpose of this study is to obtain a national projection of the incidence of injuries resulting from domestic violence, to determine the cost of such injuries to health care facilities, and to recommend health care strategies for reducing the incidence and cost of these injuries.

VAWA authorizes $120 million in grants to states, Native American tribal governments, and units of local government to encourage those entities to treat domestic violence as a serious violation of criminal law. The act provides grants to implement mandatory arrest or proarrest policies in police departments; to improve the tracking of domestic violence cases; to increase coordination among police, prosecutors, and the judiciary; and to provide education about domestic violence.

VAWA provides for the creation of a national domestic violence hot line, which was implemented on February 21, 1996. In addition, the Clinton administration created within the U.S. Department of Justice an Office on Violence Against Women. Although VAWA will certainly not end domestic violence or violence against women in the United States, it sends a powerful message and is a good start toward changing societal attitudes about such violence.

How Far Have We Come?

The fact that domestic violence is now a crime in all jurisdictions in the United States does not necessarily mean that such cases receive improved treatment in the courts. The following cases highlight that at least when a wife commits adultery, the concept of "woman as property of husband" still finds its way into judicial rulings.

On May 27, 1993, Susan Sarno, who had been separated from her husband Stephen for a year, was attacked by him when he found her and another man in bed together. Susan required 17 stitches to close her facial wounds. At Stephen's sentencing hearing, Susan told the court that she thought it was important that her husband "get a clear message that he was not justified in what he did." In response, Judge William J. O'Neil, of Concord, New Hampshire, stated that Susan was "still his wife" when Stephen found her in bed with the man. The judge concluded that although the assault was "a tragic thing, I can't conclude that it was completely unprovoked. . . . To have slapped you, might have been, you know, something more normal."[3]

In February 1994, Kenneth Peacock, a long-distance trucker, came home unexpectedly and found his wife, Sandra, in bed with another man. Hours after finding her, and after hours of drinking and arguing, Kenneth killed his wife by shooting her in the head with his hunting rifle. Following Kenneth's plea of guilty to the charge of manslaughter, Judge Robert E. Cahill of Baltimore County Circuit Court sentenced Kenneth to 18 months in jail with possible work release, alcohol counseling, and 50 hours of community service in an unspecified domestic violence program. In imposing the sentence, the judge stated:

> I seriously wonder how many married men—married five, four years—would have the strength to walk away without inflicting some corporal punishment, whatever the punishment might be. I shudder to think what I would do. . . . I'm forced to impose a sentence . . . only because I think I must do it to make the system honest.[4]

Within 2 weeks of the sentencing, Kenneth was put on work release from the detention center and was working for a trucking company from 5 a.m. to 9 p.m. (Rosenfeld, 1994).

In January 1996, following Stewart Marshall's conviction for spousal abuse, Michigan District Court Judge Joel Gehrke told Marshall to roll up his shirtsleeve and then punished him with a literal three-finger "slap" on the wrist and said, "Don't do that." The judge said that the real crime was adultery, committed by Marshall's wife. She acknowledged having had an affair with her husband's brother that resulted in the birth of a child. In reference to the Old Testament, the judge stated, "In the laws of Israel, if Mr. Marshall had come home and found his wife in this situation, the question would not be, 'Did you strike her?' It would have been, 'Well, are you ready to publicly be the first one to stone her?' "[5]

Perhaps one of the most significant historical changes in the treatment of domestic violence cases is that each of the court rulings described above was met with tremendous public outrage.

◙ SOCIETAL MYTHS AND MISCONCEPTIONS

A number of societal myths about domestic violence have developed through the ages. These are ingrained in our society today and play a significant role in current attitudes toward domestic violence victims.

Myths are beliefs not based on fact. Such beliefs can affect one's values and judgments, deter intervention, and negatively influence treatment philosophy. Belief in myths can cause numerous adverse outcomes for the patient, including failure to diagnose, victim referrals for inappropriate treatment, triage to the lowest level of emergency department care, treatment of domestic violence victimization as nonemergency, and inappropriate prescriptions for tranquilizers and pain pills (Klingbeil & Boyd, 1984). Understanding the truth about domestic violence is a powerful first step toward enabling oneself to intervene in such cases.

Myths about domestic violence are numerous. Twelve of the most common are examined here.

> *1. Myth: The victim caused the violence. She "asked for it."*
> *Fact: The batterer caused the violence; he is responsible for his actions.*

Holding the victim responsible for the batterer's attack on her is victim blaming, plain and simple. Herman (1992), in her book *Trauma and Recovery,* explained victim blaming by stating:

> It is very tempting to take the side of the perpetrator. All the perpetrator asks is that the bystander do nothing. He appeals to the universal desire to see, hear, and

speak no evil. The victim, on the contrary, asks the bystander to share the burden of pain. The victim demands action, engagement and remembering. (pp. 7-8)

Many people quickly conclude that a man acts with brutal force only because he was "provoked" by his female partner. Yet this logic would not justify violence against others outside of the home with whom that same man might come into contact. Consider that each of us is provoked by others every day of our lives. Someone cuts you off in traffic; your boss criticizes your work; the meal you order at a restaurant is bad. Violence is not an acceptable response to any of those incidents. If a man cannot punch his boss in the face for criticizing him, why is he allowed to punch his wife in the face? The answer lies in the lack of consequence for the behavior and our willingness as bystanders not to become involved.

The answer may also lie in what Lerner (1965) called the "Just World Hypothesis." According to this theory, people basically believe that good things happen to good people and bad things happen to bad people (Lerner & Simmons, 1966). "She asked for it" says that the victim is bad and *deserved* the bad thing (the beating). It also suggests that the speaker can avoid the bad thing because the victim must have done something the speaker would never do. The reaction "I don't believe her, I wouldn't stand for it if it was me" similarly says that the speaker is a good person. Because the speaker is good, he or she would not be victimized. Therefore, if the victim were a good person, she would not be victimized either. According to this logic, either the victim is a bad person or she must not have been victimized: She must like the abuse, or she is exaggerating or lying about what really happened.

2. *Myth: The victim enjoys the abuse (Gelles & Straus, 1989). This is often combined with another myth: If she didn't enjoy it, she would leave him. Fact: No one enjoys being beaten.*

Society quickly labels a domestic violence victim as masochistic (Caplan, 1985; Walker, 1979), implying that it is somehow sexually gratifying to the victim to be beaten, choked, stabbed, or otherwise assaulted. Examination of the context in which the violence occurs dispels this myth. You may find that the victim was attacked because she told the abuser she wanted to end the relationship; she cooked carrots instead of green beans for dinner; or she was late returning from night school and was beaten while being accused of having an affair.

It is telling that although the victim is readily labeled a masochist, we do not label the batterer a sadist (Caplan, 1985). An argument could certainly be made that anyone who brutally beats a person he supposedly loves must enjoy seeing that person in pain and therefore must be gratified in inflicting injury (Caplan, 1985).

The masochistic label puts the blame on the victim. It implies that something is innately wrong with her. Because something is wrong with her, she alone must be responsible for the abuse. This label reinforces the societal myth that domestic violence is an isolated problem in unusually disturbed couples (Hilberman, 1980).

> 3. *Myth: Domestic violence is a family or private matter.*
> *Fact: Domestic violence is a crime against the victim and against society.*

The repercussions and costs of domestic violence affect all of us. Dollar costs include services of the police, the prosecutors, the courts, and social services, as well as medical expenses, lost workdays, and decreased productivity. Children who witness domestic violence experience both immediate and prolonged negative outcomes (Wolfe & Korsch, 1994). They are more likely than children from nonviolent homes to repeat the cycle of such violence as adults.

> 4. *Myth: If the victim left the batterer, the violence would stop.*
> *Fact: Most victims are in greater danger of increased violence after they leave the abuser (Browne, 1987).*

For example, a Harris poll of 1,793 women in Kentucky showed that two thirds of the women who reported being abused were divorced or separated from the batterer at the time of the abuse (Schulman, 1981). According to a study conducted by Browne (1987), more than half of men who had killed their partners reported "desertion" by their wife as a major problem.

> 5. *Myth: Alcohol (Caplan, 1985; Walker, 1979) and drug abuse cause domestic violence (Gelles & Straus, 1989).*
> *Fact: Generally speaking, alcohol and drug use do not cause violent behavior.*

Unfortunately, it is socially acceptable to blame drug or alcohol use for bad behavior (Klingbeil & Boyd, 1984). If a man abuses alcohol or uses drugs and is violent, he has two distinct problems: a substance abuse problem and a violence problem.

Many people refer to alcohol or drug use as "liquid courage" or "chemical courage." They claim that the substance relaxes inhibitions in the user; therefore "He couldn't help himself."

Some drugs such as phencyclidine (PCP) can cause a user to act violently. But generally, drugs and alcohol do not cause people to act violently. If they did, everyone who drank or who used drugs would be violent. This is certainly not the case. Furthermore, alcoholics beat their wives when they are sober (Hilberman, 1980; Klingbeil & Boyd, 1984), and drug users beat their partners when they are straight. Contrary to the argument that drugs cause men to act violently, Klingbeil and Boyd (1984) reported that some victims actually find reprieve when their partners are "stoned" due to their "mellow" state.

> 6. *Myth: Domestic violence only occurs in lower socioeconomic groups.*
> *Fact: Domestic violence occurs in all socioeconomic groups (Straus et al., 1980).*

Although the highest reported incidence of domestic violence is among the poor, this may be accounted for by the fact that the poor, unlike those with economic means, have little alternative but to seek help from public agencies, which maintain statistics (Hilberman, 1980). For example, they are more likely to call the police, go to hospital emergency departments and legal clinics, and turn to shelters. Middle- and upper-class women are more likely to have resources that give them the option of using private physicians and attorneys and staying at hotels. They are therefore less visible to agencies that gather statistics on battering.

> 7. *Myth: The incidence of domestic violence is overstated. It is not that much of a problem.*
> *Fact: Regardless of the exact statistics, domestic violence is a significant problem in the United States.*

The very nature of domestic violence—a crime that occurs behind closed doors—makes it difficult to quantify. Studies that have attempted to gather data on incidence may vary widely depending on measures used, such as definitions of domestic violence. Further, individuals surveyed may be unwilling to disclose violence occurring inside their homes. Nonetheless, there have been some attempts to document this problem.

For example, according to a study by Straus et al. (1980) of 2,143 families, 50% of American homes experience violence within the family at least once per year. Conclusions drawn were that the family is a major institution of violence in our society, that violence is taken for granted, and that the marriage license could be considered a "hitting license." According to a nationally representative survey of 400,000 women conducted by the U.S. Department of Justice in 1994, it was estimated that on average, there are 572,032 violent victimizations against women perpetrated by intimates annually. Of the women surveyed, only about half reported the crime to the police (U.S. Dept. of Justice, 1994).

8. *Myth: Women are just as violent as men.*
   Fact: Men make up the overwhelming percentage of domestic violence perpetrators.

According to the U.S. Department of Justice (1994), approximately 95% of domestic violence victims are female. Consider that in 1993, approximately 575,000 men were arrested in the United States for committing crimes against women, but only 49,000 women were arrested for committing crimes against men (American Psychological Association, 1996). Nonetheless, the possibility that the health care provider may encounter male victims should not be ignored by protocol or practice. Indeed, the AMA Council on Scientific Affairs (1994) has recommended that their own Campaign Against Family Violence include male victims and that physicians be encouraged to identify male victims of abuse as well.

In terms of violent conduct by both sexes, it is men who use more dangerous and injurious forms of violence, do more damage due to their physical strength, use repeated violence (Straus et al., 1980), and, even when unarmed, pose more of a physical menace to women than vice versa (Browne, 1993). Browne (1993) pointed out that claims that women and men are equally violent ignore the fact that men are almost always the perpetrators of forced sexual assaults between partners in relationships. It is also important to recognize that the motivation for the violent acts often differs between male and female partners (Browne, 1987), as do the physical consequences (Saunders, 1988). A man may attack his partner because he did not like something she did; he did not get his way; or he did not like the way she spoke back to him, and he wanted to show her that he was in charge. Women's use of violence may more frequently be in self-defense (Browne, 1987) to stop an ongoing or threatened attack by their partner.

The U.S. Commission on Civil Rights (1982) may have summed it up best when explaining the reason for focusing on female victims of spouse abuse as opposed to both sexes. The commission discussed the dynamics of female victimization, stating:

> The incidence of abuse of women by men is much greater than the abuse of men by women. Women are, as a group, more likely to be economically dependent upon their spouses and therefore unable to escape an abusive relationship without protection from the legal system and support from various organizations. Finally, the common law legacy of women as objects of property and as incompetents unable to conduct their own legal affairs continues to color the attitudes of police officers, prosecutors, and judges. (p. v)

9. *Myth: Battered women gravitate to abusers. Even if such women leave their violent partners, they will just find other men who will beat them (Walker, 1979).*
   Fact: Women who are domestic violence victims do not seek abusive partners.

Given the statistics of battering in relationships, the odds are that most women will become involved with a violent partner at some time in their lives. However, once breaking free, many battered women avoid all relationships, concluding that they are unlikely to find a nonviolent partner. Others may have difficulty trusting their ability to choose intimate partners who will not abuse them (Graham, Rawlings, & Rimini, 1988).

10. *Myth: The assault is an isolated incident, unlikely to happen again.*
    Fact: Battering is part of a complex pattern of domination and control.

It is amazing how quickly some people are willing to respond to a man's punching his wife or girlfriend in the face with "He just lost his temper," "He's under a lot of pressure at work," or "He said he was sorry. I'm sure he'll never do it again." Contrary to this myth, studies show that the violence tends to recur and to become more frequent and severe over time (U.S. Dept. of Justice, 1986; Walker, 1979).

11. *Myth: Domestic violence is merely "a push and a shove."*
    Fact: Batterers engage in countless forms of violence (Violence Against Women, 1992).

It is true that batterers sometimes push and shove their victims. But they also punch, kick, stomp, bite, burn, stab, slash, shoot, and choke. Injuries range from superficial to lethal.

12. Myth: If he beat her up, he must be mentally ill.
    Fact: Mental illness is not a prerequisite for domestic violence.

It is true that just as there is mental illness in society at large, some men who batter their partners do suffer from mental illness. However, not everyone with mental illness is violent, and not all batterers are mentally ill. Automatically attributing a man's violence to the belief that only someone mentally ill could do such a thing excuses the batterer's conduct and relieves him of responsibility for his actions.

◈ OBSTACLES TO INTERVENTION

As I conducted the research for this book, I was surprised and dismayed to discover that findings of studies regarding obstacles to domestic violence intervention in the health care setting were almost identical to my own experiences in working with prosecutors, police officers, and other members of the criminal justice system. Given the very different missions of law enforcement and health care, I wondered how this could possibly be the case. I concluded that although the setting and semantics differed, the perceptions of battered women held by the various professions transcend professional boundaries.

Obstacles to domestic violence intervention are complex and often multidimensional. They may be on the personal, institutional, or societal level. In addition, the obstacles may operate on more than one level at the same time.

Personal obstacles include one's own values and beliefs, such as beliefs in societal myths about domestic violence. Institutional obstacles include system issues, such as the failure to allocate resources to intervention and the failure to provide training for health care providers. Finally, societal obstacles include community values and norms, such as the general myths and stereotypes about domestic violence.

Obstacles to domestic violence intervention in the health care setting are not unique. Although it is not possible to list every obstacle, those frequently discussed in recent literature are considered here.

Failure of medical professionals to recognize domestic violence is one of the first and foremost obstacles to domestic violence intervention in the health care setting. Although battered women are seen in virtually every health care setting, health care providers routinely fail to recognize domestic violence as the underlying cause of the patient's problem. The various failures to recognize and intervene appropriately are so distinct that Stark et al. (1981) described a three-stage medical-response "battering syndrome." In the first stage, the focus is on symptomatic treatment for the victim's traumatic injury and minor medical or mental health problems. In the second stage, the victim is "labeled" by the health care provider as "hysterical," "neurotic," or "hypochondriacal," or as a "well-known patient with multiple vague complaints," due to secondary psychosocial problems that result from the ongoing abuse, such as alcoholism, drug use, depression, attempted suicide, and perceived mental illness. By labeling the victim, the health care provider blames her for the problems stemming from the abuse. In the final stage, punitive interventions are used to deal with the secondary problems associated with chronic abuse. For example, a woman may be inappropriately prescribed tranquilizers or institutionalized. As a result of the inappropriate medical response, battered women make multiple medical and mental health care visits for health problems related to the battering, which goes unrecognized.

According to Flitcraft (1990), reasons for the failure of physicians to recognize domestic violence victims in their practice include a lack of routine questions to women patients about whether they are in violent relationships, concerns about possibly offending patients with questions about domestic violence, concerns about the effect on one's schedule of giving the problem the attention it needs, and frustration when the patient fails to handle the situation promptly. Flitcraft (1993) also pointed out that the individual physician determines only a small part of what takes place in the physician-patient encounter. The rest is molded by the "social and cultural context, the policies and resources of health care institutions, and the beliefs, values, and professional norms of the medical community" (p. 156). Flitcraft (1993) argued that one cannot expect considerable changes in the treatment of domestic violence victims by physicians without simultaneous changes in the other areas as well.

After conducting interviews of physicians in an urban HMO, Sugg and Inui (1992) found that physicians' barriers to recognition and intervention included lack of comfort, fear of offending, concerns about time constraints, feelings of powerlessness about the inability to fix the problem because of the complexity of the problem and their own lack of training, and lack of control over the patient's outcome. Further, physicians who identified with their patients socioeconomically were unlikely even to consider the possibility of abuse. Sugg and Inui also found that in a broad sense, physicians viewed domestic violence intervention as a process that could spiral out of control, likening it to "opening Pandora's box" or "opening a can of worms" (p. 3158).

A nationwide survey conducted by the Commonwealth Fund's Commission on Women's Health at Columbia University (1993) found that 92% of female domestic violence victims did not talk about the abuse with a physician. Further, physicians seldom identify domestic violence patients (Abbott et al., 1995).

Belief in the general societal myths about domestic violence can be a major obstacle to domestic violence intervention. Some health care professionals, as part of society at large, share these beliefs. Consider that even though the helping professions have focused on working with survivors of domestic violence since the 1970s, myth-filled rhetoric is still encountered today. Sheridan (1987) explained that many health care professionals continue to ask the traditional victim-blaming questions, such as "What did you do that made him want to hit you?" "Why did you provoke him when he was drinking?" and "Why do you stay with him?" (p. 14). According to the AMA's Council on Ethical and Judicial Affairs (1992b), physicians have a duty to be aware of the societal myths about domestic violence and to prevent these misconceptions from affecting the diagnosis and management of abuse.

Belief in the myths, as it relates to the health care provider's perception of the victim/patient, can influence whether she is offered intervention. Kurz (1987) conducted a participant observation study of the responses to battered women by emergency department staff in four metropolitan hospitals. She reviewed medical records, interviewed staff, and observed interactions between battered women and staff. Kurz found that emergency department staff were most likely to intervene when they viewed the patient as a "true victim"—someone who was polite, had no "discrediting attributes," and was perceived to be in imminent physical danger. Staff also felt sympathetic toward women who were taking action to leave the abusive relationship. Finally, women with pleasant personalities were viewed as legitimately deserving of staff time and attention.

Staff were less likely to intervene when patients were not responsive or were evasive as to the cause of their injuries. Interestingly, however, Kurz (1987) found that in 75% of these cases, women volunteered that they had been injured by a husband or boyfriend. In the other 25% of the cases, the cause of injury became known because of information provided by a relative or police officer. Kurz also found that staff were unlikely to intervene when the victim had a condition that complicated interaction with her, such as alcohol or drug use; when the victim acted "crazy"; when the victim was a "fighter"; or when staff believed they could not help her or produce results for her. Staff were totally nonresponsive when, in addition to the above reasons, they felt too busy. In addition, some staff did not view battering as a legitimate medical concern. Even volunteered information was ignored. Some staff members viewed domestic violence as a personal problem and thought that questions about it were an invasion of privacy. Also mentioned by staff were concerns about their personal legal responsibility and fears that the batterer would retaliate against them.

Bokunewicz and Copel (1992), in a study of emergency nurses' attitudes about domestic violence, found that belief in stereotypic views of battered women was common. Particularly common were the beliefs that the violence was attributable to mental illness, that the violence was a one-time incident, that the battered woman could simply leave, and that the battered woman was masochistic.

Just as belief in societal myths can be an obstacle to domestic violence intervention, one's personal values can also present an impediment to intervention. For example, beliefs about family autonomy and privacy can impede physicians' responses to domestic violence (Jecker, 1993). Traditionally, the home is regarded as sacrosanct. Hence, there is a great reluctance to do anything that is perceived as intruding into that domain. Sentiments such as "People shouldn't air their dirty laundry," "What happens behind closed doors is their business," and "They should stay together for the sake of the children" reflect commonly held beliefs. However, for a victim to escape abuse, she must often go against these beliefs, tell outsiders what has happened, and leave her abusive partner.

Allowing one's private values to affect professional behavior may prove detrimental to the patient (Bowker & Maurer, 1987). Suppose, for example, that a patient's husband has brutalized her for years and she has concluded that the only way to stop the violence is to leave him and file for divorce. What if the physician does not personally believe in divorce? Will that belief affect the advice that he or she may offer the patient?

Another obstacle to intervention is the belief that all battered women are unwilling to discuss the abuse. If the health care provider holds this belief, he or she may automatically decline to inquire about abuse with all such patients. Lack of inquiry may result in failure to gather information that may affect diagnosis and treatment.

Contrary to this belief, a clear majority of battered women are willing to discuss the abuse with their health care providers. According to Kurz (1990), 68% of battered women were neither reluctant nor evasive about disclosing the true cause of their injuries and responding to direct questions. Interestingly, however, emergency department staff nonetheless generally referred to all battered women as "evasive."

Certainly, some victim/patients are evasive with their health care providers, and this presents yet another obstacle to intervention. But there may be various reasons for such behavior. For example, a patient may have already had a negative experience with service providers such as health care professionals or persons in the justice system (Hilberman, 1980). After such an experience, the victim may be unlikely to see any point in disclosing the abuse because either it got her nowhere before, or, worse, it put her in jeopardy of retaliatory violence by the batterer.

Another reason for patient evasiveness might be that the victim finds herself in a position of having to disclose abuse to a man. Because the majority of physicians in the United States today are male, chances are that a victim will be seen by a male physician. A woman who has been victimized by her male partner may not feel safe disclosing the abuse to a male health care provider (Hilberman, 1980). This situation can be compounded if the health care provider is someone who is not of the patient's cultural or ethnic background (Klingbeil & Boyd, 1984). Of course, the demeanor of the physician and his apparent sensitivity to the issue can affect the patient's comfort level in discussing the abuse.

Health care providers may feel frustrated when a patient is evasive or when the provider takes the time to intervene and offer intervention options but the patient fails to use the resources offered. This sense of frustration can create an obstacle that discourages the professional from future intervention efforts with other patients.

In their study, Sugg and Inui (1992) noted that "many physicians were frustrated by their inability to control the patient's behavior, and the patient's inability to control the circumstances of their lives. This need to gain control and expeditiously solve the problem was one of the major obstacles to physicians' willingness to address domestic violence" (p. 3159).

Frustration is not limited to the perception of patient inaction alone. Rosenberg (1994) pointed out that physicians can become frustrated when the assistance they give a vulnerable patient is not helpful or is even harmful. For example, the failure of police to make an arrest following notification of an assault could be viewed as not helpful. Such inaction could become harmful if it leads to retaliatory violence by the batterer. Frustration from these experiences could lead to future inaction on the part of the health care provider for fear that other potential interveners will not respond appropriately.

The fact that health care providers and domestic violence victims may define differently what constitutes an emergency can also impede intervention. To the practitioner in an emergency department, "emergency" may only encompass immediate, life-threatening situations evident through examination, x-ray, or laboratory tests (Stark et al., 1981). However, abused women frequently turn to emergency care not only for help with their current physical injuries but also for help in stopping future violence. To an abused woman with a black eye sitting in the emergency department, the emergency may be her perception that if something does not happen soon to stop her abusive partner's behavior, he will eventually kill her. There is no examination or test that can confirm for the physician the actual risk of death the patient faces. Automatically dismissing less-than-life-threatening physical battering injuries as nonemergency impedes effective intervention.

Another obstacle is the difference between the expectation of the medical professional and that of the battered woman concerning the outcome of treatment. According to Bowker and Maurer (1987), although the doctor and nurse may focus on the physical injury, the victim's primary concern is ending the violence. This unfulfilled expectation leads to disappointment when extramedical services, such as referrals to social service, shelter, and counseling, are not provided.

Aside from personal obstacles that may affect the individual service provider, the institution of medicine plays a part in the actions and inactions of its members. According to Kurz and Stark (1988), the lack of appropriate and sensitive medical response includes the lack of technical knowledge about abuse, institutional sexism, and medical-model structural constraints that attribute male violence to biological, individual, or situational factors and treat domestic violence victims "by denying the abuse [occurred], discounting its clinical significance, or by locating its origin in the woman's behavior" (p. 263).

The way in which the medical profession is structured bears directly on the way in which it responds to patients who are victims of domestic violence. According to Warshaw (1992), the barriers to physician intervention include the status structure of medicine, the traditional male bias, and the strict hierarchical organization of medical training. Warshaw has suggested that the medical model, as taught and practiced, reinforces an objectification process in which the person is viewed as a mere patient who fits a certain medical or psychiatric diagnosis. It has been observed that the medical process itself mirrors the dynamics of an abusive relationship in that it sanctions hierarchies of domination and control. According to Warshaw, clinicians trained within this model may find it hard to provide the support that battered women need.

Other institutional obstacles can be attributed to policies and procedures. For example, HMO practitioners may have been instructed not to spend more than 15 minutes with each patient. It would be no wonder if a physician in such a practice was concerned about the effect of intervention on his or her time schedule. The lack of an institutional protocol for the detection and treatment of domestic violence victims is another obstacle to intervention (McLeer, Anwar, Herman, & Maquiling, 1989). In the absence of a protocol, everyone does things his or her own way, which, realistically, is probably nothing at all. According to a retrospective study of female trauma patients in a medical school emergency department, staff training and the use of a protocol to identify domestic violence injuries increased identification of such patients from 5.6% to 30% of all trauma patients. However, protocols have little meaning if use is not mandatory and compliance is not monitored. The study showed that when the emergency department stopped using the protocol and failed to have a system in place to monitor staff procedures and treatment, the identification rate dropped down to 7.7%. In short, the staff reverted to their old way of doing business: failure to diagnose a significant number of domestic violence victims (McLeer et al., 1989).

It has been suggested that the problem-oriented medical record's initial-note and progress-note formula SOAP (subjective, objective, assessment, and plan) is a barrier to intervention. Under the formula, what the patient relates about her condition is considered subjective; what the physician or laboratory states about the patient is considered objective (Donnelly, Hines, & Brauner, 1992).

In an effort to follow the SOAP format, clinicians encountering a domestic violence victim interpret a woman's objective statement about how the abuse occurred as subjective. This interpretation may account for those physician statements within medical records that I have routinely seen, such as "The patient claims . . ." or "The patient alleges that. . . ." Such statements discount the abuse to which the victim has been subjected. Labeling the patient's version of events as subjective may also account for physicians' wanting a third party or "neutral" information to corroborate a patient's disclosure of abuse before concluding that the abuse in fact occurred.

According to Donnelly et al. (1992), calling the patient's statement "subjective" but the physician's and laboratory's findings "objective" makes the patient's input suspect and gives undue weight to the input of the physician. SOAP also ignores that subjectivity enters into what the physician writes in the medical record and that a physician's work is interactive with the patient. To fix the problem with SOAP, these authors suggested a revised formula: history, observations, assessment, and plans, or "HOAP," pronounced "hope."

The structure of medical training may also present obstacles to intervention. Williamson, Beitman, and Katon (1981) faulted one-dimensional medical training, which views illness from a biomedical perspective, as creating certain beliefs that tend to perpetuate physician avoidance of the psychosocial aspects of patient care. On the basis of their observations while teaching third-year medical residents, they defined three categories of such beliefs. First are beliefs concerning the physician's role: a primary focus on the need to rule out organic disease, a failure to view psychosocial problems as "medical problems," a lack of time in the physician's schedule, and the physician's feeling that he or she will become overwhelmed and will burn out. Second are perceptions about what the patient does and does not want: the belief that discussing the psychosocial issues will be too painful for both physician and patient; that if the physician delves into this realm, the patient will never come back; that the patient will reject the physician's recommended treatment; and that the patient will become totally dependent on the physician. The final category is fears about approaching the patient as a person: beliefs that the patient's problem may be beyond the physician's competence; that it is too painful to deal with the emotions of others; and that a physician with the same problem will be unable to help the patient because the physician has not helped him- or herself.

Although avoidance of psychosocial issues may be a problem, focusing too much on issues that are obvious may distract from the underlying problem, chronic victimization. For example, Stark et al. (1979) conducted a study of medical records at a hospital in New Haven, Connecticut. They found that the staff overlooked battering and focused on psychosocial problems such as depression, substance abuse, and suicide attempts. The focus was the same even when the onset of sequelae occurred after victimization started.

Failure to look for a history of victimization can mask the true cause of the patient's problem. Without knowledge of the patient's history, the possibility of appropriate intervention is remote. Hamberger, Saunders, and Hovey (1992) studied domestic violence rates in a large, midwestern family-practice residency-training clinic by means of an anonymous questionnaire that asked women whether they had ever been physically assaulted by their partner. Of all the women who responded, 22.7% had been victims of domestic violence within the previous 12 months, and 38.8% had been victimized by a partner sometime during the relationship. Yet only 7.7% of the women who appeared for other than brief appointments were questioned about physical abuse, and only 1.7% of all patients were questioned by their physician. According to Hamberger et al., although current abuse may require crisis intervention, women who have a history of being abused may require treatment for the sequelae of abuse. They recommended training physicians to recognize and inquire about current and lifetime domestic violence victimization.

Lack of knowledge and training is another obstacle to recognizing and treating domestic violence victims. Consider that 50% of the physicians in a study by Sugg and Inui (1992) indicated frustration and feelings of inadequacy when discussing what would constitute appropriate interventions. Sixty-one percent of physicians disclosed that they had received no training whatsoever on intimate-partner violence in medical school, residency, or continuing medical education courses. Only 8% of the participants reported that they had received good training.

Although training is needed, a brief amount will not necessarily fix nonintervention problems. For example, Kurz (1990) conducted a study based on observation data at four hospital emergency departments in a large city. The study was conducted after staff at these emergency departments received some training that described how to identify battered women and how to discuss with a battered woman the intervention she might require. The staff were also instructed to give each such patient a card with telephone numbers for battered women's organizations. Following the training, four obstacles to intervention were identified. First, medical staff members who discovered domestic violence sometimes failed to pass along information to the next staff member who saw the same patient. Second, staff were unlikely to intervene in cases in which they considered the patient to have "discrediting attributes" such as alcohol or drug use, inappropriate behaviors, or reluctance to talk to staff about how they were injured. Third, some staff members moved on to work on other cases before making a determination that battering had occurred. In this regard, some staff felt they did not have enough time to spend with the patient. Others believed there was not much they could do for the battered woman. Finally, some staff did not view battering as a legitimate concern and failed to make a determination of battering. Some viewed it as a personal problem, one feared legal responsibility, and one feared retaliation by the batterer.

A limited range of intervention options also poses an obstacle (Stark et al., 1981). The health care provider may be limited because of a lack of knowledge about existing resources (including how to access them) or because such resources are deficient or nonexistent in the community.

◙ REASONS TO INTERVENE

Given all of the obstacles that can impede effective intervention efforts, why should health care providers even try? There are numerous arguments in favor of intervention.

1. It is good medicine.

Domestic violence intervention seeks to treat the actual cause of the problem, not just the symptoms or sequelae. Treating the patient without documenting that the cause is chronic victimization and without appropriate referrals to services is bad medicine (McLeer et al., 1989).

2. Intervention saves money over time.

One in five battered women seeking medical attention has sought medical treatment for abuse on 11 previous occasions (Feldman, 1992). Intervention helps the victim to avoid subsequent battering and nontrauma sequelae of abuse. A study conducted by the U.S. Department of Justice (1986) showed that once a woman is victimized by a partner, she is at substantial risk of repeat victimization. The study revealed that during the 6 months following an incident of domestic violence, approximately 32% of the victims, or 672,000 women, were victimized again. According to Stark and Flitcraft (1985), 75% of domestic violence victims who receive medical treatment are subjected to ongoing physical abuse.

3. It is the physician's ethical duty to diagnose and treat domestic violence.

Denying that abuse occurred, minimizing it, and blaming the victim further harm her and directly contradict the principles of beneficence and nonmalfeasance. According to the AMA's Council on Ethical and Judicial Affairs (1992c), physicians have an ethical duty to diagnose and treat family violence because of the principles of beneficence and malfeasance. *Beneficence* means doing good or doing the right thing for the patient. In the context of domestic violence, this means intervening to treat the true cause of injuries and sequelae, not just the symptoms. *Nonmalfeasance* means doing no harm. Failure to diagnose domestic violence can lead to ineffective and dangerous treatment. Examples include prescriptions for painkillers and sedatives for abuse victims who might be at risk for suicide and substance abuse. Treating the patient's injuries and symptoms without addressing the cause, violence in the home, is simply ineffective treatment (AMA, 1992b).

One writer has suggested that focusing on the ethical principles of beneficence and nonmalfeasance may not go far enough. According to Jecker (1993), the AMA council's analysis of physician's ethical duties should be expanded to include the ethical principle of justice. Justice is implicated because failure to intervene can further disempower and revictimize a victim while simultaneously maintaining the batterer's privilege and dominance.

4. Intervention saves lives.

Domestic violence is recurrent and tends to become more frequent and severe over time (Straus et al., 1980; Walker, 1979). Early intervention can help prevent traumatic injuries, related sequelae (including suicide), and homicide of the victim by the batterer or vice versa. It can also help prevent injury to third parties who may be injured coming to the victim's aid or those hurt in the cross fire, such as the children.

5. The lack of appropriate intervention may result in civil liability.

Battered women or their survivors may file civil lawsuits against health care providers alleging various causes of action—that is, theories of the case. One such theory could be negligence based on failure to diagnose. Note that the AMA has recognized that physicians may be held liable for failure to recognize abuse and respond to the patient's complaints (AMA, 1995b).

Consider the following illustration: A female patient presents herself for treatment in a hospital emergency department at 2:00 a.m. with signs of trauma. She has a broken nose, a black eye, and days-old black and blue marks on her back. She also has a half crescent-shaped scar on her shoulder that appears consistent with a human bite mark. When asked by medical staff what happened to her, she responds simply that she fell down some stairs. Staff are aware that the woman's husband is in the waiting room and seems overly solicitous.

No one questions her version of events. However, it is obvious that she could not have been injured in the manner she claims. Further, the approved professional practice, as it has now evolved, would be to ask her direct questions about abuse in her life. But this is not done. Her symptoms, traumatic injury consistent with blunt-force trauma inflicted by another person, are consistent with domestic battery. However, the cause of the injuries is not diagnosed as such. No one offers her information about domestic violence; no one offers her any support; no one offers her the option of referrals to an advocate, a shelter, or any legal or social services. No intervention is documented in her medical records. The staff members merely attend to the woman's wounds and send her on her way with her husband.

Three weeks later, the woman is maimed by her husband. Suit is filed against the medical facility and all staff involved on a theory of negligent treatment for failure to diagnose. The argument might go that the victim was battered and sought medical treatment; that the health care providers knew or should have known that the patient was a victim of domestic violence; that anyone who treats domestic violence victims should know that domestic violence is recurrent and tends to escalate over time; that the health care providers should have anticipated and foreseen that the patient would be battered again; that the health care providers owed the patient a duty to provide appropriate treatment; that appropriate treatment should have included identifying the cause of her injuries as chronic victimization due to domestic violence; and that appropriate treatment should have included intervention with referrals and safety planning.

Instead, the health care providers willfully disregarded the obvious. The true cause of the injuries was not diagnosed. No intervention was offered or provided. If intervention had been offered, the patient might not have returned to the batterer, might have begun to take steps to leave him, or at least would have known what to do when he began to attack her again.

As a result of the failure to diagnose and intervene, the patient was permanently crippled. She could argue that the damages she suffered included actual damages for the cost of medical treatment, pain and suffering, and loss of future productivity.

◈ WAYS TO FACILITATE INTERVENTION

Domestic violence cases require intervention that does not fit the biomedical model. One of the keys to fostering effective intervention efforts may simply be the recognition that domestic violence injuries stem from sociological causes. There is no quick fix, no prescription that will cure the problem immediately, and no "cookie cutter" answer that will work for every victim who walks through the door.

These cases are different from other kinds of cases. They are labor intensive in what seems to be a nonmedical way, they are emotionally draining, and the success of the intervention is not always immediately evident. It may take years for a victim to break away from the batterer and start a new life. Although somewhere down the road the patients you help may be grateful to you, in the short term, you may find this a thankless job. How then do you perform well and feel good about doing this difficult work? How do you motivate yourself and encourage others?

1. Change your expectation and definition of success.

Do not expect immediate results. The intervention you provide to the victim today will help her to become empowered and hopefully to escape future injuries. View a victim who has turned down help in the past as someone who is more likely to accept help from others now. If a battered woman with whom you have intervened returns to her abusive partner, it does not mean that the health care intervention has failed (Stark et al., 1981). Rather, it may mean that the victim believes her safety cannot be ensured today unless she goes back to him for the time being.

2. Look for the small victories.

A patient who is willing to talk about the abuse or to take a card with crisis resource information may be taking the first steps toward ending the violence in her life and the lives of her children. Remember that the help you provide is like a building block for the patient.

3. Expect the battered woman to be less than "the perfect patient."

She is human, and she has been victimized. You may see her when she is in crisis, is in denial, or has basically resigned herself to the belief that being abused is her lot in life. The effects of repeatedly having been battered may have taken a toll on her. Her self-esteem may be quite low, and she may have no sense of hope. Perhaps she lives in abject poverty and her life choices in the best of circumstances are quite limited.

4. Set realistic goals.

The violence in her life did not start overnight, and it is not likely to end overnight. It may take months or longer for the victim to leave her abuser or for other interventions to take place and produce results. Detection and diagnosis of battering are the beginning of treatment, not the cure (Klingbeil & Boyd, 1984).

5. Create treatment teams in hospitals, clinics, and practices.

The team might consist of a physician, a nurse, and a social worker or other professional trained in family violence interventions (Bowker & Maurer, 1987). The team approach spreads the work around and allows specialization. A team approach also fosters a sense of camaraderie, helps reduce burnout, and adds efficiency to the process. For example, social history can be gathered by one member of the team while the medical examination and treatment are being rendered by others (Klingbeil & Boyd, 1984). This approach, if properly conducted, leads to an efficient use of resources.

6. *To ease time constraints, delegate tasks to other health professionals.*

Delegation can be implemented in conjunction with a team approach or, if a team is not feasible, by itself. According to McLeer and Anwar (1987), it is the responsibility of the physician to see to the patient's quality of care. This responsibility includes obtaining an adequate trauma history; making a determination of the battered woman's medical and emotional status; determining the risk of future harm to her and to her children, which may include the need for emergency shelter and legal information; developing a follow-up plan that includes safety planning; and documenting findings and recommendations in the medical records. However, the physician need not personally perform all of these tasks.

Regardless of who carries out the delegated tasks, it is important that the health care provider acknowledge the abuse and convey a supportive attitude to the patient. Let the patient know that you believe what she is telling you, you support her, you are on her side, and you are there to help her. Male health care providers should be careful not to trigger accidentally fears of violence and domination in the patient by invading the patient's personal space, shaking their finger in her face to make a point, or raising their voice for emphasis (Koss et al., 1994). A more detailed interview and follow-up can be conducted by a nurse, social worker, volunteer (McLeer & Anwar, 1987), or physician's assistant. The person conducting the detailed interview and intervention should be trained in crisis intervention and domestic violence advocacy. This person should also be familiar with state reporting requirements, the legal options of family members, and community services and entitlements.

7. *Provide a means for health care staff to deal with their own issues in working on these cases.*

Staff members may have experienced violence and abuse in their own lives as children or as adults. They may find themselves reliving their own traumatic experiences while hearing about the experiences of others. This may affect their ability to help others. In addition, recognizing the abusive dynamics in health care education, training, and treatment settings can help health care providers recognize abuse in patients (Feldman, 1992).

8. Streamline and standardize intervention.

A uniform approach to domestic violence intervention allows all personnel involved to know what is expected of them. It also provides for a consistent quality of service to patients regardless of the particular staff members working on a given day. One option is to create a standardized domestic violence intake form that suggests referral options. Staff may be receptive to using such a device. In Kurz's (1990) study, staff felt that completing an approved form and making a referral were simple tasks and not too time consuming.

9. Provide training, and make attendance mandatory.

An educational program, which includes periodic in-service programs, can alter stereotypical attitudes about domestic violence held by staff. Such training can also increase health care providers' confidence in intervention (Bokunewicz & Copel, 1992). If training is not provided for you, seek out training on your own. Alternatively, read literature on the subject. Knowledge will help you feel more competent to help others.

10. Create a mandatory protocol and monitor compliance.

Lack of protocol justifies inaction. Without a protocol, no one knows what is considered appropriate or what he or she is expected to do. Without compliance monitoring, people tend to deviate from the protocol as they see fit. Everyone does his or her own thing, which may be nothing at all.

11. Participate in coordinated community organizations designed to address domestic violence in a systemic manner.

If your community lacks meaningful social service referrals, work institutionally or individually to improve them. Even if there are good service provider options available, the medical community should network with representatives of such organizations to ease and expedite patient referrals. Many cities have begun to develop domestic violence coordinating councils to improve the overall system response to domestic violence. Health care plays a vital role in such a mission and should be well represented in community efforts.

◙ NOTES

1. From "Battered Wives: Help for the Secret Victim Next Door," August 1976, *Ms. Magazine.* Reprinted by permission of Ms. Magazine, © 1976.

2. From "Spousal Abuse a Thorny Issue for Churches: Catholics' Condemnation Highlights Approaches to Dealing With Problem," by T. Weber, November 5, 1992, *Orange County Register,* p. A-1. Copyright 1992 by the Orange County Register. Reprinted with permission.

3. From "Victim 'Stunned' by N.H. Judge: Comments, Sentence in Domestic Violence Assault Prompt Outrage," by L. A. Kiernan, June 5, 1993, *The Boston Globe,* p. 1. Copyright 1993 by The Boston Globe. Reprinted courtesy of the Boston Globe.

4. "Mercy for a Cuckolded Killer: Women Outraged Over Judge's Light Sentence," by M. Rosenfeld, October 28, 1994, *The Washington Post,* p. C-1. © 1994, The Washington Post. Reprinted with permission.

5. "Spousal Abuse Earns Slap on the Wrist; Judge Says Real Crime Was the Adulterous Wife," January 18, 1996, *Detroit News,* p. A-1. Copyright 1996 by the Associated Press. Reprinted with permission.

3

THE DYNAMICS
OF ABUSE

◆ CHARACTERISTICS OF
THE ABUSIVE RELATIONSHIP

An abusive relationship is one that is primarily characterized by power and control. The abusive partner seems to have all of the power and seeks to exercise control over his partner. Areas over which the abusive partner may seek to control his mate may include many aspects of life: economic decisions and access to the family's financial resources, the pursuit of educational advancement, spending time with friends and relatives, decisions regarding one's leisure time, wearing the type of clothing one chooses, and developing and maintaining one's sense of self-esteem.

In an abusive dynamic, the abusive partner may use several types of coercion to force the victim to behave as he wishes: both to do things he wants her to do and not to do things he wants her to refrain from doing. The types of abuse are not always obvious; indeed, some tactics may be quite subtle. For example, suppose the abuser wants to control all of the family finances. He knows that if his partner lacks access to the bank accounts, she will have to come to him for every purchase or financial decision. Further, without access to money, there is little chance that his partner can leave him no matter how badly he treats her.

The abuser will not tell his partner that he wants her to have her paycheck regularly deposited into his bank account so that he can control all of her money

46

and leave her with no freedom, thereby leaving her helpless without him. This approach, though quite honest, would never work. Abusers are manipulators, and they use the tools that orchestrate the results they want to achieve.

The abuser will wait for the opportunity to make it seem as if he is looking out for the victim's or the couple's best interests. He may wait until she bounces a check. Countless adults have, at one time or another, mismanaged their check ledger and bounced a check. Assuming that one is not knowingly writing bad checks, bouncing a check is nothing more than an innocent mistake, easily remedied.

However, her mistake gives the abuser his opportunity. He may humiliate her by telling her that she is incompetent and stupid—that she cannot even keep a simple bank account straight. He may tell her that thanks to her, the couple's finances will be destroyed and that they will not be able to obtain goals for which they have planned, such as buying a new house. He may take the opportunity to humiliate her in front of friends or family by commenting about the bounced check.

Once she feels utterly terrible and degraded, he will move in for the kill. He may tell her that even though she is incompetent and worthless, he is still willing to help her out. He will graciously offer that if she gives him all of her bank records, he will redo her accounting and straighten out the account. At this point, he may suggest that she have her paychecks deposited directly into his account or into a joint account. Of course, in either event, only he will have access to the checkbook. Every week he will give her all the money she needs—*an allowance.* If she needs more money, *all she has to do is come to him and ask.* He will even offer to pay all of the bills.

Sounds like a good idea, right? After all, she cannot seem to keep her account balanced. She does not want to destroy their credit. That new house is a dream they have both had for a long time. Besides, now she will not have the headache of having to write all the checks for the bills. The problem is that the abuser's motivation is not to help her; it is to control her. Keeping her dependent gives him control.

An abusive relationship does not start out with violence. It begins with Prince Charming riding over the hill to rescue the waiting princess from her life of drudgery. He may be handsome and charming. He may be the first man in her life to compliment her repeatedly. He may shower her with attention. Her interests may "coincidentally" be the exact things he has been interested in for years but has never had the time to pursue. He may quickly fall in love with her and not be able to bear being apart from her, not even while she goes to the grocery store. He may tell her things such as "You are the only woman who has ever really understood me" and "My life was so empty before I found you."

He will not tell her that he wants to isolate her from friends. He will tell her that her friends are snobs who treat him badly. He will say that it is obvious they do not want him to be with her. Besides, they are *her* friends, not his friends. If she really loved him, he will add, she would not want to be with them.

He will not tell her that he wants to isolate her from her family. He will tell her that her parents constantly try to drive a wedge between them. He will claim that they are always making him feel as if he is not good enough for her. If she really loved him, he will add, she would not want to be around them so much. He may throw a tantrum the night before a family gathering or treat her so badly afterwards that soon spending time with her family is not worth the consequences she will have to endure.

All families have conflict. However, not all families are violent. In some families, conflict is resolved by discussion or argument (Straus et al., 1980) without punching, hitting, or other violence. According to Browne (1987), aggression that is used as the primary method of response to everyday situations is a damaging pattern that tends to get more frequent and severe over time.

According to Browne (1987), a cycle occurs when the perpetrator becomes desensitized over time and needs to justify his violence by degrading the victim. The denigration can lead to more violence as the perpetrator perceives that the victim "deserves" the abusive treatment. Browne theorized that when a victim complies with an abusive partner's demands or shows pain, his aggression is reinforced. Therefore, the victim may actually reinforce the pattern of victimization. Victims eventually stop responding as dramatically to abuse. This failure to respond as before adds to the abuser's aggression because he tries to attain the previous degree of impact. Finally, although people may think of domestic violence as repeated instances of physical abuse, one-time physical violence can change the power balance in the relationship and leave the victim in fear of future violence (Browne, 1993).

Power and Control

The Domestic Abuse Intervention Project of Duluth, Minnesota, created two different diagrams in the shape of wheels to explain violent relationships based on "Power and Control" versus nonviolent relationships based on "Equality" (see Figures 3.1 and 3.2).

As the Power and Control Wheel illustrates, the tools of power and control include not only physical and sexual violence but the use of intimidation; emotional abuse; isolation tactics; minimizing, denying, and blaming; the children; male privilege; economic abuse; and coercion and threats. In sharp

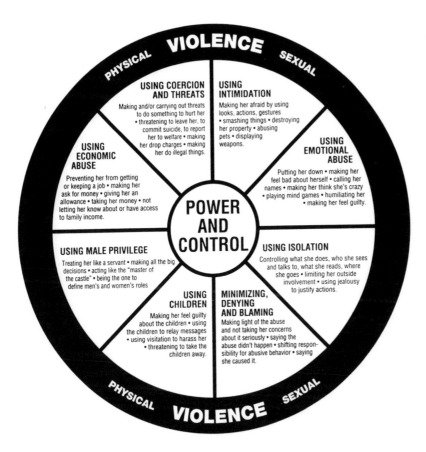

Figure 3.1. "Power and Control" Wheel Describing Violent Relationships

SOURCE: From *Power and Control: Tactics of Men Who Batter,* by E. Pence and M. Paymar, 1986, Duluth, MN: Domestic Abuse Intervention Project. Copyright 1986 by Minnesota Program Development, Inc. Reprinted with permission.

contrast, equality is characterized by nonviolence and by nonthreatening behavior; respect; trust and support; honesty and accountability; responsible parenting; shared responsibility; economic partnership; and negotiation and fairness.

Victim and Batterer Characteristics

Do victims or batterers have any common characteristics? Some of those who have studied domestic violence believe that they do. Some readers may disagree with the items listed. However, it is important to consider such charac-

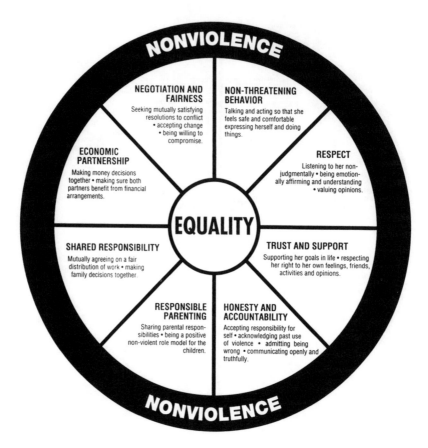

Figure 3.2. "Equality Wheel" Describing Nonviolent Relationships

SOURCE: From *Power and Control: Tactics of Men Who Batter*, by E. Pence and M. Paymar, 1986, Duluth, MN: Domestic Abuse Intervention Project. Copyright 1986 by Minnesota Program Development, Inc. Reprinted with permission.

teristics for a clearer, more meaningful understanding of the dynamics that may occur in the context of abuse.

In her study, Walker (1979) identified nine common characteristics of women who had been battered. According to Walker, a battered woman commonly

1. Had low self-esteem and a related underestimation of her ability to do anything
2. Believed all of the myths about battering relationships
3. Was a traditionalist about her role in the home, viewed the man as the head of the family, and strongly believed in family unity and the prescribed feminine

sex-role stereotype in which she was taught to believe that she was incapable of taking care of herself and had to be dependent upon a man

4. Believed that she could keep the batterer from becoming angry and accepted responsibility for the batterer's actions
5. Suffered from guilt but denied the terror and anger she felt
6. Presented a passive face to the world but had the strength to manipulate her environment enough to prevent further violence and being killed
7. Had severe stress reactions with psychophysiological complaints
8. Used sex as a way to establish intimacy
9. Believed that no one would be able to help her resolve her predicament but herself[1]

Boyd and Klingbeil (1993) identified 21 common characteristics of domestic violence victims. They found that a domestic violence victim

1. Had long-suffering, martyr-like endurance of frustration, passively accepted the batterer's behaviors, and internalized anger
2. Displayed stress disorders and psychosomatic complaints, sadness, and depression
3. Had economic and emotional dependency and was at high risk for secret drug and alcohol use and "home accidents"
4. Had unlimited patience for discovery of a "magic combination" to solve marital and abusive problems and would "travel miles" on tiny bits of reinforcement
5. Was unsure of her own ego needs and defined herself in terms of partner, children, family, job, and other external components
6. Had low self-esteem and continued faith and hope that her battering partner would get a "lucky" break
7. Had an unrealistic hope that change was imminent and believed in "promises"
8. Experienced gradually increasing social isolation, including loss of contact with immediate family and friends
9. Experienced an inability to convince her partner of her loyalty, futilely guarded against accusations of "seductive" behavior toward others, and was often compliant, helpless, and powerless
10. Experienced constant fear and terror (even when danger was not imminent), which gradually became cumulative and oppressive, and experienced hypervigilance
11. Helplessly "allowed" containment or confinement/restriction by her partner and usually misinterpreted it as a sign that her partner "cared"
12. Gradually lost sight of personal boundaries for herself and her children, was unable to assess danger accurately, and accepted all of the blame
13. Believed that transient acceptance of her partner's violent behavior would ultimately lead to a long-term resolution of family problems and believed "If only . . ."

14. Accepted guilt for her partner's behavior, thought her partner "couldn't help it," considered her own behavior provocative, and blamed herself

15. Had a generational history of witnessing abuse in her family and may have also been abused

16. Participated in "pecking-order" battering

17. Learned which behavioral events would either divert or precipitate partner's violence, but her level of carelessness increased, and her judgment of lethality potential deteriorated over time

18. Had a poor sexual self-image and assumed that her role was to accept totally her partner's sexual behavior, and her attempts to punish partner with abstinence resulted in further abuse

19. Was at high risk for assault and other abuse during pregnancy

20. Frequently contemplated suicide, had a history of minor attempts, and occasionally completed suicide; frequently wished that her partner was dead and occasionally completed homicide in self-defense

21. Was powerless in child custody issues, lived in terror that children would be "kidnapped," struggled to maintain rights of children and self, and might use an "underground" to escape[2]

According to studies, batterers also exhibit commonalities. Walker (1979) identified nine common characteristics of batterers. She found that the abusive man commonly

1. Had low self-esteem

2. Believed all of the myths about battering relationships

3. Was a traditionalist believing in male supremacy and the stereotyped masculine sex role in the family, and many, as children, witnessed their father beat their mother or were themselves beaten

4. Blamed others for his actions

5. Was pathologically jealous

6. Presented a dual personality

7. Had severe stress reactions, during which he used drinking and wife-beating to cope

8. Frequently used sex as an act of aggression to enhance self-esteem in view of waning virility, and may have been bi-sexual

9. Did not believe that his violent behavior should have negative consequences[3]

Boyd and Klingbeil (1993) also identified 21 common characteristics of batterers. They found that a batterer

1. Had poor impulse control, a limited tolerance for frustration, and an explosive and unpredictable temper; flew into rages; and constantly demonstrated but often successfully masked his anger
2. Displayed stress disorders and psychosomatic complaints, and his success at masking dysfunction varied with his level of social and educational sophistication
3. Was emotionally dependent and subject to secret depressions known only to his family
4. Had a limited capacity for delayed reinforcement and was very "now" oriented
5. Had insatiable ego needs and displayed a quality of childlike narcissism that was not generally detectable to those outside the family group
6. Had low self-esteem, perceived unachieved ideals and goals for himself, and was disappointed in his career, even if he was successful by other people's standards
7. Had qualities that suggested a great potential for change and improvement (i.e., frequent "promises" for the future)
8. Perceived himself as having poor social skills, described his relationship with his partner as the closest he had ever known, and remained in contact with his own family
9. Was excessively jealous, frequently accused his partner of infidelity, voiced great fear of being abandoned or "cheated on," and engaged in controlling, hovering, and harassing behaviors
10. Was fearful that his partner and/or children would abandon him and was afraid of being alone
11. Contained/confined his partner and employed espionage tactics against her (e.g., checked mileage and timed errands), with his cleverness depending on his level of sophistication
12. Violated others' personal boundaries and rejected responsibility for marital, familial, or occupational failures or for his violent acts
13. Believed that his coercive behavior was aimed at securing the family nucleus "for the good of the family"
14. Lacked guilt or remorse on an emotional level even after an intellectual recognition
15. Had a generational history of abuse
16. Frequently participated in "pecking-order" battering
17. Had assaultive skills that improved with age and experience and were accompanied by a rise in danger potential and lethality risks to family members over time
18. Was demanding and often assaultive in sexual activities, sometimes punished his partner with abstinence, sometimes experienced impotence, and may have sexually abused children, relatives, and strangers
19. Had increased assaultive behavior when his partner was pregnant, with pregnancy often marking the first assault

20. Exerted control over his partner by threatening homicide and/or suicide, often attempted one or both when his partner separated from him, and was known to complete either or both

21. Frequently used the children as "pawns," exerted power and control through custody issues, and might have kidnapped or held the children hostage[4]

◆ THEORIES THAT EXPLAIN WHY A VICTIM MIGHT STAY WITH AN ABUSIVE PARTNER

It is often difficult for outsiders to understand why domestic violence victims act certain ways: why, for example, the victim denies or minimizes the abuse, blames herself for a beating, fails to call the police to report the beating she has endured, fails to leave her abusive partner, or, having left him, soon returns to him. In working with victims, it is important to recognize that there are no pat answers to explain the responses of victims as a class. Victims may experience a wide range of emotions in response to victimization, which include anger, sadness, grief (Dutton, 1992), and denial. Each victim is different, and she brings to the moment of crisis a life time of her own experiences that may affect her reaction and response to violence.

Many victims do leave abusive partners. Numerous issues may affect a victim's decision to leave. For example, how long has she been in the abusive relationship? How many times has she been battered? Have the battering incidents been pushes and slaps or life-threatening assaults? How severe does the victim perceive the violence to be? Did she, as a child, witness her father beating her mother? Was she sexually or physically abused as a child? What are her beliefs about the roles of husband and wife or about divorce? Has she previously separated from him? Does she abuse alcohol or use drugs? Does she have children with the batterer? Are the children also being physically or sexually victimized? Does she have financial resources, family or friends to whom she can turn for help, or other avenues of assistance? Does she have anywhere else to stay? Has she experienced secondary victimization in the past—when, for example, she called the police but was greeted with hostility and disbelief? Does she still love her abusive partner? Has he threatened her that if she ever tries to leave, he will take the children or harm them? Has he threatened her that if she ever leaves him, he will hunt her down and kill her?

The list above is by no means a complete inventory of the diversity of experiences and life factors that affect the victim's decision-making processes. However, even with these limited examples, it is clear that numerous factors can affect a victim's perception of her reality, the possibility of escape, and the likelihood of survival away from the abusive partner.

Tolerance for any bad situation is a question of context. For example, some women have put up with the abuse of sexual harassment in the workplace for many years. Why does a woman not quit her job the first time her boss makes an inappropriate comment, sexual innuendo, or proposition? Maybe she has worked there for years. Maybe she depends on her job to put food on the table for her family. Maybe it might not be so easy to find another job. If she did quit, there is no guarantee that a new boss would behave any differently than her current one. Is this not just what women have to put up with at work? Maybe he did not mean it, and it was just the way she took his comments, but how else would one have taken them? Maybe he was just kidding, even though she did not think it was funny. Besides, if she complained, who would believe her? It would be her word against his, and he could be a respected long-term employee, perhaps even a married man.

Women put up with abuse at work every day and stay in those jobs. Ordinarily, there is much less connection to and investment in a job than in a husband or live-in partner. Is it any wonder women stay with abusive partners? Is it not more surprising when someone finds the wherewithal to leave?

No studies conclusively identify the factors that cause a victim to decide to leave an abusive partner. Unfortunately, due to the difficulties in studying family violence, research in this area has a number of problems. According to Strube (1988), problems include the selective nature of study samples (e.g., victims who sought shelter for battered women), the retrospective nature of the studies, the over-reliance on self-reported data, and the lack of consistency regarding the type of variables examined that are related to relationship status. Nonetheless, a number of theories have been developed.

The Cycle of Violence

Walker (1987) coined the phrase "the cycle of violence" to describe a three-part cycle in battering relationships that may explain the reason some women stay with their abusive partners. The cycle consists of a tension-building phase; an acute phase, which may include a battering incident; and a tranquil, loving, nonviolent phase. During the tension-building phase, minor violence, such as slaps and pushes, may occur; the batterer may also use verbal putdowns and blaming. During this phase, the woman may attempt to placate the batterer by doing things his way or simply by trying to stay out of his way. The second phase, the acute phase, is the violent outburst. During this phase, the batterer may destroy property and brutally attack and injure the woman. The attacks may be physical and/or sexual. The batterer may use a weapon against the woman. During the third and final "tranquil" phase, the batterer may express remorse and shower the victim with gifts. He may beg forgiveness and promise not to be violent in the future. Walker described the third phase as the illusion of bliss because the woman may convince herself that the batterer means what he says and will change his violent ways. As time goes by, the cycle may become more frequent, with less time between each phase. The violence may also become more severe.

There is no set time between the phases in the cycle. A victim who is experiencing the tension-building phase does not know exactly when the batterer may attack her or what he may do to her. Many victims describe a feeling of constantly holding their breath or "walking on eggshells" during this time. It is not uncommon to hear stories from battered women that while the tension was mounting, they intentionally provoked the batterer to escalate his conduct, thereby speeding up the next phase and getting the violence over with (Dutton & Painter, 1981).

The March of Dimes Birth Defects Foundation has illustrated the cycle of violence through the depiction of a coming rainstorm (Phase 1, the tension-building phase), followed by rain and thunder (Phase 2, the acute phase) and then emerging sunshine (Phase 3, the tranquil or calm phase) (see Figure 3.3).

Although an acute battering incident may land a victim in a hospital emergency department, a woman may seek clinical care during the other phases of the cycle as well. Hilberman (1980) pointed out that a woman is more likely to see her clinician toward the end of the tension-building phase or during the end of the tranquil or "honeymoon" phase. Hilberman cautioned that without understanding where the victim is in the cycle of violence, the health care provider may view the woman as a masochist. This is because a woman in the honeymoon phase of the cycle, who is being treated well by her partner, may appear to be unconcerned about the violence and because a woman in the tension-building phase, who is under severe anticipatory anxiety and who provokes the batterer to bring about the inevitable assault, may appear gratified by the violence.

Traumatic Bonding and
Intermittent Reinforcement

Dutton and Painter (1981) theorized that a bonding, which they referred to as "traumatic bonding," occurs in relationships involving domestic violence.

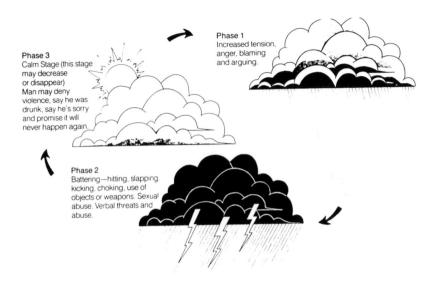

Phase 3
Calm Stage (this stage
may decrease
or disappear)
Man may deny
violence, say he was
drunk, say he's sorry
and promise it will
never happen again.

Phase 1
Increased tension,
anger, blaming
and arguing.

Phase 2
Battering—hitting, slapping,
kicking, choking, use of
objects or weapons. Sexual
abuse. Verbal threats and
abuse.

Figure 3.3. The Cycle of Violence
SOURCE: From Helton, A.: *A Protocol of Care for the Battered Woman.* White Plains, NY: March of
Dimes Birth Defects Foundation, 1987, p. 8. Reproduced with permission of the copyright holder.

This bonding is similar to what occurs in other relationships such as hostage/
captor, abused child/abusive parent, cult member/leader, and prisoner/guard.
Dutton and Painter defined traumatic bonding as the formation of strong emotional
ties between two individuals, one of whom, the abusive person, intermittently
harasses, beats, threatens, abuses, or intimidates the other, the victim.

There are two common primary characteristics of the social structure in each
such relationship. First, there is a power imbalance in the relationship that causes
the victim to perceive him- or herself as dominated by the abuser. Second, the
abuse is not continuous but, rather, is intermittent (Dutton & Painter, 1981).

When the violence and other abuses are not occurring in such a relationship,
there can be seemingly normal times. In fact, battered women often focus on
what they perceive to be "the good times" in the relationship. For example, a
victim who had been severely and repeatedly beaten and abused during her
20-year marriage tried to explain to me that her husband really was not so bad.
She added, "When he isn't drinking or using drugs, when he doesn't get
frustrated about money, and when I don't make him angry, he's really a nice guy.
Besides, he never hit me when I was pregnant." This women had separated from
and returned to her abusive partner many times during their marriage.

Walker's cycle-of-violence theory fits well with the concept of intermittent abuse and traumatic bonding. After the acute battering incident, the violence and abuse may cease, and the batterer may be apologetic and remorseful and make promises to change his ways. He may be kind and gentle, the way he was when the woman first met him. His seemingly improved behavior may cause the victim to hope that his promises of nonviolence are meaningful. She may bond to the affectionate side of her abuser's personality that meets her healthy need to be loved and cared for (Caplan, 1985). She may stay with him or return to him, holding fast to the belief that he will change.

The Stockholm Syndrome

Graham et al. (1988) likened the situation of battered women to the Stockholm syndrome, a theoretical construct of traumatic bonding. The syndrome was named after a 1973 bank robbery in Stockholm, Sweden. During the crime, bank tellers were taken hostage by the robbers and held for 6 days. The captors intermittently treated their hostages very badly and quite well. The hostages displayed an aversion toward outsiders who tried to help them. They had identified completely with their captors. After the hostage situation was neutralized, some of the hostages had so bonded with their captors that some visited their captors in jail, and one woman became engaged to one of the perpetrators (Gentry, 1991).

Graham et al. (1988) suggested that some of the psychological reactions of battered women may be best explained as a result of their experience of being trapped in situations similar to those of hostages. They suggested that within the context of the Stockholm syndrome, the battered woman's behavior, including depression, may be seen as a normal adaptive survival mechanism.

Both hostages and battered women feel fear as well as love, compassion, and empathy toward a captor who has shown them any kindness. In the hostage situation, following the violent taking or kidnapping, the victim feels frightened and vulnerable. Any kindness the captors show the hostages eases the emotional pain the captors themselves have created. Graham et al. (1988) noted that in Walker's cycle-of-violence theory, following the battering phase, the woman may not only be in physical pain but also feel helpless and needy. The batterer is the most readily available person to provide comfort and support. The battered woman thereby learns to depend on the batterer to ease the emotional pain that he himself has created. Considering the context of isolation in which most battered women find themselves, the greatest source of the battered woman's pain, in effect, becomes the sole source of her comfort.

According to Graham (quoted in Gentry, 1991, p. A-1), the Stockholm syndrome is characterized by four conditions. First, people believe that their survival is threatened. Second, they are shown some small kindness by the person terrorizing them. Third, they are isolated from any views other than those of their captor. Fourth, they believe that they have no escape.[5]

Among battered women, signs that the Stockholm syndrome has developed include that the victim "is grateful for any act of kindness shown to her, denies the abuse, is hypervigilant to the abuser's needs, is suspicious of people trying to help her, finds it difficult to leave the abuser, and fears the abuser will come back to get her if she leaves."[6]

Learned Helplessness

During the 1960s, experimental psychologists Seligman, Maier, and Geer experimented on hundreds of dogs (Seligman, 1975) and developed the theory of learned helplessness (Seligman, Maier, & Geer, 1968). In the experiments, electric shock tests were performed on two sets of dogs, referred to as the "naive dogs" and the "pretreated dogs." The naive dogs were put in a cage with a shoulder-high barrier that, if the dog jumped over, would cause the shock to cease. Shock pads were hooked to the dogs' rear paws. The cages were dimly lit. Each had a solid surface on which the dog could stand and a small window that the experimenter could open to view the dog. When initially shocked, the naive dogs ran around, howled, and defecated until they discovered that they could avoid the shock by jumping over the barrier. On repeated tests, the naive dogs became more efficient at avoiding the shock by jumping over the barrier more quickly. The other group of dogs, referred to as the pretreated dogs, were so named because before they were subjected to the experiments, they were strapped into hammock-like harnesses from which their legs essentially dangled and were given inescapable shock at unpredictable intervals for a period of 24 hours.

According to Seligman et al. (1968), when the pretreated dogs were tested under the same conditions as the naive dogs, they initially ran but soon stopped running and remained silent until the shock terminated. In sharp contrast to the naive dogs, the pretreated dogs did not cross the barrier but rather seemed to give up and accept the shock. They repeatedly endured 50 seconds of severe pulsating shock.

After the initial tests, the pretreated dogs were taught to escape the shock by shuttling over the barrier. The test was then readministered. All but one of the four pretreated dogs failed to escape the shocks, even when the barrier between the shock area and the safe area was removed.

From these experiments, it was theorized that learned helplessness occurred when the dogs learned that the end of the shock had nothing to do with their response (Seligman & Meier, 1967). The experimenters speculated that in humans, "maladaptive passive behavior in the face of trauma" or exposure to traumatic events in situations in which the individual cannot eliminate or mitigate the trauma results in passive responding to future aversive events (Seligman et al., 1968).

In 1978, the learned helplessness theory was criticized and reformulated (Abramson, Seligman, & Teasdale, 1978). The reformulation was based on attribution theory and was intended to correct two defects of the earlier theory. First, the original theory failed to take into account that there are some situations no one can control (helplessness is "universal") and other situations in which some people can exercise control (helplessness is "personal"). Second, the original theory did not distinguish between general and specific, or chronic and acute, helplessness.

Walker (1979) applied the original learned helplessness theory to the situation of battered women as a theoretical construct deduced from her interviews with battered women (p. xvi). According to Walker, repeated batterings, like electrical shocks, cause a decrease in the victim's motivation to respond. The woman becomes passive, does not believe that her response will benefit her, believes that she has no power to alter the outcome of the situation, and becomes more prone to depression and anxiety.

Although a battered woman's behavior in staying with her abusive partner may be a sign of "helplessness," it may be something else entirely. As noted by Browne (1993), staying with an abusive partner may be a realistic evaluation of the batterer's potential for violent retaliation and the victim's perception of the inability of others to guarantee her safety should she attempt to leave. What appears to be passive and compliant behavior may be the victim's way of reducing her immediate danger (AMA, 1995a).

In seeming contradiction to the learned helplessness theory, not all battered women are passive when responding to violence. They employ a variety of alternatives to survive or to minimize abuse. For example, they call the police, they try to avoid behaviors they perceive to be triggers for their partner's violent behavior, they try to stay away from places in the house where weapons are kept, they apply for civil protection orders, and they often fight back to try to stop an attack and protect themselves. In fact, some victims kill in situations in which death of the batterer may appear to be the only option to stop the violence (Dutton, 1992).

In my own experiences with battered women, I have observed that it is often at the time a woman comes to the realization that nothing she can do will make her abuser stop his violent behavior that she leaves him or tries to escape from him as a means of stopping the violence.

Psychological Entrapment

According to this theory, the victim gets caught up in the process of trying to make the abusive relationship work. She continues to try in order to justify her previous efforts (Strube, 1988). Giving up would mean that she was a failure and that all of her efforts were for naught.

Reasoned Decision Making

A victim's decision to leave or to stay may simply be based on rational decision making. For some women, there may be no realistic alternative to living with their partner, no matter how badly they are treated. A woman may have no money, no job, and no life choices. For example, she may believe that it would be more traumatic for their children to be uprooted and face an uncertain future than for her to endure her partner's abuse. In essence, she weighs the pros and cons and makes a rational decision. Issues may include economic variables, religious beliefs (Fortune, 1987; Pope-Lance & Chamberlain-Engelsman, 1990), family pressure and/or support, evaluation of the future risk of harm from the abusive partner to her and to her children, and the responsiveness of social services or other potential interveners, such as the police or the courts.

On the basis of a survey of family violence literature, Strube (1988) noted that a woman was more likely to stay with an abusive partner than to leave him when she lacked economic means; was willing to put up with the abuse as long as the children were not also being abused and/or the violence did not become too severe; and was very committed to making the relationship last.

Change Is a Process

Brown (in press) used the "transtheoretical model" of behavioral change to explain how domestic violence victims work to overcome abuse. The model, originally refined in the context of smoking-cessation research, has been applied to numerous other kinds of behavioral change. The transtheoretical model assumes that changing one's behavior is a dynamic process that advances through stages. The central constructs of the model are *stages of change* (readiness to make change), *processes of change* (experiential or behavioral techniques used to bring about change), *decisional balance* (weighing the pros and cons), and *self-efficacy* (measured by temptations that may lead to relapse). The model assumes that there are measurable cognitive and emotional aspects to change.

According to Brown (in press), leaving the batterer is a slow and incremental process that encompasses various stages of change in the victim's life. During the process of change, a victim may leave and return to an abusive partner a number of times before ending the relationship. This is viewed as a normal part of the process. Brown noted that even while still involved with the batterer, victims can make extremely important change in their lives. When a victim remains with a batterer, it does not mean that intervention has been ineffective or that the victim is not taking action. Rather, cognitive and behavioral changes occur in the victim that cause her to view her situation and herself differently. These changes prepare the victim to take action in ending the abuse. Brown pointed out that considering the context in which the abuse occurs, a better question than "Why doesn't she just leave?" is "How does she go about making changes in her life to free herself from violence and abuse?"

◈ SECONDARY OUTCOMES OF DOMESTIC VIOLENCE TRAUMA

A comprehensive discussion of every possible secondary outcome that victims of domestic violence may experience is beyond the scope of this book. However, some of the outcomes most commonly equated with domestic violence trauma are presented here.

This discussion should serve to highlight the need for mental health intervention, where appropriate, in conjunction with medical intervention. Unfortunately, victims who suffer psychological consequences as a result of victimization are often blamed for the abuse. Dutton (1992) suggested that rather than blaming the victim, it is useful to start with the perspective that psychological distress is due to the trauma that the victim has experienced.

Posttraumatic Stress Disorder

Much like combat veterans, victims of disasters, and victims of other kinds of violent personal assaultive crimes, battered women may suffer the anxiety disorder known as Posttraumatic Stress Disorder (PTSD). The distinguishing feature of this disorder is the development of certain symptoms after exposure to an extreme life-threatening stressor. Such stressors include events that involve one's threatened death, serious bodily injury, or the threat to one's physical integrity. The stressor can also be witnessing or learning about a threat, injury, or the death of a family member or close friend.

The abuses to which battered women are subjected are often cruel and sadistic. A health care provider may encounter such victims who have been beaten, choked, bitten, burned, stomped on, stabbed, slashed, shot, raped, thrown down the stairs, had their hair ripped out or cut off, had chemicals or boiling water thrown on them, or been subjected to any combination of abuses. A woman may have been threatened that she or her children would be killed, or that her children would be taken away and she would never see them again if she ever tried to leave or if she called the police. Victims may have witnessed batterers destroying treasured belongings, demolishing furnishings, punching holes in the wall, ripping a door off the hinges, or hurting or killing a beloved family pet.

In domestic violence situations, the violence and abuse are not isolated. A victim may be subjected to violence repeatedly at unpredictable intervals over a period of years. The "human volcano" may erupt without warning at any time. Hilberman (1980) has observed that domestic violence victims live in a state of paralyzing terror in which the stress is without end and the threat of assault is constantly present.

PTSD was first used to describe the symptomatology of some combat veterans (Dutton & Goodman, 1994). The diagnosis was derived from the observation of soldiers with combat neurosis (Frances, First, & Pincus, 1995). The diagnosis was of tremendous significance. First, it meant that war veterans suffered a *real* problem for which there was a name and for which they could be treated. Second, it meant that veterans could develop symptoms that were normal reactions to terrifying situations.

It has since been recognized that other stressful situations can produce PTSD. These situations include being held hostage, kidnapped, raped, robbed, or mugged; being tortured; being diagnosed with a life-threatening illness; and being in a serious automobile accident (American Psychiatric Association, 1994). It has also been recognized that many domestic violence victims may experience PTSD (Houskamp & Foy, 1991). However, such recognition is a recent phenomenon (Dutton & Goodman, 1994).

Two diagnostic features of PTSD seem particularly noteworthy when considering the stressors to which a battered woman is subjected. First, the American Psychiatric Association (1994) noted that PTSD may be especially severe or long-lasting when the stressor is of human design. This would include the situations of rape, torture, and other violent personal attacks. In cases of domestic violence, the stressor, that being the battering and other abuse, is always of human design, as the violence is perpetrated by the victim's current or former spouse or other intimate partner. Second, the likelihood of developing PTSD may increase as the intensity of and physical proximity to the stressor increase. In cases of domestic violence, the victim is often subjected to repeated attacks that increase in frequency and intensity with the passage of time.

In terms of physical proximity, during the relationship the victim usually lives with the source of the stress, the batterer. Even after separation, she may be forced into repeated contact with the batterer through family or criminal court proceedings, child custody arrangements, or the abuser's continued assaults, threats (Houskamp & Foy, 1991), and harassment. According to Houskamp and Foy, continued exposure to the abuser *after* the acute violence can affect the prevalence of symptoms and warrants recognition.

According to the American Psychiatric Association (1994), the diagnostic criteria for PTSD are as follows:

A. The person has been exposed to a traumatic event in which both of the following were present:
   1. The person experienced, witnessed, or was confronted with an event or events that involved actual or threatened death or serious injury, or a threat to the physical integrity of self or others.
   2. The person's response involved intense fear, helplessness, or horror. Note: In children, this may be expressed instead by disorganized or agitated behavior.
B. The traumatic event is persistently re-experienced in one (or more) of the following ways:
   1. Recurrent and intrusive distressing recollections of the event, including images, thoughts, or perceptions. Note: In young children, repetitive play may occur in which themes or aspects of the trauma are expressed.
   2. Recurrent distressing dreams of the event. Note: In children, there may be frightening dreams without recognizable content.
   3. Acting or feeling as if the traumatic event were recurring (includes a sense of reliving the experience, illusions, hallucinations, and dissociative flashback episodes, including those that occur on awakening or when intoxicated). Note: In young children, trauma-specific reenactment may occur.
   4. Intense psychological distress at exposure to internal or external cues that symbolize or resemble an aspect of the traumatic event.
   5. Physiological reactivity on exposure to internal or external cues that symbolize or resemble an aspect of the traumatic event.

C. Persistent avoidance of stimuli associated with the trauma and numbing of general responsiveness (not present before the trauma), as indicated by three (or more) of the following:

1. Efforts to avoid thoughts, feelings, or conversations associated with the trauma.
2. Efforts to avoid activities, places, or people that arouse recollection of the trauma.
3. Inability to recall an important aspect of the trauma.
4. Markedly diminished interest or participation in significant activities.
5. Feeling of detachment or estrangement from others.
6. Restricted range of affect (e.g., unable to have loving feelings).
7. Sense of a foreshortened future (e.g., does not expect to have a career, marriage, children, or a normal life span).

D. Persistent symptoms of increased arousal (not present before the trauma) as indicated by two (or more) of the following:

1. Difficulty falling or staying asleep.
2. Irritability or outbursts of anger.
3. Difficulty concentrating.
4. Hypervigilance.
5. Exaggerated startle response.

E. Duration of the disturbance (symptoms in Criteria B, C, and D) is more than 1 month.

F. The disturbance causes clinically significant distress or impairment in social, occupational, or other important areas of functioning.[7]

The American Psychiatric Association (1994) also noted a "constellation of symptoms" that may occur and are more commonly seen in conjunction with interpersonal stressors such as domestic battering:

- Impaired affect modulation
- Self-destructive and impulsive behavior
- Dissociative symptoms
- Somatic complaints
- Feelings of ineffectiveness, shame, despair, or hopelessness
- Feeling permanently damaged
- A loss of previously sustained beliefs
- Hostility
- Social withdrawal
- Feeling constantly threatened

- Impaired relationships with others
- Change in the individual's previous personality characteristics[7]

According to Dutton and Goodman (1994), the avoidance symptoms of PTSD can help explain why domestic violence victims might not act as others would expect, as when they fail to call the police after being beaten. They pointed out that when a woman is numb, in denial, or minimizing the abuse, she is not likely to recognize the behavior as abusive or to seek help from others.

Note that unlike situations of surviving a one-time disaster or an isolated instance of a stranger-perpetrated personal assaultive crime, domestic violence subjects the victim to repeated, continuing, and escalating life-threatening assaults. For such a victim, the situation would seem more accurately described as one of continual traumatic and post-traumatic stress. One must wonder whether each preceding traumatic event adds to the impact of the new trauma. It is known that when PTSD is present before a particular stressor, the stressor may excerbate the already present condition of PTSD (Skodol, 1989).

Acute Stress Disorder

In the immediate aftermath of an extreme stressor, an individual may develop Acute Stress Disorder in which there is a brief episode of symptoms similar to those of PTSD. The early development of Acute Stress Disorder symptomatology is a predictor of the subsequent development of PTSD (Frances et al., 1995). Two key features of this disorder distinguish it from PTSD. First, the symptoms of Acute Stress Disorder last at least 2 days but less than 1 month. Second, dissociative symptoms are present; these may be common in PTSD as well but are not required for a PTSD diagnosis (American Psychiatric Association, 1994).

The diagnostic criteria for Acute Stress Disorder are as follows:

A. The person has been exposed to a traumatic event in which both of the following were present:
   1. The person experienced, witnessed, or was confronted with an event or events that involved actual or threatened death or serious injury, or a threat to the physical integrity of self or others.
   2. The person's response involved intense fear, helplessness, or horror.
B. Either while experiencing or after experiencing the distressing event, the individual has three (or more) of the following dissociative symptoms:

      1. A subjective sense of numbing, detachment, or absence of emotional responsiveness

      2. A reduction in awareness of his or her surroundings (e.g., "being in a daze")

      3. Derealization

      4. Depersonalization [e.g., feeling like "being in a dream"]

      5. Dissociative amnesia (i.e., inability to recall an important aspect of the trauma)

C. The traumatic event is persistently reexperienced in at least one of the following ways: recurrent images, thoughts, dreams, illusions, flashback episodes, or a sense of reliving the experience; or distress on exposure to reminders of the traumatic event.

D. Marked avoidance of stimuli that arouse recollections of the trauma (e.g., thoughts, feelings, conversations, activities, places, people).

E. Marked symptoms of anxiety or increased arousal (e.g., difficulty sleeping, irritability, poor concentration, hypervigilance, exaggerated startle response, motor restlessness).

F. The disturbance causes clinically significant distress or impairment in social, occupational, or other important areas of functioning or impairs the individual's ability to pursue some necessary task, such as obtaining necessary assistance or mobilizing personal resources by telling family members about the traumatic event.

G. The disturbance lasts for a minimum of 2 days and a maximum of 4 weeks and occurs within 4 weeks of the traumatic event.

H. The disturbance is not due to the direct physiological effects of a substance (e.g., a drug of abuse, a medication) or a general medical condition [such as head trauma], is not better accounted for by Brief Psychotic Disorder, and is not merely an exacerbation of a preexisting Axis I or Axis II disorder.[7]

Depression

Depression (Kemp, Rawlings, & Green, 1991) and anxiety (Dutton & Goodman, 1994) have been identified to coexist along with many symptoms of PTSD. Depression is a serious mood disorder that may lead an individual to attempt suicide (American Psychiatric Association, 1994). The fourth edition of the *Diagnostic and Statistical Manual* lists a number of characteristics of depressive disorders that are identical to some of the common somatic complaints a health care provider may hear from a patient who has been chronically abused by a partner. These include

- Depressed mood
- Loss of interest or pleasure

- Weight loss or weight gain
- Sleeplessness, insomnia, or hypersomnia
- Fatigue
- Changes in motor activity and the rate of thinking (psychomotor agitation or retardation)
- Moving or thinking as if in slow motion or pacing/inability to sit still
- Feelings of worthlessness or excessive or inappropriate guilt
- Inability to concentrate
- Suicidal thoughts or behavior (American Psychiatric Association, 1994, p. 320)

A high percentage of domestic violence victims may develop depression as a result of the abuses to which they have been subjected. Consider a study by Cascardi and O'Leary (1992) of a group of 33 battered women who sought support and counseling services in Nassau County, New York. The women had been battered for an average of 5 years. Of the study group, 52% were found to suffer from severe levels of depressive symptomatology. In addition, as the abuse increased or worsened, in terms of the number of incidents, type, and consequences, the women's depression increased, and their self-esteem decreased.

Changes in Brain Chemistry

According to Charney, Deutch, Krystal, Southwich, and Davis (1993), acutely severe psychological trauma may actually cause biological changes in the brain. They pointed out that soldiers can have flashbacks to trauma that occurred many years earlier. The flashback causes hyperarousal and fear similar to what was experienced at the time of the actual trauma. They theorized that a relationship exists between dysfunctional parts of the brain, neurochemical systems, and clinical symptoms of PTSD.

Alcohol and Drug Use

Women who endure abuse may self-medicate through the use of drugs or alcohol to dull their pain. Unfortunately, such substance abuse makes the victim more vulnerable to future abuse (Blount, Silverman, Sellers, & Seese, 1994) and the compounded difficulty of having a substance abuse problem (Herman, 1992).

◙ NOTES

1. From *The Battered Woman,* by Lenore E. Walker. Copyright (c) 1979 by Lenore E. Walker. Reprinted by permission of HarperCollins Publishers, Inc.

2. From *Family Violence: Behavioral Characteristics in Spouse/Partner Abuse* (revised; chart), by V. D. Boyd and K. S. Klingbeil, 1993. Copyright 1993 by Vicki D. Boyd. Adapted with permission.

3. From *The Battered Woman,* by Lenore E. Walker. Copyright (c) 1979 by Lenore E. Walker. Reprinted by permission of HarperCollins Publishers, Inc.

4. From *Family Violence: Behavioral Characteristics in Spouse/Partner Abuse* (revised; chart), by V. D. Boyd and K. S. Klingbeil, 1993. Copyright 1993 by Vicki D. Boyd. Adapted with permission.

5. From "Women, Abusers Bond," by C. Gentry, August 18, 1991, *St. Petersburg Times,* p. 1-A. Copyright 1991 by The St. Petersburg Times. Adapted with permission.

6. From "Abused Women May Be 'Hostages,' " by S. Roan, August 20, 1991, *The Los Angeles Times,* p. E-1. Copyright, 1991, Los Angeles Times. Reprinted with permission.

7. From *Diagnostic and Statistical Manual of Mental Disorders* (4th ed., pp. 427-429), by the American Psychiatric Association, 1994, Washington, DC: Author. Copyright 1994 by the American Psychiatric Association. Reprinted with permission.

4

THE MEDICAL RESPONSE

◧ THE POWER OF HEALTH CARE INTERVENTION

Health care providers hold a unique position of trust and confidence with their patients that gives them the power either to help domestic violence victims significantly or to victimize them further. The Domestic Violence Project, Inc., of Kenosha, Wisconsin, has developed the "Medical Power and Control" and "Advocacy" Wheels from the "Power and Control" and "Equality" Wheels (Pence & Paymar, 1986) presented in Chapter 3. These wheels represent behaviors on the part of professionals that may either escalate the danger of victims of domestic violence or empower them to help themselves (see Figures 4.1 and 4.2).

As the Medical Power and Control Wheel illustrates, the health care provider has the power to escalate the victim's entrapment and place her in increased danger by violating confidentiality, trivializing and minimizing the abuse, blaming the victim for the violence, failing to respect her autonomy, ignoring her need for safety, and treating her victimization as a normal occurrence (Cosgrove, 1992). On the other hand, as illustrated by the Advocacy Wheel, health care providers have the power, through patient advocacy, to empower the patient by respecting confidentiality, believing and validating the victim's experiences, acknowledging the injustice of the situation, respecting her autonomy, helping her plan for future safety, and promoting her access to community services (Cosgrove, 1992).

The goals represented in the Advocacy Wheel are consistent with the views of the AMA. According to the AMA's Council on Ethical and Judicial Affairs

ARE WE PART OF THE PROBLEM?

ESCALATING DANGER

Violating Confidentiality...
Interviewing in front of family.
Telling colleagues issues
discussed in confidence
without her consent.
Calling the police
without her consent.

**Trivializing
and minimizing
the abuse...**
Not taking the danger she feels
seriously. Expecting tolerance
due to the number of years in
the relationship or recent
illness.

**Normalizing
victimization...**
Failing to respond to her
disclosure of abuse.
Acceptance of intimidation as
normal in relationships. Belief
that abuse is the outcome of noncompliance with patriarchy.

**MEDICAL
POWER
&
CONTROL**

**Ignoring her need
for safety...**
Failing to recognize her sense of
danger. Being unwilling to
ask "is it safe to go home?
do you have a place
you could go if
the situation
escalates?"

**Not
respecting
her autonomy...**
"Prescribing" divorce, sedative
medicines, going to a shelter,
couples counseling, c : law enforcement involvement. Punishing
the patient for not taking your
advice.

Blaming the victim...
Asking what she did to provoke
the abuse. Focusing on her as
the problem "why don't you
just leave? why do you
put up with it? why do
you let him do
that to you?"

INCREASED ENTRAPMENT

Figure 4.1. The Medical Power and Control Wheel
SOURCE: *Medical Power and Control Wheel*, by A. Cosgrove, 1992, Kenosha, WI: Domestic Violence
Project, Inc. Copyright 1992 by Domestic Violence Project, Inc. Reprinted with permission.

(AMA, 1992b), primary responsibilities for physicians dealing with domestic violence include identifying and acknowledging the abuse; providing sensitive support; clearly documenting the abuse; providing information about options and resources; and, with the patient's consent, making necessary referrals.

▣ INTERVENTION STEPS

Outlined here are the steps one may take to meet the responsibilities outlined by the AMA. I believe these steps are also necessary to aid in the successful prosecution of the batterer.

OR PART OF THE SOLUTION?

EMPOWERMENT

Respect Confidentiality...

All discussions must occur in private, without other family members present. This is essential to building trust and ensuring her safety.

Promote access to community services...

Know the resources in your community. Is there a hotline & shelter for battered women?

Believe & validate her experiences...

Listen to her and believe her. Acknowledge her feelings and let her know she is not alone. Many women have similar experiences.

ADVOCACY

Help her plan for future safety...

What has she tried in the past to keep herself safe? Is it working? Does she have a place to go if she needed to escape?

Acknowledge the Injustice...

The violence perpetrated against her is not her fault. No one deserves to be abused.

Respect her autonomy...

Respect her right to make decisions in her own life, when she is ready. She is the expert in her life.

EMPOWERMENT

Figure 4.2. The Advocacy Wheel
SOURCE: *Advocacy Wheel,* by A. Cosgrove, 1992, Kenosha, WI: Domestic Violence Project, Inc. Copyright 1992 by Domestic Violence Project, Inc. Reprinted with permission.

Show Caring, Nonjudgmental Support

It is important to remember that people generally trust their health care providers. They look to them for help, comfort, support, and guidance. However, a frightened victim may distrust anyone asking her questions about the abuse. Therefore, the first step in intervention is to attempt to develop trust.

When you are dealing with a patient who you suspect is being battered, simple body language communicating openness and confidentiality may help her relax. Look her in the eyes and tell her that you are concerned about her well-being and health. Tell her that you want to know what happened to her and that it is important, medically, that she tell you the truth. Ask her in a sympathetic way, "Are you in danger?" This will make her realize that other people are abused too (Glazer, 1993, p. 172). Similarly, do not react with shock when the patient discloses violence. Your surprise at the violence she has endured will only add to her feelings of isolation and belief that the abuse she suffered is unique.

If a victim opens up and tells you that she has been battered, do not ask questions such as "Why do you stay with him?" "Why don't you just leave?" or "What did you do to make him hit you?" Such questions indicate that you blame the victim for her abuser's violent actions in attacking her. Alternatively, letting the victim know that it is safe to talk to you, that you are knowledgeable about the dynamics of domestic violence abuses, and that you have information regarding resources and options for her will be empowering to her. Supportive comments that encourage the victim to disclose more information include statements such as "I'm sorry this has happened to you" and "You've really been through a lot."

Do not suggest to the patient that her concerned, teary-eyed partner seems so remorseful that she should simply forgive and forget. Such statements minimize the violence and relieve the batterer of accepting responsibility for his actions. This may also further empower the abuser to believe he can get away with anything, even fooling medical professionals. More important, it does nothing to guarantee the victim/patient's future safety.

Do not seek to verify the patient's statements of abuse through conversations with her companion, whether a spouse, a partner, or some third person (Flitcraft, 1992). Such disclosures violate confidentiality and may lead to retaliation by the batterer against the patient or against medical staff. In any event, accusatorial conversation with the batterer, which would probably take the form of "Your wife says you beat her up, is that true?" would accomplish little. The batterer has motive to deny, minimize, and blame the victim for the abuse because admission of committing a battery could subject him to criminal sanction.

Some kind words and a little information may well be a first step for the victim/patient to reclaim her own life. If she engages in self-blame with such comments as "I always talk too much and make him mad," tell her that nothing she says can justify someone else's battering her. If she minimizes her injuries, point out just how serious the injuries really are, and say that the next time she might not be so lucky. If she attempts to justify the batterer's behavior with comments such as "He only gets this way when he drinks," tell her that drinking is only one of his problems; the other is violence.

Address the Violence:
Ask the Pertinent Questions

Doctors must treat the injuries and address the cause. Otherwise, the treatment is superficial and ineffective to prevent future injury. Rosenberg (1994) analogized such failures to "a malaria eradication program that repeatedly treats the afflicted with medication but fails to hang mosquito netting or drain the mosquitos' breeding swamp" (p. 4).

All physicians should routinely question female patients about violence in their lives. To accomplish this objective, the AMA (1992a) suggested that practitioners first make an opening supportive statement such as "Because abuse and violence are so common in women's lives, I've begun to ask about it routinely" (p. 4). Six basic questions that can assist the health care provider to conduct an abuse assessment screen of all female patients are as follows (the first five are from Parker & McFarlane, 1991):

1. Within the last year, have you been emotionally or physically abused by your partner or someone important in your life? If so, how many times?
2. Within the last year, have you been hit, slapped, kicked, or physically hurt by someone? If so, how many times?
3. Within the last year, has anyone forced you to have intercourse or engage in sexual activities you did not want to do? If so, how many times?
4. Are you afraid of your partner or anyone else?
5. If the patient is pregnant, add: Since you've become pregnant, has anyone hit, slapped, kicked, or physically hurt you?
6. Where is the person who harmed you, and what is his name?

Some health care providers may anticipate that they will have great difficulty in getting the patient to open up and talk about the abuse and therefore may be apprehensive about asking such questions. In one study of primary care physicians designed to explore the barriers to domestic violence recognition and intervention, 55% of the doctors indicated that they refrained from asking about abuse for fear of offending the patient (Sugg & Inui, 1992). However, a study of female patients showed that abused women readily responded to questions about abuse and were relieved that someone had directly asked them how they had been hurt. Further, the majority of nonbattered women did not appear to mind being asked the questions (McLeer & Anwar, 1989).

Although difficulty may be encountered with patients at times, the health care provider's concerns can be readily allayed if there is a standard approach used by all members of the health care organization. For example, the Dart-mouth-Hitchcock Medical Center of Lebanon, New Hampshire, has developed straightforward strategies for interviewing patients suspected to be domestic violence victims (see Figure 4.3).

Provide Complete Documentation
in the Medical Records

As a career prosecutor who has handled countless domestic violence cases, I have seen the many problems a prosecutor must overcome when medical records are in some way deficient. The deficiencies may be due in part to some health care providers' lack of knowledge and training in domestic violence and their general lack of understanding of the importance of medical records to law enforcement intervention efforts.

A first step is recognition of injuries that are characteristic of domestic violence and recognition of inconsistent or false explanations for injuries. Typical domestic violence injury patterns include bruises, contusions, or minor lacerations to the head, face, neck, breasts, or abdomen. In contrast, accidental injuries are more likely to involve the periphery of the body (AMA, 1992c). Refer to Chapter 1 for an in-depth discussion of characteristic domestic violence injuries. Health care providers should suspect assault as the cause of injury whenever the women's explanation regarding how the injury occurred does not seem plausible or when there has been a delay in seeking treatment (AMA, 1992a). Note also that abused women have been found to be twice as likely as nonabused women to delay commencing prenatal care until the third trimester (McFarlane et al., 1992).

Bearing these points in mind, what follows are my suggestions for improv-ing the quality of medical records for domestic violence patients. These sugges-tions are consistent with the 1996 JCAHO standards (JCAHO, 1995), which recognize that victims of abuse have special needs in the medical assessment process that include the gathering of information and evidentiary materials that could be used in future legal proceedings. These standards require that hospital policies and procedures define the hospital's responsibility for the collection, retention, and safeguarding of information and evidence.

Document the Entire Patient Examination

The encounter of health care provider and patient comprises a number of elements. Documentation of each of these elements has significance in mak-

Ask the patient direct, nonthreatening questions in an empathetic manner. You may find it difficult to ask these questions. However, asking the questions and identifying the woman as battered is the first step toward appropriate treatment. Examples follow:

1. I noticed you have a number of bruises. Could you tell me how that happened? Did someone hit you?
2. You seem frightened of your partner. Has your partner ever hurt you?
3. Sometimes patients tell me they have been hurt by someone close to them. Could this be happening to you?
4. You mention that your partner loses his temper with the children. Does he lose his temper with you? Does he ever hurt you physically when he loses his temper?
5. Have there been times during your relationship when you have had physical fights?
6. Do your verbal fights ever include physical contact?
7. Have you ever been in a relationship where you have been hit, punched, kicked, or hurt in any way? Are you in such a relationship now?
8. You mentioned your partner uses drugs/alcohol. How does your partner act when drinking or on drugs?
9. Does your partner consistently control your actions or put you down?
10. Sometimes when others are overprotective and as jealous as you describe, they react strongly and use physical force. Is this happening in your situation?
11. Your partner seems very concerned and anxious. Was he responsible for your injuries?

If the patient states battering has occurred, give her time to verbalize openly before beginning your physical assessment. Allow her to control the timetable of the discussion.

Assure the patient that this information will be addressed after the medical examination and testing are complete. Remain nonjudgmental, supportive, and relaxed. Reassure her that no one has the right to hurt others and that she is not responsible for someone else's abusive behavior.

Figure 4.3. Interviewing Strategies for Patients With Suspected Domestic Violence
SOURCE: Dartmouth-Hitchcock Medical Center, 1994, p. 5.

ing medical records complete and can aid in the successful prosecution of a batterer. To ensure complete medical records:

1. *Identify the patient by her full name, date of birth, and social security number.* Primarily, this information will assist in proving that the medical records offered at the trial pertain to the victim in the case. An issue can arise if the victim has a common surname and the records lack complete identifying information.

2. *Mark each page with patient identification.* Each page of the patient's medical records should include the patient identification number or some other unique identifier, such as a social security number. The lack of internal identification can pose a problem in the legal proceedings.

3. *Provide the full name of the attending physician(s) and his or her specialty.* The prosecutor can experience a real dilemma trying to figure out from the records the identity of the treating physician(s) and how a particular physician was involved in the patient's care. This can be a particular problem when a doctor enters the emergency department to assist in some significant way and is not reflected in the records at all. The most frustrating thing that can happen is for a doctor who was referenced in the records to come all the way to court, only to discover that he or she is not in fact the needed witness.

4. *Document the nature and location of all injuries.* It is important to document all current injuries as well as healed or healing injuries. The body can be as much of a crime scene as the physical location of the assault. When a pattern of multiple injuries is seen in a woman, particularly in combination with evidence of old injury, physical abuse should be suspected (AMA, 1992c). In the presence of more severe injuries, old injuries, as well as fresh bruises or scratches, may be overlooked. However, documenting such injuries could be important in subsequent legal proceedings. Note that the health care provider should not attempt to date old injuries on the basis of his or her observations alone. As discussed in greater detail in Chapter 7, such attempts at dating injuries can cause problems in future legal proceedings.

5. *Document the diagnosis and treatment.*

6. *Document the date(s) and time(s) of treatment.*

7. *Record a brief statement from the victim/patient regarding how she was injured and who caused her injuries.* For example, the medical records could state, "Ms. Durham reports that her boyfriend, John Edwards, punched her in the left eye with his fist at approximately 10 p.m. tonight." The name of the batterer and his relationship to the victim/patient should be documented for prosecution purposes, for facility security reasons, and to record the true cause of the victim's injuries.

8. *Record a brief statement from the victim/patient regarding the history of violence.* For example, "This is the fourth incident of physical violence by her boyfriend, John Edwards. Prior episodes have involved slapping and pushing. Abuse is becoming more severe."

9. *Record a brief statement from the victim/patient as to the cause of any old injuries observed.* If the patient recalls the approximate date that she received a particular old injury, such information should be included as part of her statement. Some victims have been battered so frequently that they cannot recall the exact date on which a beating took place. Descriptive information such as "He kicked me in the ribs around Thanksgiving" would be sufficient.

10. *If a suspected false statement is given by the victim/patient and if she maintains this position after being confronted, document the inconsistency of her statement in relation to the injury observed.* In a firm but nondemeaning tone of voice, the health care provider should simply tell the patient, "What you are saying does not make sense. I know you were not injured in the manner you are claiming. It is important for you to tell me how this happened to you because it may affect the treatment I prescribe." If the victim persists in the false explanation, the records should reflect that in the doctor's opinion, the injuries presented are inconsistent with the explanation given, and should state a conclusion as to the cause of the injuries if such an opinion is within the doctor's area of expertise. For example, the entry might read, "Injuries are not consistent with bumping into a door but are consistent with blunt-force trauma to the head."

11. *Record completely and accurately all statements made by the victim/patient.* All of the victim/patient's statements made for the purpose of medical diagnosis and treatment, as reflected in the medical records, have evidentiary significance and may be used by the prosecution at trial. Note that failure to document accurately all patient statements concerning the injury can adversely affect the prosecution's case. See Chapter 7 for a more detailed discussion. In addition, the doctor may need to rely on the records to refresh his or her recollection of the examination if called to testify. A criminal case can sometimes take a full year to come to trial.

12. *Use nonjudgmental terms in describing the patient's statements as to the cause of her injuries.* Use phrases such as "the patient reports . . ." or "according to the patient . . ." Such language sounds neutral and accurate. Avoid phrases such as "the patient claims . . . ," "the patient alleges . . . ," or "the patient contends. . . ." Such language sounds judgmental and implies that the writer does not believe what the victim/patient has reported.

13. *Use active, not passive language.* For example, the statement "Ms. Durham reports that her boyfriend, John Edwards, punched her in the left eye with his fist" is much better than "Patient was punched in the left eye with a fist." Passive language minimizes the violence that the patient has actually experienced.

14. *Record all information in the medical records legibly.* Illegible records are virtually worthless. If the jury cannot read and decipher the contents of the records for themselves, they may not believe testimony provided concerning the entries in the records.

15. *Stick to your area of expertise.* If a surgeon recovers a bullet from a patient's body, for purposes of the medical records, it is "a bullet." It should be referred to as "a .45 caliber bullet" only if the surgeon also happens to be a firearms expert. When a surgeon guesses that the bullet's caliber is .45, but in fact it is a .38, this

causes needless evidentiary issues in the criminal case. The government will seek to prove at the trial that the bullet presented in court is the same bullet that was recovered from the victim's body. If the medical records conflict with the actual description of the evidence as provided by a firearms examiner, the defense will argue that the government has the wrong evidence.

16. *Avoid editorializing.* Jurors believe everything a doctor says as the gospel truth. Whatever a doctor writes in the records can have profound impact in subsequent court proceedings. As a prosecutor, I have reviewed numerous medical records for domestic violence victims in which health care providers have written negative comments concerning the victim's demeanor. These comments can negatively affect a jury's evaluation of the victim's credibility at the trial. It is important for health care providers to realize that the domestic violence victim may not behave in the way one would expect. Instead of being teary-eyed and hapless, she may seem angry or emotionally absent or may have flat affect. Simply because she does not fulfill expectations of "victim" does not mean that she has not been victimized. Her accumulation of suffering, exhaustion, or numbness from having been battered and from having to tell her story repeatedly to law enforcement personnel and/or others may place her beyond tears. According to Dotterer (1992), a physician and herself a formerly battered woman, "Don't expect [the patient] to be emotionally raw just because you're shocked to hear her story. . . . Don't assume she's lying just because she doesn't cry."[1] Consider how long a patient has been awake, the traumas to which she has been subjected, and her emotional state. Before a doctor writes in the medical records, "patient uncooperative," "patient hostile," or "patient appears intoxicated," the doctor should be sure it is not really a case of "patient exhausted, traumatized, and unable to give full details at this time."

Document Injuries With Photographs

Photographic documentation of traumatic injuries can be the most dramatic evidence presented at a criminal trial or other proceeding in connection with domestic abuse. The court proceedings may occur many months after the assault. By then, injuries will have healed and bruises will have faded away. The chance to document the injuries photographically is fleeting. Once the opportunity to preserve the image of a brutal assault is lost, it is lost forever.

The potential uses of photographic evidence highlight its tremendous importance. First, a photograph can be used in the legal proceeding as direct evidence of the injury. The photograph captures the violent result of the brutal assault. As direct evidence, the photograph can also be used to prove intent of the defendant. For example, a photograph depicting strangulation marks around a victim's neck tends to prove a batterer's intent to kill. The photograph can be especially useful as direct evidence of guilt if the victim becomes uncooperative at trial and refuses to testify.

Second, a photograph can be used as corroborating evidence of the injury at trial. The photograph can complement the victim's or witnesses' testimony as to the fact of the assault, the character of the injuries, the brutality of the beating, and the extent of the injuries.

Third, a photograph can be used to refresh a witness's recollection as to the violence of the moment. Just as wounds heal, memories fade. A victim may not recall the full extent of her injuries, or she may minimize the injuries. Even cooperative witnesses may tend to minimize the assault as time goes by waiting for the case to go to court. A photograph can bring the moment back. A photograph can also be particularly helpful to the medical professional who faces the prospect of testifying.

Fourth, a photograph can help a prosecutor convince a reluctant victim to cooperate with the criminal prosecution. For many batterers, the only thing that will deter their future violence is criminal prosecution and sanction. A good-quality photograph enables the prosecutor to show it to the victim and say, "Look what he did to you."

Fifth, a photograph can convince a jury as to the violence of the crime. Usually by the time of trial, the victim's injuries have healed. Listening to testimony engages only the jury's imagination about the injury. Photographs engage the sense of sight, giving the injuries scope and dimension.

Sixth, photographs of the victim's injuries can be used to contradict the testimony of a defendant who asserts that no injury occurred, that the injury was not serious, or that he was acting in self-defense. For example, the defendant may claim that he simply slapped the victim. A photograph depicting a black eye would tend to prove that the assault was more consistent with a punch and that the defendant is lying. A photograph depicting bruises on a victim's forearms would tend to prove that she was injured while trying to deflect blows and that her partner was the true aggressor.

Finally, photographs can be used at the sentencing of a batterer to show the judge the seriousness of the injury. Often, criminal cases are resolved by a guilty plea. In such an instance, the judge may not see the victim until the time of sentencing. This is usually long after the date of the offense. She is likely to show no sign of physical injury by then.

Before taking a photograph of a victim's injuries, the health care provider should obtain informed consent. The AMA's Council on Ethical and Judicial Affairs (AMA, 1992b) has stated that informed consent must be obtained from all competent adult abuse victims for nonemergency interventions, which include taking photographs. A model consent form is shown in Figure 4.4.

[On facility letterhead]:

_____

(Date)   Addressograph

I, _____, a patient in the
                    (Patient's full name)

care of the above-referenced medical facility, do hereby consent to
having my photographs taken. I understand that these photographs will
become part of my official medical records and will be maintained by
this facility. I further understand that under no circumstances will these
photographs be released to anyone except with my written consent, by
court order, or as otherwise provided by law.

_____

(Signature of patient)

Medical Record Number: _____

Witnessed by: _____
              (Name and title of witness)

Figure 4.4. Consent for Photography

Intervention, however helpful it might be in the long run, should not be
forced on a patient who does not want it. Going against the wishes of a patient
who has refused the intervention option violates the ethical principle of respect
for the patient's autonomy (AMA, 1992b). Respect for the choices of a domestic
violence victim has important therapeutic ramifications. However, overriding
such a victim's wishes further victimizes and disempowers her.

Invariably, when the medical provider tells the patient that he or she wants
to photograph the patient's injuries, the patient will ask why photographs are
needed. An explanation could be offered as follows:

There are several reasons that we would like to take photographs of your injuries
today. First, as they say, "A picture is worth a thousand words." The photographs

that are taken today will be made part of your medical records. The images captured in the photos are a visual representation of your injuries. The photos are more descriptive than anyone could provide by simply writing an observation in those records (for example, "patient has a black eye"). Second, if you ever have to go to court for any of a variety of reasons, these photos may be important to you. Civil attorneys use the photos to show to judges when they request civil protection orders. Prosecutors use the photos to prove how severely you were injured. Finally, after we take the photos, we will give you a copy of at least one photo for your own records. After you leave here today, your injuries will start to fade away. If you start to forget how serious the situation you are in really is, we want you to take that photo out and look at it.

   The health care provider should then seek to have the patient sign a written consent form. This form assures the patient that the photographs will be made part of her official medical records. She is further assured that the photographs will not be released unless she consents to the release of her medical records or any part of them in writing, unless the photographs are ordered to be released by a court, or unless the law otherwise requires it, as in the case of a duly authorized subpoena in connection with a civil or criminal proceeding. Note, however, that the patient generally signs an insurance form authorizing the release of her medical records to her insurance company. The patient's insurance carrier could request such photographs as part of the patient's medical records. Some patients may refuse consent when they learn that their insurance company will have access to such photographs. Because the need to capture the victim/patient's injuries photographically is great and the need of the insurance company to obtain such photographs seems questionable at best, this is an area in which insurance reform may be required.

   One issue health care providers will face regarding the use of cameras is whether to use instant or standard film. Instant photography is preferable to standard film for a number of reasons. First, instant cameras are easy to operate with minimal training and photographic ability to get good results (Hinds, 1993). Second, there are no negatives to develop. Negatives can be lost, damaged, or destroyed. Negatives also require film processing. This means that photographs cannot normally be placed in a patient folder quickly. Third, with instant film, the photographer knows whether he or she has captured the desired image only moments after taking the photograph. Fourth, standard 35-mm film has 24 or 36 exposures per roll. The health care provider might deem it necessary to take only two or three photographs per patient. Therefore one roll of film could have numerous photographs of various patients. There would be no practical way to identify, per patient, who the patient is, who actually took the photographs, and when the photographs were taken. Attempts to match up photographs with patient files would be time consuming and an administrative nightmare. Fifth, instant film gives health care providers the option of providing a photograph to the victim on the day of treatment. After she leaves the medical facility, the victim may need to speak with a police officer, a prosecutor, a civil attorney, and/or a judge to seek the remedies she requires. Simply stated, a photograph of her injuries may help the victim secure assistance from the justice system. Finally, instant film ensures patient confidentiality. No third-party developer will see the photographs.

When photographing the victim, one should take photographs of new injuries and healed or healing injuries (Polaroid Corporation, 1992). Documenting a series of offensive injuries in various stages of healing tends to prove a pattern of abuse. Such photographs can be effectively used by prosecutors and civil attorneys to prove an ongoing, escalating pattern of abuse.

Before taking a photograph of the victim, the photographer should ask him-or herself, "What am I trying to document?" Nothing is more frustrating for a prosecutor than to look at a photograph and wonder what it is supposed to represent. This occurs frequently when photographs lack context or the depiction is out of focus.

To aid in creating a valuable image, when possible, photographs of the victim should be taken from three perspectives (Polaroid Corporation, 1992):

1. *Full body.* Make sure that at least one photograph shows the victim's face for purposes of identification. Otherwise, at the trial the defense may claim, for example, that the shoulder depicted in the photograph could be anyone's shoulder, not necessarily that of this victim.
2. *Midrange.* Such photographs should show the portion of the body wounded.
3. *Close up.* If a close-up lens is an option, one-to-one ratio photography is an excellent way to document the injury. *One-to-one* means that the depiction in the photograph is the exact size it was in real life. If a close-up lens is not available, the photographer should still attempt to take a photograph as close up as the camera equipment permits.

The photographer should be mindful that the photographs may be viewed by numerous individuals outside of the medical field. Although a patient may not be embarrassed about her doctor or nurse seeing her disrobed in a photograph, she may be extremely embarrassed about the prospect of strangers, such as police officers, lawyers, and jurors, seeing the same photographs. Therefore, if injuries are located on parts of the body normally covered by clothing, a sheet should be used to cover portions of the victim's body not relevant to the photograph.

Photographs must fairly and accurately represent the injury depicted. With that in mind, the photographer should avoid angles that create perspective distortion, which is distortion of the true size of the wound. An example of such distortion includes the classic all-nose photograph one gets when trying to take a photograph of oneself. Photographers should also be aware of the potential for color distortion when taking photographs in fluorescent lighting. (See Chapter 7 for more information regarding legal problems associated with photographic distortion.) Try to use a reference in the photograph, such as a coin or a ruler, so that the size of the injury may be appreciated.

The photographer should always print his or her name and the date the photographs were taken on the back of each photograph in an area that will not deface, alter, or otherwise damage the photograph. With instant film, the best place to write is the bottom margin. The photographer's name should be legible, and the date should include the month, day, and year.

If the depiction in the photograph is not readily identifiable in terms of which way is up, the photographer should write "top" on the reverse side of the photograph in the upper center portion. For example, this procedure may be necessary for a close-up photograph depicting an injury to a portion of the victim's back. In such a photograph, all that may be depicted is a mass of flesh and a wound. The directional marking on the back of the photograph helps give it context. If the victim has multiple injuries across large body-mass areas and it is not apparent from close-up photographs what portion of the body is depicted, the photographer should also make a note as to the body part on the reverse side of the photograph. For example, a notation could read, "top—right shoulder."

All photographs should be placed in a special envelope marked "PHOTO-GRAPHS" and secured in the patient's medical record file sequestered in the appropriate section of the medical record department.

Document Injuries
With an Injury Location Chart

All injuries, new and old, should be identified on a female injury location chart. If such a chart is used, the injury number indicated on the chart could be marked on the back of the photograph that depicts the same wound. This process will eliminate the need for the photographer to label the back of the photographs descriptively, as discussed above. Also, this procedure will enable police officers, the prosecutor, the health care witness, and jurors to relate the photographic depiction easily to injuries discussed in the written patient medical records. This

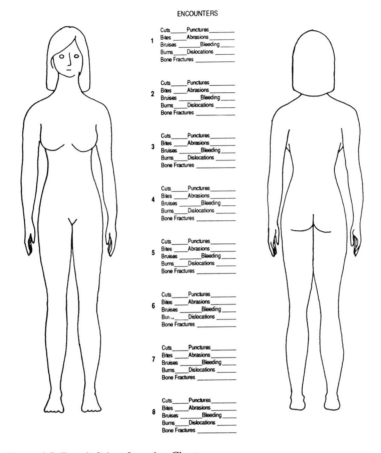

ENCOUNTERS

1
Cuts_____Punctures_____
Bites_____Abrasions_____
Bruises_____Bleeding_____
Burns_____Dislocations_____
Bone Fractures _____

2
Cuts_____Punctures_____
Bites_____Abrasions_____
Bruises_____Bleeding_____
Burns_____Dislocations_____
Bone Fractures _____

3
Cuts_____Punctures_____
Bites_____Abrasions_____
Bruises_____Bleeding_____
Burns_____Dislocations_____
Bone Fractures _____

4
Cuts_____Punctures_____
Bites_____Abrasions_____
Bruises_____Bleeding_____
Burns_____Dislocations_____
Bone Fractures _____

5
Cuts_____Punctures_____
Bites_____Abrasions_____
Bruises_____Bleeding_____
Burns_____Dislocations_____
Bone Fractures _____

6
Cuts_____Punctures_____
Bites_____Abrasions_____
Bruises_____Bleeding_____
Burns_____Dislocations_____
Bone Fractures _____

7
Cuts_____Punctures_____
Bites_____Abrasions_____
Bruises_____Bleeding_____
Burns_____Dislocations_____
Bone Fractures _____

8
Cuts_____Punctures_____
Bites_____Abrasions_____
Bruises_____Bleeding_____
Burns_____Dislocations_____
Bone Fractures _____

Figure 4.5. Female Injury Location Chart

SOURCE: From Helton, A. *A Protocol of Care for the Battered Woman.* White Plains, NY: March of Dimes Birth Defects Foundation. (1987). Reproduced with permission of the copyright holder.

procedure will also aid in interpreting the depiction in the photograph. A sample female injury location chart is shown in Figure 4.5.

Document Physical Evidence

During the examination of the victim/patient, medical staff may recover physical evidence of the crime. Such evidence could include things such as a bullet or bullet fragment(s) or the victim's torn, bullet-riddled, or blood-splattered clothing. Hospital security may occasionally recover from the batterer, who has accompanied the victim to the hospital, the weapon used in the crime, such as a knife or gun. Weapons and other physical evidence of the crime have tremendous significance in the prosecution of the perpetrator. Because recovery of evidence is bound to happen, all medical facilities should develop standard operating procedures and policies for the identification, recording, and temporary retention of evidence recovered from the victim/patient and/or the batterer.

When should medical staff preserve evidence, and what should the facility do with such evidence? If a police officer has accompanied the victim/patient to the facility, the officer can determine what evidence, if any, should be collected from the victim and can take immediate custody of such items. If hospital security recover a weapon believed to have been used in a crime, they should immediately release it to the officer who has accompanied the victim/patient.

What should facility personnel do when the police are not present? They should collect evidence that is important to proving that a crime occurred and to proving who committed the crime. In performing this task, the health care provider should understand that there are two categories of evidence: that which has independent significance in proving the abuse and that which merely corroborates the abuse.

All instrumentalities of crime, such as the gun, the knife, and the bullet, have independent significance to the criminal case. Such items may be subjected to scientific examinations that may tend to prove how the crime was committed or who perpetrated it. For example, a bullet may be examined to determine the type of firearm from which it was fired or to match it to a particular firearm. A shirt with a bullet hole may be subjected to a gunshot powder residue examination. Such a test tends to prove whether the shot was fired from a distance of inches away or from more than a few feet. Evidence of firing at a distance tends to undercut the shooter's claim that the gun discharged during a struggle. All evidence of this nature should be collected and temporarily retained for law enforcement.

In general, items such as torn or bloody clothing merely corroborate the crime. Consider a patient who was punched in the face by an abusive husband. The blow caused her nose to bleed. The blood splattered on her shirt. Is the shirt evidence? Yes, it is. However, in this example, the shirt merely corroborates the fact that the victim bled. A photograph depicting the victim/patient's injuries, whether or not she is wearing the shirt, is fully satisfactory to prove the fact that she bled. The shirt itself has little evidentiary value. Note, however, that this may not hold true if the case involves more serious injuries or death. For example, in a case in which the victim dies as a result of injuries sustained, there may be a need for DNA testing or hair and fiber analysis of her clothing. In such a case, all clothing should be preserved as evidence.

If evidence has been collected by the health care staff and no police officer is present at the facility to collect it, a number of steps should be taken. First, notify the police that there is evidence at the hospital that should be collected. Describe the evidence, and request that the police take custody of it within a set period of time, such as within 4 hours. Hospitals are not in the business of long-term evidence storage. It is unreasonable for law enforcement to expect otherwise. It should be noted, however, that if the police indicate that they intend to collect the evidence but are unable to respond within the agreed-on time, the evidence should not be destroyed by the facility. Destruction of important evidence could possibly be considered obstruction of justice.

Second, all evidence collected should be documented in the patient's medical records. This documentation should include the chain of custody: that is, the individuals through whose hands the evidence has passed. The records should reflect the names of all staff who recovered the evidence, where the evidence was stored while it was in the medical facility, and to whom the evidence was released.

The law enforcement officer should sign a receipt or similar documentation to reflect that certain items were provided to him or her by the medical facility. The receipt can be written on facility letterhead. It should include at a minimum the patient's name; the medical records number; the date; a description of the evidence; and the name, badge number, and agency of the law enforcement officer taking custody of the property. The officer should date and sign the document. To expedite and standardize this process, every facility should prepare its own "Property Release Form."

Educate the Patient
About Domestic Violence

When domestic violence is suspected or disclosed, the health care provider has an excellent opportunity to educate the patient about such violence. In addition to conveying messages that let the patient know that the abuse is not unique, that it is not her fault, and that she is not responsible for the violence, the patient should be informed about the dynamics of abusive relationships and the health risks that violence may pose to her and to her children. The patient should be told that domestic violence can cause serious physical and psychological problems. In addition, she should be told that abuse can lead some victims to self-medicate and develop alcohol and drug dependencies, thereby complicating an already serious situation.

Provide Information
Regarding Options and Resources

Providing information so that the victim can begin to help herself should not be confused with ordering the patient to take a certain course of action. In fact, the last thing a victim needs is to be told what to do. In a truly abusive and controlling dynamic, she is always being told what to do. What she needs is the tools to make choices for herself.

Put together a referral list of resources available for battered women in your community. The list should include telephone numbers for hot lines, shelters, legal clinics, advocacy groups, and criminal justice and social service agencies. The list should also provide a brief description of the services offered by each organization. If there are no local service providers in your area, list the names and telephone numbers of state or national organizations and agencies.

Obtain brochures about domestic violence, if available, from local service providers and national organizations. An excellent patient education pamphlet entitled *The Abused Woman* has been produced by the American College of Obstetricians and Gynecologists (1995). In addition or as an alternative, facilities can create their own brochures about domestic violence. The referral list of resources and any appropriate brochures should be offered to each patient who is suspected to be a victim of domestic violence. These materials should specifically address the needs of battered women (Lee, Letellier, McLoughlin, & Salber, 1993) and should be translated into other languages as required to best serve the diverse populations in your community. In addition, written information should be placed in three separate locations: the waiting room, the treatment area (AMA, 1992a), and the rest rooms. The batterer may have accompanied the victim/patient for treatment, and she may be unable to take information in his presence. Placing the materials in locations the batterer will not access, such as the women's rest room, gives the victim the opportunity to obtain the information she needs.

One resource that can make a world of difference to a victim is a victim advocate. Generally, a victim advocate is a volunteer, often herself a survivor of domestic violence. A victim advocate has special training in the field of domestic violence, is sensitive to the needs of victims, is extremely knowledgeable about resource options and legal procedures, and offers support to the victim. Generally, victim advocates may be identified through battered women's shelters or through local or state domestic violence coalitions. A woman contemplating leaving an abusive relationship may have to deal with the criminal legal process, family court, divorce court, and difficult issues such as child support, custody, and visitation. A knowledgeable victim advocate can provide vital information and encouragement. The victim advocate can also perform a needs assessment for the victim, which may range from basic needs, such as where the victim/ patient and her children will sleep that night, to longer term safety planning, legal options, and available resources.

If finances allow, the creation of an advocacy program at the medical facility, staffed by specially trained volunteers, would provide continuity and consistency of services to victims. Some universities that have programs focusing on family violence or social work may be willing to make students available to fulfill this function in an intern capacity. Additional sources for such volunteers include law schools and the local bar association. Facility social workers knowledgeable in this field could also fulfill this role.

The victim should also be provided information about her legal rights and options. According to the National Council of Juvenile and Family Court Judges' Model Code on Domestic and Family Violence (National Council of Juvenile and Family Court Judges, 1994), all health care providers who become aware that a patient is a domestic violence victim should provide that patient with a written statement of rights and available services. They suggest that the state public health agency develop the form. The Model Code suggests the notice shown in Figure 4.6.

Although the form provides information sufficient to enable a victim to contact shelters, it absolutely should not contain the addresses of the shelters unless that information is already a matter of public information. The National Council of Juvenile and Family Court Judges also suggested that the form be available in languages other than English, as needed.

A civil protection order (CPO; referred to as an order for protection in Figure 4.6) is a court order, usually issued by the family court, that may provide any number of many possible remedies. Some of those remedies are referenced in Figure 4.6. The parties in this type of a proceeding are referred to as the *petitioner* (the person who files for the CPO) and the *respondent* (the person against whom the CPO is sought).

The types of interpersonal relationships over which a court has jurisdiction to issue a CPO vary from state to state, as do the remedies available pursuant to such laws (Klein & Orloff, 1993). A judge may issue a CPO after a court hearing. Such an order may last up to 6 months. A violation of a CPO may be prosecuted as a contempt of court. The punishment for contempt may include a

If you are the victim of domestic or family violence and you believe that law enforcement protection is needed for your physical safety, you have the right to request that an officer assist in providing for your safety, including asking for an emergency order for protection. You may also request that the officer assist you in obtaining your essential personal effects and locating and taking you to a safe place including but not limited to a designated meeting place for a shelter, a family member's or a friend's residence, or a similar place of safety. If you are in need of medical treatment, you have the right to request that the officer assist you in obtaining medical treatment. You may request a copy of the report[a] at no cost from the law enforcement department.

You may ask the prosecuting attorney to file a criminal complaint.[b] You also have the right to file a petition in *insert name of court* requesting an order for protection from domestic or family violence which could include any of the following orders:[c]

(a) An order enjoining your abuser from threatening to commit or committing further acts of domestic or family violence;

(b) An order prohibiting your abuser from harassing, annoying, telephoning, contacting or otherwise communicating with you, directly or indirectly;

(c) An order removing your abuser from your residence;[d]

(d) An order directing your abuser to stay away from your residence, school, place of employment, or any other specified place frequented by you[e] and another family or household member;

(e) An order prohibiting your abuser from using or possessing any firearm or other weapon specified by the court;

(f) An order granting you possession and use of the automobile and other essential personal effects;

(g) An order granting you custody of your child or children;

(h) An order denying your abuser visitation;

(i) An order specifying arrangements for visitation, including requiring supervised visitation; and

(j) An order requiring your abuser to pay certain costs and fees, such as rent or mortgage payments, child support payments, medical expenses, expenses for shelter, court costs, and attorney's fees.

Figure 4.6. Statement of Rights and Available Services for Victims of Domestic Violence
SOURCE: From *Family Violence: A Model State Code* (pp. 42-43), by the National Council of Juvenile and Family Court Judges, 1994, Reno, NV: Author. Copyright 1994 by the National Council of Juvenile and Family Court Judges. Reprinted with permission.

The forms you need to obtain an order for protection are available from the *insert clerk of the court or other appropriate person.* The resources available in this community for information relating to domestic and family violence, treatment of injuries, and places of safety and shelters are: *insert list and hotline numbers.* You also have the right to seek reimbursement for losses suffered as a result of the abuse, including medical and moving expenses, loss of earnings or support, and other expenses for injuries sustained and damage to your property. This can be done without an attorney in small claims court if the total amount claimed is less than *fill in the amount required by statute.*

a. I suggest referring to this document as the "police" report.
b. I suggest inserting, "The prosecuting authority in this jurisdiction is *insert name of City or District Attorney's Office, address, contact person, and telephone number.*
c. I would also include among the listed orders "an order directing your abuser to stay away from you."
d. I would note, "even if both of you own or rent that property."
e. This could also include, for example, one's place of worship.

Figure 4.6. *Continued*

fine and/or a period of imprisonment. It is usually up to the petitioner to file for contempt.

Most states do not include mere dating partners who have never resided together or people who do not have children in common within the scope of those who may seek a civil protection order. Likewise, most states do not cover gay or lesbian partners. Prior to creating a form such as the one depicted in Figure 4.6, local law should be researched thoroughly. No one would want a patient to leave the medical facility believing that she has a particular legal remedy when in fact she does not. For this reason, I suggest that after paragraph "j" in Figure 4.6, you insert other terms the court in your jurisdiction can order, such as that the abuser be ordered to attend a batterer counseling program; that the victim be permitted to maintain possession of jointly owned property, such as the car; or that certain property not be sold, transferred, encumbered, or destroyed by the abuser.

The health care provider should document in the patient's medical records all resource materials offered and all referrals made. JCAHO (1995) requires that hospitals document referrals to private or public community agencies in patient medical records. Likewise, a patient's refusal to accept resource infor-

mation should be noted in the medical records. Should a liability issue subsequently arise, the medical facility and staff can establish through medical
record documentation that all concerned acted appropriately by trying to intervene. The facility might consider the creation of a standard checklist for
available resource options. Such a list could easily be completed by the appropriate health care provider and made part of the patient's medical records.

Develop Safety Plans

According to the AMA (1992a), medical staff should discuss the patient's
safety with her before she leaves the medical facility. Eight issues that they
recommend one discuss with the victim/patient are:

1. Does she have friends or family with whom she (and her children) can stay?
2. Does she want immediate access to a shelter for herself (and for her children)?
3. If there are no available shelters, or if there is no space available, can she be
   admitted to the hospital?
4. If she does not want immediate access to a shelter, she should be given written
   information about shelters and other resources. She should also be alerted to
   keep the information in a safe place where her abusive partner will not find it.
   She may feel that it is unsafe for her to take the written information with her
   because, for example, her partner is likely to look through her purse when they
   leave the facility. If he finds such material, she may fear that he will batter her
   again. When such a situation occurs, she should be asked whether there is a safe
   address where the material can be mailed, such as that of a friend or relative
   who will not disclose the article of mail to the batterer.
5. Does she need immediate medical or psychiatric intervention?
6. Does she want immediate access to counseling to help her deal with the stress
   caused by the abuse?
7. Does she want to return to her partner, with a follow-up appointment at a later
   date?
8. Does she need referrals to local domestic violence organizations? Such organizations can provide information concerning social service, legal, and criminal
   justice resources and options.[2]

Advocates in the field of domestic violence take the issue of victim safety
one step further. They suggest that before a patient is released from the medical
facility, a safety plan be developed for the patient and provided to her. Such a
plan serves a twofold purpose. It can help a victim learn what to do when the
next incident of violence arises and can assist her as she begins to make plans
to escape from her abusive partner.

A safety plan need not be specially designed for each person the health care provider assists. Rather, general information can be distributed in a preprinted form. For example, the District of Columbia Coalition Against Domestic Violence prepared a two-sided information card that measures $3\frac{5}{8}$ inches by 4 inches. A perforation in the center of the card allows it to be folded so that the card becomes the size of a business card. One side of the card lists information of "Who To Call." This side provides telephone numbers for the police, battered women shelters, homeless shelters, and legal services and support groups for battered women. The reverse side of the card provides a minisafety plan. Information contained on the card is reproduced in Figure 4.7.

A safety plan should be printed in various languages, as needed. If the option of printing a card is used, I suggest printing the cards on white paper with black ink that is relatively inconspicuous. There is no need to give a battered woman a card that will stand out from her other belongings. Batterers have been well known to retaliate against the victim when they learn that she is contemplating leaving.

As an alternative to the brief preprinted card, a very thorough safety plan can be developed for each patient. Although time consuming to prepare, such a plan can greatly help a victim think through and plan how and when to leave an abusive partner. The Pennsylvania Coalition Against Domestic Violence has developed an excellent tool entitled "Personalized Safety Plan" (Hart & Stueling, 1992). The plan is intended to be completed by a victim working with an advocate.

Conduct Danger Assessments

Clinicians may want to consider conducting danger assessments for domestic violence patients who have sought treatment in their facilities. A danger assessment, sometimes referred to as a *lethality assessment,* is a device used to evaluate whether a domestic violence victim is at risk either for being killed by or for killing her abusive partner.

A few cautions go along with use of danger assessments. The assessment is not meant to be used by the domestic violence victim alone. It is intended to be administered by a nurse, social worker, or victim advocate who will discuss the result of the assessment with the victim. Providing this tool to a patient without administration by a knowledgeable person could cause the patient to panic when confronted with the result.

Predictive validity of the danger assessment has not been established (Campbell, 1995). The assessment is based on retrospective research that has

---

Don't Be Another Statistic:
Be Safe and Free From Violence

1. **Break the Silence.** Tell a family member or friend what's going on and keep this card with you at all times.
2. Plan **NOW** for your escape; think about all possible escape routes—not only doors, but first-floor windows and basement exits.
3. Plan **NOW** for a safe place for you and your children to go.
4. Have a backup plan in case the first plan doesn't work.
5. Let someone you trust keep your spare set of keys, clothes, birth certificates, passports, divorce/custody/separation agreements, protection orders, prescriptions, bank cards, and money.
6. Try not to let the abuser trap you in a kitchen with potential weapons or in small places like a bathroom.
7. If you are injured, go to a hospital or doctor, tell them what happened, and make sure they write it in your medical records.
8. Try to start a savings account in your own name. Save $10 from each check, or save some cash for an emergency. Keep it in a safe place near an escape exit. Keep your savings account book with a friend, and have statements sent to the friend's address.
9. Know your rights. Contact the District of Columbia Coalition Against Domestic Violence to find out about your legal rights and what resources are available in the community.
10. **If you are in immediate danger, don't wait, call 911.**

Figure 4.7. Information Card Safety Plan
SOURCE: *Safety/Exit Plan,* by the District of Columbia Coalition Against Domestic Violence, 1994, Washington, DC: Author. © 1994 District of Columbia Coalition Against Domestic Violence. Reprinted with permission.

identified factors associated with homicide (Campbell, 1986). The factors are correlates, not causative factors of homicide (Campbell, 1995). No combination of factors in the assessment will conclusively establish that a woman will be killed or that she may kill. At the other extreme, a batterer with only one positive characteristic may kill his victim.

Nonetheless, the assessment has value in the clinical setting. According to Barbara Hart, an attorney and leading victim advocate in the field of domestic violence, the danger assessment "is not a tool for certain prediction but rather one for risk assessment and safety planning or interventions in light of apprehended risk" (Hart & Gondolf, 1994, p. 7). The tool is designed simply to alert domestic violence victims that there may be a risk of homicide in their relationship and to help them assess that risk (Campbell, 1995). A danger assessment is shown in Figure 4.8.

Conduct Follow-up

In domestic violence cases, it is important that the health care facility, perhaps through the victim advocate, follow up with the victim/patient. Follow-up is needed for several reasons. First, at the time of treatment, a patient may be in crisis. If she was provided a large amount of resource information, she may not have understood it all. Second, some patients will need encouragement to follow through. Third, some patients simply need to know that someone cares about their well-being.

Follow-up can be accomplished in person or by telephone. Before the patient is released from the medical facility, a subsequent appointment can be scheduled to discuss the patient's options further or to discuss the progress of referrals. If telephone contact is used, care should be exercised. It is not unheard of for a batterer to listen in on telephone conversations. Even if he is not listening in, his nearby presence may prevent the victim from participating fully in the telephone conversation. Also, use caution in mailing materials to the victim. Mailed matter may be easily intercepted by an abusive partner so that the patient does not receive the materials sent to her. Further, such material may agitate a batterer and prompt a retaliatory beating. This means of contact should be used only if a safe address for the receipt of mail has been previously arranged with the patient.

◙ NOTES

1. From "Breaking the Cycle of Domestic Abuse," by C. S. Dotterer, June 30, 1992, *The Washington Post,* Health Section, p. Z-9. Copyright 1992 by C. S. Dotterer. Reprinted with permission.

2. From *Diagnostic and Treatment Guidelines on Domestic Violence* (p. 12), by the American Medical Association, 1992, Chicago: Author. Copyright 1992 by the American Medical Association. Adapted with permission.

Several risk factors have been associated with homicide (murder) of both batterers and battered women in research conducted after the killings have taken place. We cannot predict what will happen in your case, but we would like you to be aware of the danger of homicide in situations of severe battering and for you to see how many of the risk factors apply to your situation. (The *he* in the questions refers to your husband, partner, ex-husband, or whoever currently is physically hurting you.)

A. On the calendar, please mark the approximate dates during the past year when you were beaten by your husband or partner. Write on that date how long each incident lasted in approximate hours and rate the incident according to the following scale:

  1. Slapping, pushing; no injuries and/or lasting pain
  2. Punching, kicking; bruises, cuts, and/or continuing pain
  3. "Beating up"; severe contusions, burns, broken bones
  4. Threat to use weapon; head injury, internal injury, permanent injury
  5. Use of weapon; wounds from weapon

  (If any of the descriptions for the higher number apply, use the higher number.)

B. Answer these questions yes or no.

_____ 1. Has the physical violence increased in frequency during the past year?

_____ 2. Has the physical violence increased in severity during the past year, and/or has a weapon or threat with weapon been used?

_____ 3. Does he ever try to choke you?

_____ 4. Is there a gun in the house?

_____ 5. Has he ever forced you into sex when you did not want to have sex?

_____ 6. Does he use drugs? (By *drugs,* I mean "uppers" or amphetamines, speed, angel dust, cocaine, crack, street drugs, heroin, or mixtures).

Figure 4.8. Danger Assessment

SOURCE: *Danger Assessment,* by J. C. Campbell, 1985. Copyright Jacquelyn C. Campbell, Ph.D., RN, FAAN, Johns Hopkins University School of Nursing. Reprinted with permission. Please correspond with the author before using for research purposes.

_____ 7. Does he threaten to kill you and/or do you believe he is capable of killing you?

_____ 8. Is he drunk every day or almost every day? (In terms of quantity of alcohol).

_____ 9. Does he control most or all of your daily activities? (For instance, does he tell you whom you can be friends with, how much money you can take with you shopping, or when you can take the car?) (If he tries but you do not let him, check here _____).

_____ 10. Have you ever been beaten by him while you were pregnant? (If never pregnant by him, check here _____).

_____ 11. Is he violently and constantly jealous of you? (For instance, does he say, "If I can't have you, no one can"?)

_____ 12. Have you ever threatened or tried to commit suicide?

_____ 13. Has he ever threatened or tried to commit suicide?

_____ 14. Is he violent toward your children?

_____ 15. Is he violent outside the home?

_____ TOTAL YES ANSWERS

THANK YOU. PLEASE TALK WITH YOUR NURSE, ADVOCATE, OR COUNSELOR ABOUT WHAT THE DANGER ASSESSMENT MEANS IN TERMS OF YOUR SITUATION.

Figure 4.8. *Continued*

5

ASCERTAINING THE TRUE CAUSE OF INJURY AND COMPLIANCE WITH INJURY-REPORTING REQUIREMENTS

◈ THE IMPORTANCE OF OBTAINING TRUTHFUL INFORMATION

Getting a truthful explanation from a patient regarding the cause of her injuries has obvious medical significance because it may affect both diagnosis and treatment. Failure to ascertain how the patient was actually injured can lead to horrific results, as illustrated in the following case.

On February 9, 1994, the *Washington Post* reported the tragic August 31, 1993, death of 2-year-old Danny Carter, Jr. Apparently, Danny's mother had brought the child to the hospital claiming that a sibling had pushed him down a flight of stairs. On the basis of this information, doctors treated the child for a concussion. In truth, Danny's father, angered at Danny for wetting his bed, had picked his son up by the throat, punched him in the chest, and then thrown him to the ground. An autopsy revealed that the child suffered a bruised heart. Although it is not known if the correct information would have saved his life,

98

Danny's treatment surely would have been different if doctors had known the truth about his injuries.

Danny's mother eventually told the truth, but not until a month after Danny's death, while her husband lay dying from an overdose of Extra-Strength Tylenol. She was charged in connection with her son's death for providing false information. In her defense, her lawyer claimed that she had been severely battered by her husband over a long period of time, that she had been terrified of him, and that she had lied about her son's injuries out of fear of her husband.[1]

Could the hospital staff have determined that Danny's mother was a battered woman and that she lied out of fear of her husband? Studies show that in 45% to 59% of child abuse cases, the child's mother is also abused (McKibben, Devos, & Newberger, 1989). This case highlights the need for all medical care providers to screen routinely for abuse. Unfortunately, few hospitals have developed such intervention programs. Excellent programs are in place at Children's Hospital in Boston and the Children's Center for Child Protection in San Diego.

Medical staff should stress to all patients that information given regarding the cause of injury may affect treatment and that false information may endanger the patient's life. These points should be impressed on parents and caretakers of injured children as well.

Getting a truthful explanation from a patient regarding the cause of her injuries can also affect the success of a criminal prosecution of the batterer. However, as discussed in Chapter 7, incomplete or false patient statements in the medical records, or just the complete absence of patient statements from the medical records, may lead a jury to disbelieve a victim when she testifies truthfully at trial about the cause of her injuries.

◙ FACTORS THAT MAY AFFECT THE HEALTH CARE PROVIDER'S ABILITY TO ASCERTAIN THE TRUTH

A victim's fear of retaliation by the batterer may intimidate her from disclosing the abuse to anyone. A victim's love for the batterer or her misguided belief that she is in some way to blame for the violence can similarly affect her willingness to disclose abuse. Chapter 3 provides an in-depth discussion of the dynamics of an abusive relationship, many aspects of which are relevant to this issue.

As discussed in Chapters 2 and 4, the health care provider's mannerisms, attitudes, perceptions, and degree of sensitivity may affect the patient's willingness to disclose abuse.

Others present during the physician-patient encounter may influence the patient's ability to disclose. The most likely person to cause such interference is the batterer. A victim will not be able to tell the truth about how she was injured if her batterer is standing over her while she is being treated. If the victim does not speak English fluently, health care staff may unquestioningly use anyone accompanying her who is bilingual to interpret for them. However, her "interpreter" may well be her attacker. In such a case, not only is the batterer able to maintain a threatening atmosphere around the victim, but he may relate only such information to the victim as he wants her to hear. Likewise, he may substitute his own statements as answers to questions posed by the staff to the victim/patient.

The existence of mandatory injury-reporting laws may affect the victim/patient's willingness to make a truthful disclosure about abuse. Unlike victims of stranger-on-stranger crime, many victims of domestic violence do not necessarily want the crime to be reported to the police.

Another obstacle to a patient's willingness to disclose abuse could be fear that her health insurance will be canceled. It has recently come to light that some of the largest insurance companies in the United States routinely deny life and health coverage, and cancel coverage, for women who have been beaten by their husbands (Powers, 1994).

The justifications for such practices include viewing the battering as a "preexisting condition," likening a battered woman to a diabetic who refuses to take her insulin or to a skydiver or race car driver who voluntarily puts herself in a position of great risk, and seeing the insurance as providing the husband/beneficiary with a motive to kill his wife: the insurance proceeds.

The logic of such analogies is faulty. Domestic violence is not an illness and therefore is not like diabetes. There is no medication the victim can take to make the batterer stop attacking her. Domestic violence is not an activity one engages in for pleasure, money, or fame. Finally, battering is not about economic gain, it is about power and control. Even if economic gain were the motivation for violence, all states have "slayer rules" that bar murderers from taking their victims' property or from benefiting in any economic way from the premature death of their victim (Fellows, 1986).

In May 1994, the staff of Representative Charles E. Schumer (D-N.Y.) found that of 16 insurance companies, half admitted that they might reject an insurance applicant because she had been beaten by a husband or partner. Representative Schumer called on the insurance companies to end the practice voluntarily, adding that if they did not he would introduce legislation requiring them to do so.[2]

According to Schumer, the companies that denied coverage to battered women included State Farm, First Colony, and the Prudential. The Prudential denied having such a policy. The eight companies that would insure battered women were Allstate, Blue Cross of New York and Pennsylvania, Cigna, CNA, Mutual of Omaha, New York Life, The Travelers, and Wausau.[3] Following adverse publicity, the *New York Times* reported on June 1, 1994, that "weeks after receiving adverse publicity on the issue, State Farm Insurance announced today that it would no longer deny life insurance or health insurance to the victims of domestic violence."[4] The *Boston Globe* identified Nationwide, Allstate, Aetna, Metropolitan Life, the Equitable Companies, and the Principal Financial Group as additional companies that denied or canceled coverage to battered women.[5]

Several states have passed legislation to prohibit insurance companies' discrimination against victims of domestic violence. Some of the state laws apply to all kinds of insurance; others cover only health, life, or disability insurance. In 1995, California, Connecticut, Delaware, Florida, Iowa, and Massachusetts enacted laws to prohibit such insurance discrimination. Pennsylvania and Minnesota passed legislation in 1996. Legislation is currently pending in Alaska, Arizona, California, Georgia, Illinois, Indiana, Kansas, Maine, Maryland, Michigan, New York, Utah, Washington, West Virginia, Wisconsin, and Wyoming (Women's Law Project and the Pennsylvania Coalition Against Domestic Violence, 1996).

Federal bills have been sponsored by Senator Paul Wellstone, D-Minn. (H.R. Res. 1191, 1995, and H.R. Res. 1201, 1995), Representative Ron Wyden, D-Ore., and Senator Schumer (S. Res. 524, 1995). The Federal bills provide criminal and civil liability for insurers who treat domestic violence as a preexisting medical condition. The bills also prohibit insurance companies from "engaging in a practice that has the effect of denying, canceling or limiting health insurance benefits, or establishing, increasing or varying the premium charged for the coverage of benefits" for domestic violence victims (S. Res. 524, 1995; H.R. Res. 1191, 1995; H.R. Res. 1201, 1995).

A panel of the National Association of Insurance Commissioners heard testimony on March 14, 1995, and is also drafting model legislation to prohibit such insurance discrimination. The model legislation is expected to have great weight when presented by state insurance commissioners to state legislators.[6]

◙ STATE MANDATORY INJURY-REPORTING LAWS

A health care provider may be obligated by state law to report certain types of injuries to law enforcement. Laws that dictate such reporting are commonly referred to as *injury-reporting laws*. The obligation to report, however, may be in direct conflict with the wishes of the domestic violence victim. Where a mandatory reporting law is in effect, the wishes of the victim/patient are not controlling. If the criteria of the statute are met, the health care provider has no discretion; the report must be made. The only exception to the mandatory reporting law is where the state law conflicts with Federal law. In that event, Federal law is controlling. This topic is discussed later in the chapter.

State injury-reporting laws were created to provide a mechanism for alerting law enforcement that a suspected criminal is or was present at a health care facility. A classic scenario is that of the bank robber who is shot during the course of a robbery, who gets away, and who goes to a hospital for treatment of the gunshot wound. A mandatory injury-reporting law that covers injuries received by firearms would be likely to assist law enforcement in the apprehension of the bank robber.

Mandatory injury-reporting laws vary greatly from state to state in terms of what injuries must be reported, the form of the report and its contents, who must make the report, and to whom the report must be made. Some states do not have mandatory injury-reporting laws. At the other extreme, a few states have not only the general mandatory injury-reporting laws but also laws that specifically target the reporting of domestic violence.

Most states have injury-reporting laws mandating that certain health care providers make a report to law enforcement when a patient has suffered an injury caused by a firearm, accidental or otherwise. Most states also require reporting when a patient has suffered an injury caused by some other dangerous weapon when the injury was incurred as a result of a crime. In some states, the duty to report certain injuries to law enforcement is based solely on the injury, regardless of the context in which it was received. For example, in a jurisdiction that requires the health care provider to report all injuries caused by a knife, treatment of a patient who has suffered a slash wound must be reported to the authorities.

A few states have reporting laws that address domestic violence specifically. Ohio law (Reporting Felony: Medical Personnel to Report Gunshot, Stabbing, and Burn Injuries and Suspected Domestic Violence, 1993) mandates that certain medical professionals who know or have reasonable cause to believe that a patient has been a victim of domestic violence make note of that information in the patient's medical records. The professionals covered by the law include doctors, osteopaths, interns, residents, and registered or licensed practical nurses. California law (Injuries by Firearm; Assaultive or Abusive Conduct, 1995) explicitly includes spouse and cohabitant abuse in its general mandate regarding health care provider reports to law enforcement of injuries inflicted as "the result of assaultive or abusive conduct" (§ 11160(b)(3)(d)(18)). Colorado law (Injuries to Be Reported, 1995) mandates that physicians report injuries that the physician has reason to believe involved a criminal act, including domestic violence.

The reporting statutes generally impose the duty to report on the first specified individual to receive a request for, or actually to render, treatment to a person suffering from an injury or wound caused by the means or instrumentality specified in the reporting law. If the person rendering treatment works for a hospital or other specified institution, the obligation to report may fall on the administrator, superintendent, or other person in charge of the facility.

Generally, a report, where required, must be made to a specified law enforcement agency in the county where treatment is sought or rendered. In some states, however, health care providers report to non-law-enforcement officials. For example, Kentucky law (Rules and Regulations; Reports; Cabinet Actions, 1991) stipulates that they report to the Cabinet for Human Services. The cabinet notifies law enforcement. New Mexico law (Duty to Report, 1992) requires a report of adult abuse, neglect, or exploitation to the Human Services Department or other appropriate agency. Rhode Island law (Medical Data Collection Reports, 1993) provides for medical data collection reports when either the patient discloses domestic violence or the medical provider has reasonable cause to believe that the injuries resulted from it. The reports are filed quarterly with the court.

In some states, the failure to report or comply with the reporting law is a misdemeanor criminal violation punishable by fine and/or imprisonment. Other states do not specify that failure to report is a crime but provide a fine for nonreporting.

Some states explicitly provide civil and/or criminal immunity from liability, in connection with the required report, for the reporting person and the facility for which that person works. Many of the immunity laws presume that the mandated report is made in "good faith." Such laws generally state that immunity is provided except where "bad faith" or "malice" is shown. In other states, although immunity is not explicitly provided by statute, case law and rules of evidence that govern legal proceedings are clear that the physician-patient privilege is suspended in favor of mandatory reporting.

◙ STATE VOLUNTARY
INJURY-REPORTING LAWS

Some states have voluntary reporting statutes for acts of abuse. For example, Pennsylvania law (Protection From Abuse, 1991) provides that a voluntary report may be filed with the local police department by anyone having reasonable cause to believe that a person is being abused (§ 6115). *Abuse* is defined to include acts between family or household members and intimate partners. It includes, among other things, acts of intentional bodily injury, rape, and sexual assault (§ 6102). The contents of a report in Pennsylvania should include the name and address of the abused person, information concerning the nature and extent of the abuse, and any other information that the reporting person believes might be helpful to prevent further abuse. Any person who files a voluntary report in Pennsylvania is immune from civil and criminal liability unless the reporting person acted in bad faith or with a malicious purpose (§ 6115).

Mississippi law (Protection From Domestic Abuse, 1993) provides that a written report of known or suspected domestic abuse, between family or household members, may be made to the Department of Public Welfare. The reports and the identity of the reporting person are confidential (§ 93-21-25). *Abuse* includes intentional bodily injury (§ 93-21-3). Certain participants in the making of such reports are presumed to have acted in good faith and are immune from civil and criminal liability. The named participants include doctors, dentists, interns, residents, and nurses. Institutions are also covered (§ 93-21-23).

◙ FEDERAL LAWS THAT AFFECT
STATE INJURY REPORTING

When there is a conflict between Federal and state law, Federal law is controlling. Therefore, when a Federal law conflicts with a state injury- or domestic violence-reporting law, mandatory or otherwise, the Federal law must be followed. Such a conflict may arise when a victim of domestic violence seeks treatment from certain alcohol or drug treatment programs.

Title 42 of the U.S. Code ("Confidentiality of Records") prohibits the disclosure of patient records that are maintained by and relate to any federally assisted or regulated substance abuse program. The prohibition covers the patient's identity, diagnosis, prognosis, and treatment (§ 290dd-2(a)). These prohibitions apply to such patient records regardless of whether the person is currently or was formerly a patient (§ 290dd-2(d)).

The only permitted disclosures provided under Title 42 are those with a patient's written consent; those needed by other medical personnel to meet a medical emergency; those needed by qualified personnel for the purpose of conducting scientific research, audits, or program evaluation, provided that the patient's identity is not disclosed in any manner; or those pursuant to an appropriate court order granted for "good cause." Good cause involves a determination by a court that the public interest and the need for disclosure outweigh the potential injury to the patient, to the physician-patient privilege, and to the treatment services. No exception is provided for compliance with state injury-reporting laws (§ 290dd-2).

During recent years, Congress has voiced concern regarding the growing trend involving the release of patient information. This concern arose in the context of the movement of patients and their health information across state lines, automated data banks, and multistate health care providers.

In 1995, Congress passed model legislation entitled the Uniform Health-Care Information Act (61 Am. Jur. 2d *Physicians, Surgeons, Etc.* § 165.3, Supp. 1995). The act provides "model" law that Congress suggests be enacted in every state. However, it is up to the individual states to enact it if they see fit to do so. At present, only Montana and Washington have adopted the legislation.

The act was designed to provide uniform laws, rules, and procedures governing the use and disclosure of health care information. In the act, Congress identified multiple needs for such legislation. One such need is a recognition of the personal and sensitive nature of health care information that, if improperly used or released, could do significant harm to the patient's privacy, health care, or other interests (§ 165.3). The act places restrictions on the release of such information.

Section 2-101 of this act provides that

> except as authorized in § 2-104, a health-care provider, an individual who assists a health-care provider in the delivery of health-care, or an agent or employee of a health-care provider may not disclose health-care information about a patient to any other person without a patient's written authorization. A disclosure made under a patient's written authorization must conform to the authorization. (§ 171.5)

One authorized disclosure provided by the act is that a health care provider may disclose health care information about a patient without the patient's consent if the disclosure is to federal, state, or local law enforcement authorities, to the extent required by law (§ 171.5). This provision would include the disclosure of information to law enforcement pursuant to mandatory injury-reporting laws.

Under the act, *health care information* is defined as any information, oral or recorded, in any form or medium, that identifies or can be readily associated with the identity of a patient and relates to the patient's health care. It also includes any record of disclosures of such information (§ 163.5). *Health care provider* is broadly defined to include any person who is licensed, certified, or authorized by law to provide health care in the ordinary course of business or practice of a profession. It does not include, however, one who provides health care solely via the sale or dispensing of drugs or medical devices (§ 165.3). *Patient* is defined to include any person who receives or received health care. The term also includes a deceased individual who received health care (§ 165.3).

Under the act, for a patient's consent for disclosure to be valid, it must be in writing, be dated, be signed by the patient, identify the nature of the information to be disclosed, and identify the person to whom the information is to be disclosed (§ 171.5).

A disclosure authorization that would meet the requirements of the model act is provided in Figure 5.1. Under the act, the patient's authorization must be retained with the medical records or with any other health care information from which the disclosures were made. The patient may revoke a waiver at any time, unless given to effectuate payments for health care already provided, or unless substantial action has been taken in reliance on the authorization (§ 171.5).

The act provides criminal and civil penalties for the willful disclosure of information in violation of the act when the person making the disclosure knew or should have known that such disclosure was prohibited. A violation may be criminally punished by a fine and/or imprisonment (§ 165.3). In addition, a person who is aggrieved by a violation of the act may bring a civil action for damages and for pecuniary loss sustained as a result of the violation. The aggrieved party may recover damages if the violation resulted from willful or grossly negligent conduct. Attorney's fees and other expenses may also be awarded (§ 165.3). Note that in this model legislation, Congress referenced the amount of the fine and length of jail time in brackets. This indicates that it is up to the individual state legislatures to determine the appropriate penalties.

◧ COMPLIANCE ISSUES

Various questions surround compliance with mandatory injury-reporting laws: How does the physician-patient privilege figure into such laws? Exactly what information should the health care provider report? Is it better to give more information than is required by law? What would be a case of "bad-faith" reporting? If a patient consents to the notification of law enforcement, how does that consent affect the health care provider's ability to report to law enforcement and the scope of the disclosure? Is oral consent to disclose sufficient, or should it be in writing?

The Physician-Patient Privilege

The physician-patient privilege is a purely legislative creation. These laws did not exist at common law (81 Am. Jur. 2d *Witnesses* § 435 (1992)). Today, every state in the United States has such a law. The purpose of physician-patient privilege laws is to foster the free flow of information between the physician and the patient to facilitate treatment and to encourage individuals in need of medical care to seek it. These laws generally provide that information concerning the fact of treatment, communications between a physician and patient for the purpose of treatment, and all medical records are confidential and not subject to disclosure absent patient consent, court order, or statutory mandate. Third parties present during treatment may also be covered by the privilege if either their presence was required to assist the physician or they facilitated communication between the doctor and patient (81 Am. Jur. 2d *Witnesses* § 449 (1992)). Other professionals may be covered by the privilege, as provided by law.

An injury-reporting law that dictates the disclosure of information that would otherwise be prohibited by the physician-patient privilege reflects a societal determination that the need to identify certain crimes outweighs the rights and needs of the individual patient to confidentiality in obtaining treatment. Such laws are generally considered legislative exceptions to the physician-patient privilege (61 Am. Jur. 2d *Physicians, Surgeons, Etc.* § 170 (1981)).

What to Report

When a mandatory report is required, the reporting person should disclose as much of the statutorily requested information as is available, but no more than that. If the statute mandates that the report include the injured person's name, address, whereabouts, and the character and extent of the injuries, only that information should be disclosed, unless that patient has given written consent for a broader disclosure. If the law mandates reporting but does not specify the type of information that is to be provided, the reporting person can report broadly because the law does not explicitly limit the type of information to be provided. The report to law enforcement must be made in good faith. As a general rule, information that would be helpful in establishing that a crime was committed or

[On Facility Letterhead]

RECORD OF INJURY DISCLOSURE
TO LAW ENFORCEMENT

_____ This disclosure was made pursuant to the patient's written consent, a copy of which was provided to the law enforcement officer referenced below, OR

_____ This disclosure was made pursuant to state law.

On _____, the following patient
     (Date)

information was disclosed to _____
                        (Name of Law Enforcement Officer)

_____, _____, _____
(Badge No.) (Law Enforcement Agency) (District or Precinct)

This notification was made: (circle appropriate response)

in writing: by *mail* **or** by *fax* to (__)_____-_____ **or**

orally: *by telephone* to (__)_____-_____ **or** *in person*

Patient name: _____

Patient addresses:

Home: _____, _____, _____
        (Street)   (City)   (State)

Work: _____, _____, _____
       (Street)   (City)   (State)

Patient telephone numbers: *H:* (__)_____-_____
                          W: (__)_____-_____

Date of assault: _____, _____

Location of assault: _____, _____, _____
                 (Street)   (City)   (State)

Approximate time of assault: ____:____ a.m./p.m.

Date(s) of treatment: _____

Nature or description of injury: _____

Weapon used during assault, if any: _____

Figure 5.1. Sample Form for Reporting Patient Injury to Law Enforcement

Name of perpetrator, if known: _____

Home and/or work address of perpetrator, if known:

Home Address: _____, _____, _____
                     (Street)   (City)   (State)

Work Address: _____, _____, _____
                    (Street)   (City)   (State)

Relationship between victim and perpetrator, if any:

_____

Other identifying information about perpetrator, if known:

Sex: _____

Date of Birth: _____

Social Security Number: _____

Race: _____

Approximate Height: _____ Approximate Weight: _____

Other important information:

_____

_____

_____

This information was reported by:

_____

(Name of Reporting Person, Print)

_____

(Title of Reporting Person, Print)

(__)_____-_____

(Telephone Number of Reporting Person)

_____

*Notice: The information in this Disclosure to Law Enforcement was provided in compliance with the laws of the state of [insert name of state] pursuant to Code Section [insert code section] and/or patient authorization. Under no circumstances should any of the information provided here be disclosed to any non-law-enforcement individual or entity or to the person named as the perpetrator or any of his representatives.

Figure 5.1. *Continued*

in identifying a perpetrator would probably be considered disclosed in good faith.

All facilities should maintain written documentation of all patient consents to disclosure, compliance with applicable laws, and any disclosures made. The 1996 JCAHO standards (JCAHO, 1995) require hospitals to maintain such documentation. A suggested record of disclosure is shown in Figure 5.1. Note that such a form should be tailored to track the types of information required to be disclosed pursuant to the state injury-reporting law in your jurisdiction. Figure 5.1 assumes that the facility is located in a jurisdiction that mandates reporting of the injury under treatment but does not specifically limit the kind of information that may be disclosed to law enforcement. This form would also be satisfactory for a situation in which the patient has consented to the release of such information.

Bad-Faith Reporting

A report made in bad faith could include the following situations: A reporting person intentionally discloses information beyond the scope of the reporting law and without patient consent; a reporting person deliberately reports false or inaccurate information; or a report is submitted that contains editorial comments of personal opinion not relevant to determining whether a crime occurred or who committed it.

Consider the following example. Suppose that a female patient, age 32, is brought into the emergency department by a male companion. She has severe bruises on her face and head, consistent with blunt-force trauma. She has also been doused in kerosene. The patient discloses to staff that her companion beat her with his fists and that during the course of that beating, he poured the kerosene on her and threatened to set her on fire. The patient is extremely frightened but is very forthcoming about the facts of the incident and the extensive history of violence she has endured. However, the patient does not want the police to be notified, and she does not want to press criminal charges. She refuses to consent to the release of information to law enforcement authorities. The perpetrator, her live-in boyfriend, is seated in the waiting room adjacent to the treatment area.

Should this incident be reported to the police even though the patient does not want it to be reported? The answer to this question depends on the following variables.

Does the jurisdiction have a mandatory injury-reporting law? If not, absent patient consent, no report should be made to law enforcement. Absent consent or a statutory mandate, the physician-patient privilege prohibits the disclosure. If there is a mandatory reporting law, proceed to the next question.

Under the mandatory reporting law, what injuries or wounds must be reported? Does the injury or wound in question come within the scope of the law? The answer to this question depends on the jurisdiction in which the woman is treated.

In jurisdictions that mandate only the reporting of burns or injuries caused by a firearm, knife, axe, or sharp or pointed instrument, no report should be made to law enforcement. The injuries described do not fall within such reporting mandates.

Other language in the statute might require the report nonetheless. For example, consider whether a report on this incident would be mandatory in a jurisdiction that provided for the reporting of injuries inflicted by means of a "dangerous weapon." Clearly, kerosene as used in this illustration is a dangerous weapon. Although kerosene has legitimate uses, when intentionally poured on another person coupled with the threat to set that person on fire, it becomes a substance likely to cause death or serious bodily injury. Here, the perpetrator in the scenario did in fact threaten that he would set the victim on fire. Had he carried out his threat, the combination of kerosene and fire could have caused death or severe bodily injury to the victim.

However, in the illustration, the threat of setting the victim on fire was not carried out. Absent serious injury caused by the chemical substance itself, such as a corrosive burn, the victim's only physical injuries were those caused by the perpetrator beating her with his fists. In this situation, no report should be made to law enforcement.

If the state law provides for a more general reporting of wounds or injuries such as those "inflicted by means of violence," "resulting from assaultive or abusive conduct including abuse of spouse or cohabitant," "in violation of the state penal law," "resulting from illegal or unlawful conduct," "received in connection with a criminal offense," or "resulting in actual or threatened bodily injury," this case should be reported to the appropriate law enforcement authority.

If injuries were caused by chemical burn, reporting may be required under statutes mandating the reporting of certain burns. If a perpetrator throws a corrosive chemical substance such as lye, drain opener, or bleach onto the victim or douses the victim with an accelerant and sets her on fire, resulting injuries may come within the provisions related to burns, injuries received by means of dangerous weapons, or injuries received in violation of the state penal laws.

Some state laws require the reporting of wounds or injuries that are likely to result in death. But if we assume that the injuries in the example above are not life threatening, no report should be made on this basis either.

Patient Consent to
Law Enforcement Notification

If a patient consents to law enforcement notification, the health care provider may disclose any information within the scope of that consent, regardless of the reporting law in the jurisdiction. However, because a patient may subsequently claim that no consent was given or that due to her injuries she was not in the frame of mind to comprehend and therefore gave the consent involuntarily, it would be prudent for the health care provider always to obtain the patient's consent to the disclosure in writing. A standardized form should be used for this purpose. A model Disclosure Authorization Form is shown in Figure 5.2. Once the consent form is signed, it should be maintained as part of the patient's medical records.

Should the medical facility incorporate language into its general patient disclosure authorization form concerning the release of information related to substance abuse programs? In my opinion, the facility should not. If current treatment involves substance abuse treatment, the model form that I have suggested, Figure 5.2, covers such a disclosure. However, the form does not specifically highlight such treatment. A patient who is being treated today for a broken jaw suffered during an attack by a battering partner may be perfectly willing to consent to the release of her medical records concerning the current treatment. However, this patient may not want to consent to the disclosure of medical records that reflect that she received alcohol abuse counseling at the same facility 3 years ago. These are issues best addressed by the prosecutor.

When the prosecutor interviews the victim concerning the case, he or she will probably learn about the victim's history of substance abuse. Under certain circumstances, a full discussion of which is beyond the scope of this book, a prosecutor may be required by law to disclose the fact of the patient's prior substance abuse treatment to the defense. However, the disclosure to the defense, the extent of that disclosure, and the admissibility of this information at trial are issues that the prosecutor may want to litigate. This issue may have tremendous significance to the victim because evidence introduced at trial becomes public information. If the treatment occurred some time prior to the battering incident, which is the subject matter of the case, and if there is no indication that the patient was delusional or suffered certain memory problems, such as the ability to recall information sequentially, it is likely that a court would prohibit the disclosure or use of the records.

A physician would violate the physician-patient privilege and could be held liable if he or she disclosed patient information concerning a crime to law enforcement when no duty to report existed and if the patient did not want the matter reported to the police. Consider, for example, a patient who is reassaulted by the batterer following the physician's report to the police. The patient could allege that if the doctor had not made an unauthorized report to the police, the batterer would not have retaliated. She might maintain a legal action for damages against the physician and the medical facility. Because the physician was under no obligation to report, the physician would not be immune from liability for the disclosure. Indeed, under these facts, it could be inferred that the physician acted in bad faith. The bottom line is that medical staff should report domestic violence crimes to the police only when required to do so by law or when the patient consents in writing and requests assistance in contacting the police.

Issues Regarding Mandatory Injury Reporting of Domestic Violence

Although the soundness of mandatory injury-reporting laws for stranger-on-stranger crime seems clear, the soundness of such laws for domestic violence is questionable. First, unlike most victims of stranger-perpetrated crime, victims of domestic violence may not want the crime reported. Second, mandatory reporting in the context of domestic violence may incite retaliation by the batterer at a time when the victim is physically injured and is not prepared emotionally or financially to leave him. Third, after the first mandatory report triggers police contact, a batterer may interfere with the victim's ability to seek medical treatment in the future.

Health care providers who want to help the patient but also want to obey the law may experience an ethical dilemma when the wishes of the patient conflict with the state mandatory reporting requirements. As a means of avoiding this conflict, the AMA (1995b) suggested that mandatory reporting requirements be explained to the domestic violence patient at the outset so that she can make a decision about whether she feels safe to make a disclosure.

Inasmuch as reports to law enforcement may incite retaliation by the batterer, such reports should always be coupled with safety planning for the patient. Refer to Chapter 4 for a discussion of safety planning.

[On Facility Letterhead]

DISCLOSURE AUTHORIZATION

_____

(Date)

I, _____, hereby state as follows:
(Patient Name)

I was assaulted on _____, 19___,
                      (Date)

by _____
   (Name of Perpetrator, if known)

_____, _____-_____-_____, _____
(Date of Birth)   (Social Security No.)   (Race)

Approximate Height: _____ Approximate Weight: _____

Home: _____

Work:_____
         (home and/or work address of perpetrator, if known)

The assault occurred at _____,
                            (Street Address)

_____, _____, at approximately ____:____ a.m/p.m.
(City)   (State)

My relationship to the perpetrator is _____.
                           (Relationship)

In connection with injuries I received during the assault, I sought medical treatment at the facility indicated above. I want this incident to be reported to law enforcement authorities.

I hereby give consent to this facility and _____
                             (Name of Reporting Person)

Figure 5.2. Model Disclosure Authorization Form

to disclose to appropriate law enforcement authorities [which may include the Sheriff's Office or Chief of Police] any and all information that may be helpful in establishing that a crime was committed and in identifying the perpetrator of the crime. This disclosure authorization covers all information concerning my identity and the examination, diagnosis, prognosis, and treatment I have received in connection with the crime that has been committed. **Under no circumstances, however, should this document be released to any non-law-enforcement person or entity absent court order or my written consent.**

I understand that this Disclosure Authorization will be maintained as part of my medical records.

My identifying information is as follows:

Home Address:

_____

Home Telephone Number: (__)_____-_____

An alternative telephone number at which I can be reached is:

(__)_____-_____

Work Address:

_____

Work Telephone Number: (__)_____-_____

Date of Birth: _____

Social Security Number: _____-_____-_____

Dated: _____

Signed: _____

_____

(Name of patient should be printed below signature)

Witnessed by: _____

_____

(Name of witness should be printed below signature)

Figure 5.2. *Continued*

◙ NOTES

1. From "Woman Pleads Guilty in Death of Son, 2," by P. Davis, February 9, 1994, *The Washington Post*, p. B-1. Copyright 1994 by The Washington Post. Adapted with permission.

2. From "Insurers Admit Denying Policies to Battered Women," by R. Powers, May 13, 1994, *The Patriot News*, p. A-5. Copyright 1994 by the Associated Press. Adapted with permission.

3. From "Some Battered Women Denied Health Coverage," by S. Thomma, May 14, 1994, *The Orange County Register,* p. C-5. Reprinted by permission: Tribune Media Services.

4. From "In Shift, State Farm Will Insure Battered Women," by K. Q. Seelye, June 1, 1994, *The New York Times*, p. A-19. Copyright © 1994 by The New York Times Company. Reprinted by permission.

5. From "Domestic Violence Victims Are Routinely Rejected by Major Insurers," by J. Gaines, March 12, 1995, *The Boston Globe*, p. 1. Reprinted courtesy of The Boston Globe.

6. From "Domestic Violence Victims Testify They Were Denied Insurance," by J. Pacenti, March 15, 1995, *The San Diego Union-Tribune*, p. A-26. Copyright 1995 by the Associated Press. Adapted with permission.

◆ 6

SAFETY ISSUES

◆ VIOLENCE IN THE MEDICAL SETTING

Violent crime in the medical setting, particularly in hospitals, is a serious problem that is on the rise in the United States. There are many potentials for such violence. Domestic violence aftermath is one. Other catalysts may include illness in psychiatric patients, drug- or alcohol-abusing patients, combative trauma patients, patients and visitors who have endured long waiting periods for treatment, distraught family members, and individuals involved with drug and gang violence.

Although no one at a medical facility, employee or otherwise, is immune from violence, a 1992 study by the International Association for Healthcare Security and Safety (IAHSS) noted that physicians are increasingly the focus of the anger and frustration of patients and visitors (cited in Stultz, 1993).

Studies have documented a high incidence of violence in hospital emergency departments. According to Saxton Mahoney (1990), there are four primary reasons that the emergency department is conducive to violence: (a) there is unlimited accessibility to the public; (b) the physical environment is noisy or full of activity conducive to unrest; (c) patients or family members may become fearful, or the injury or illness may lead to a violent outburst; and (d) characteristics of the nursing staff, such as long hours, understaffing, and repeated harassment, increase frustrations. In addition, due to the increasing number of people who lack insurance, the demand for treatment in public hospitals may exceed the providers' ability to keep pace. Longer waits for treatment may lead to anger ("Doctor Shootings," 1993).

A survey conducted by Saxton Mahoney (1990) found that of 1,209 emergency department nurses surveyed from 124 hospitals in Pennsylvania, 36% reported having been the victims of job-related violence in the previous 12-month period and 63% reported at least one job-related assault during their careers. These crimes were perpetrated by patients, visitors, and family members of patients. The study also concluded that violence occurs in all hospital settings: urban, suburban, and rural.

A 1991 study conducted by Smith and Wichelman (M. Smith, personal communication, September 28, 1995) surveyed 494 directors of emergency nursing whose hospitals had 300 or more beds. The study showed that during the preceding 5-year period, 18% reported shootings or people being held at gunpoint, 38% reported use of knives or razorblades to threaten staff, and 43% reported armed threats with miscellaneous objects such as furniture and equipment. Of the gun-related incidents, 64% took place in an urban setting, 28% in a suburban setting, and 8% in a rural setting. Most of these directors indicated dissatisfaction with the security measures at their facilities. Eighty-three percent wanted to see improvement.

A 1992 study conducted by the California Emergency Nurses Association found that of 103 hospitals in California, 70% reported injuries suffered by staff, visitors, or patients. The most lethal weapons, knives and loaded guns, were those most commonly brought into the emergency department. Unloaded guns and makeshift weapons were also reported (Keep & Gilbert, 1992).

With regard to all patient treatment, the foremost issue should be to provide an environment where the patient, medical staff, and others in the medical facility are safe. The development of an appropriate safety protocol can help to provide such an environment. Although planned specific responses to all types of perpetrators may be important, Isaac, Cochran, Brown, and Adams (1994) documented that a planned response is particularly important in domestic violence cases. They reviewed the characteristics of men who batter and concluded that all clinical settings should have protocols for response to domestic violence, including guidelines ensuring on-site safety of staff and clients.

What particular danger does domestic violence present at the medical facility? In some cases, it is the batterer and his likely presence at the facility following a domestic violence episode. Why does the batterer often come to the medical facility with the patient or after her treatment has begun? His behavior is driven by the fear that if he is not present to maintain a threatening, controlling environment, his abusive conduct will be reported to the authorities. With this in mind, all health care providers should consider at the outset that unless the domestic violence victim is brought in by the police or comes in alone, her escort could be her batterer. In such situations, caution should be exercised. Remember, if the victim is seeking treatment for trauma, the batterer has already demonstrated his capacity for physical violence.

These issues are not new to the medical arena. Domestic violence victims have always sought treatment. However, health care recognition of the actual cause of the trauma and effective treatment of the cause through intervention are new. The job hazards related to the treatment of domestic violence patients should be recognized, examined, and minimized to the extent possible. This area is actually a subissue of visitor or family member violence. The potential danger a visitor can cause in an emergency department is a recognized hazard (American College of Emergency Physicians, 1988).

From a liability perspective, medical facilities should take all steps reasonably necessary to ensure a safe environment. According to Taliaferro (1988), if it can be shown that a hospital administrator knew that violence might reasonably be expected to occur but failed to do anything, the administrator could be held liable for negligence and willful disregard. Taliaferro further pointed out that negligence is difficult to defend but is covered by malpractice insurance, whereas willful disregard is not covered by malpractice insurance.

◈ SAFETY STANDARDS

Every medical facility should have a safety protocol. Such a protocol should include policies, procedures, and practices concerning precautions, responses, reporting, and follow-up to criminal activity and violent behavior. Written guidelines ensure clear communication and consistent, fair application of the rules (54 Fed. Reg. § 3912, 1989). In deciding whether to establish such a protocol or in evaluating the sufficiency of an existing protocol, there are certain recognized medical guidelines and workplace regulations to consider. For example, JCAHO's security standards are contained in the *1996 Comprehensive Accreditation Manual for Hospitals* (CAMH; JCAHO, 1995) and appear in Figure 6.1.

As a second consideration, the General Duty Clause of the Occupational Safety and Health Act of 1970 provides that an employer must "furnish to each of his employees employment and a place of employment which are free from recognized hazards that are causing or are likely to cause death or serious physical harm to his employees" (29 U.S.C. § 654 (a)(1) (1988)) and must "comply with occupational health and safety standards promulgated" under the act (29 U.S.C. § 654 (a)(1)-(2) (1988)).

Standard EC.1.4: A management plan addresses security.

Intent of EC.1.4:

A security management plan describes how the organization will establish and maintain a security management program to protect staff, patients, and visitors from harm. The plan provides processes for:

a. leadership's designation of personnel responsible for developing, implementing, and monitoring the security management program;
b. addressing security issues concerning patients, visitors, personnel, and property;
c. reporting and investigating all security incidents involving patients, visitors, personnel, or property;
d. providing identification, as appropriate, for all patients, visitors, and staff;
e. controlling access to sensitive areas, as determined by the organization; and
f. providing vehicular access to urgent care areas.

In addition, the plan establishes:

g. a security orientation and education program that addresses:
   1. processes for minimizing security risks for personnel in security-sensitive areas,
   2. emergency procedures followed during security incidents, and
   3. processes for reporting security incidents involving patients, visitors, personnel, and property;
h. performance standards for
   1. staff security management knowledge and skill,
   2. the level of staff participation in security management activities,
   3. monitoring and inspection activities,
   4. emergency and incident reporting procedures that specify when and to whom reports are communicated, and
   5. inspection, preventive maintenance, and testing of security equipment; and

Figure 6.1. JCAHO 1996 Security Standards for Medical Facilities
SOURCE: From *1996 Comprehensive Accreditation Manual for Hospitals.* Oakbrook Terrace, IL: Joint Commission on Accreditation of Healthcare Organizations, 1995, pp. 345-347 and 359.

i. emergency security procedures that address
1. actions taken in the event of a security incident or failure,
2. handling of civil disturbances,
3. handling of situations involving VIPs or the media, and
4. provision of additional staff to control human and vehicle traffic in and around the environment of care during disasters.

The objectives, scope, performance, and effectiveness of the security management plan are evaluated annually.

Examples of the implementation of EC.1.4 would include the establishment of performance standards that promote an environment of care in which employees, staff, visitors, and patients are protected from harm. The performance standards may include those that access:

— staff members' knowledge and skill requirements regarding their role in the security management program and their expected level of participation;
— monitoring and inspection activities;
— routine emergency and incident reporting procedures including when and to whom such reports are to be communicated; and
— inspection, preventive maintenance, and testing of security equipment.

Evidence of performance for EC.1.4 are management plans, performance standards, and emergency procedures for the issues addressed in the standard, and staff interviews.

Standard EC.2.3: The security management plan is implemented.

Intent of EC.2.3:

The organization implements the security management plan and performance standards, including all features described in EC.1.4.

Examples of evidence of performance for EC.2.3 are building and ground tours, observation of visitor security procedures, and staff interviews.

Figure 6.1. *Continued*

A third consideration is the OSHA Safety and Health Program Management Guidelines. These guidelines, which are voluntary, went into effect on January 22, 1989. They are intended for employer use in preventing occupational injuries and illnesses. Identified in these guidelines are four elements that OSHA believes are necessary for an effective occupational safety and health program:

1. the commitment of management and employee involvement,
2. effective worksite analysis to identify existing and potential hazards,
3. hazard prevention and control, and
4. safety and health training that addresses the responsibilities of all personnel (54 Fed. Reg. § 3909 [1989]).

The comments to the OSHA guidelines indicate that these four elements have been observed in exemplary workplaces where safety and health programs were well maintained and injury rates were exceptionally low (54 Fed. Reg. § 3910, Commentary, 1995). OSHA is in the process of developing health-care-environment-specific guidelines entitled "Guidelines for Workplace Violence Prevention Programs for Health Care Workers in Institutional and Community Settings" (S. Fox, personal communication, September 1, 1995).

Litigation to date involving OSHA standards and the General Duty Clause suggest that an employer has the duty to establish and maintain management practices necessary to ensure that safe and healthful working conditions are maintained and that corollary work practices are followed. A violation of the General Duty Clause may be established by proving that the employer failed to render the workplace free of a recognized, preventable hazard that caused or was likely to cause death or serious bodily harm. Criminal sanctions are provided for willful violations of the act.

OSHA may be on the road to becoming more aggressive in holding health care facilities accountable for workplace violence. In 1993, OSHA used the General Duty Clause to cite Charter Barclay Hospital, a Chicago psychiatric institution, for failing to protect workers from recognized hazards regarding physical assaults by violent patients. This was the first time OSHA had used the General Duty Clause against a health care facility for failure to protect its employees from workplace violence. The institution was fined, and OSHA proposed an abatement program that included increased identification of potential risks, communication between management and employees to identify the best way to respond to risks, and development of risk prevention techniques (Howard-Martin & Howard, 1994).

The state of California has taken the lead in enacting laws to deal proactively with hospital workplace violence. The laws require licensed hospitals to conduct safety and security assessments and to develop plans to deal with workplace violence (Security and Safety Assessment, 1993). California law also mandates security training and education for all emergency department employees and medical staff who are regularly assigned to assist in that department and other departments identified in the security plan (Security Training and Education, 1993). Education and training topics must include general safety measures, personal safety measures, the assault cycle, aggression- and violence-predicting factors, obtaining patient history from a patient with violent behavior, characteristics of aggressive and violent patients and victims, verbal and physical maneuvers to defuse and avoid violent behavior, strategies to avoid physical harm, restraining techniques, appropriate use of medications as chemical restraint, and any resources available to employees for coping with incidents of violence, including critical-incident stress debriefing or employee assistance programs.

Safety protection helps keep injuries and liability down. There are other positive benefits as well. OSHA notes that the effective management of safety protection not only improves employee morale and productivity but reduces worker's compensation costs and other costs of work-related injuries (Safety and Health Program Management Guidelines, 1989). No one can absolutely prevent the violence of another person. However, medical facilities can take preventive measures to deter violence.

◖ RECOMMENDED HOSPITAL SECURITY MEASURES

In keeping with OSHA's four major program elements, recommendations are made here for improving safety in the medical setting as related to the treatment of domestic violence patients. The suggestions and precautions that follow will also help strengthen hospital security regarding other types of criminal activity. If a comprehensive safety program is already in effect, facility administrators should ensure that their program recognizes the treatment of domestic violence patients as another area of potential risk and that appropriate protections are integrated into the current safety program.

The following case example highlights dangers that may occur in the absence of certain basic security measures.

One day "Mary" told "Robert"[1] that she wanted to end their relationship, and he subsequently moved out. Weeks later, while Robert was visiting their daughter at Mary's home, Mary received a telephone call from a friend. Robert flew into a rage, jumped on top of Mary, and told her that he loved her but had to kill her. Robert stabbed her repeatedly and slit her throat nearly ear to ear, severing her jugular vein. A witness summoned the police, who arrived to find Robert still on the scene. He was placed under arrest.

An ambulance transported Mary to the hospital, where she underwent life-saving surgery. Meanwhile, Robert was taken to the police station, where he was booked, then transported to the courthouse to await arraignment on the criminal charges filed against him. At the arraignment, Robert was released to third-party custody pending trial. On his release, he headed straight for the hospital. Mary awoke from anesthesia, unable to speak, to find Robert standing over her. When she opened her eyes, he said, "See, I could finish the job at any time." To all appearances, he was absolutely right.[2]

Fortunately, Robert did not carry out his threat. However, what if he had harmed Mary? Would the hospital have been liable for damages for failure to provide her with appropriate security while she was in their care? The potential danger could have extended to hospital employees as well. Suppose a member of housekeeping or the nursing staff had happened to walk into the room just as Robert was making his threat. What if he had attacked that person? Would the hospital be liable? After all, even if the hospital was unaware of the identity of the perpetrator, the facility was on notice by the very nature of the injuries that a crime victim was in their care.

Hospitalized trauma patients are particularly vulnerable to attack. Such a patient's hospital room door is unsecured, allowing easy access to anyone who makes his way through the facility. The fact that the patient is already in an injured condition and may be medicated makes her less able to protect herself (Colling, 1992).

Ideally, a hospital should be notified by local law enforcement that charges have been filed against an individual or that a specific person is believed to pose a threat to a patient in their care. This notification should include the perpetrator's name; alias, if any; physical description; and a photograph or other likeness, if available.

Ordinarily, if a batterer who has been charged with a crime is released from custody pending trial, the court will issue a stay-away/no-contact order directing the defendant not to go near the victim/patient. A hospital should be notified of the existence of such an order.

Unfortunately, hospitals may be left out of the information loop due to the absence of a coordinated community response to domestic violence. A coordinated approach is one that should involve the medical community and other agencies, including the police and the prosecutor's office. In the absence of a coordinated approach, hospitals should take the lead in establishing a liaison with local law enforcement to facilitate receiving the kind of information discussed above. Once received, such information should be flagged in the patient's chart and provided to appropriate hospital personnel, including the security office, the nursing station on the floor where the patient is located, and any visitor check-in points.

Caution should be exercised in disseminating information concerning domestic violence victim/patients, because an employee of the facility will not always know with whom he or she is speaking. It may be the batterer or a third party acting on his behalf attempting to ascertain information. Even seemingly innocuous information, such as the time a patient will be released, may be helpful to a batterer who intends to retaliate. Information that a victim intends to stay at a local shelter should never be disclosed to anyone. This protects the victim's well-being, as well as that of the other shelter residents.

Extra care should be used in releasing information over the telephone concerning these victim/patients. According to Klingbeil and Boyd (1984), batterers have been known to impersonate family members, police officers, ambulance attendants, and others to try to get information about their partners.

According to Scott (1994), if there is a fear that the perpetrator will seek the patient out to retaliate or "finish the job," staff should maintain the patient under an alias "Jane Doe" identity. Dissemination of information within the hospital regarding the true identity of this patient should be minimized and disclosed on a need-to-know basis. Outside callers or visitors asking for this patient should be told that no such person is registered at the facility. A telephone should not be placed in the room of an "AKA" (also known as) patient, as such patients may unknowingly compromise their own safety by calling friends, who then disclose their whereabouts to the perpetrator. This is particularly important in today's age of telephone caller identification.

Uncontrolled visitor access to the facility is another safety issue. Where outsiders may enter freely, there is no opportunity to bar even a known perpetrator. One solution would be for all visitors to sign in and be issued visitor passes while on hospital grounds. The issuing of visitor passes, in and of itself, has a preventive component. An individual who goes through the process of obtaining a visitor pass often assumes there is more control in the facility than there actually is (Colling, 1992). In addition, this written record of the visitor's presence at the hospital may serve as a deterrent to inappropriate behavior.

A visitor pass should be a bright color and can be either clip-on or self-adhesive. It should be worn on the visitor's shirt in plain view. The date of issue should be clearly displayed on the badge. Another feature is for each of the badges to boldly display a number. This number could be cross-referenced to the visitor sign-in log. These security measures allow for a restricted visitor list, which is another security option. Such lists, if used, should be maintained by security, nurse stations, and visitor sign-in areas (Simonowitz, 1993).

Aside from the issue of visitor passes, all employees should wear photo ID badges. These badges should be a color obviously different from that of visitor identification badges. In considering whether to implement such a system, note that anyone can look official in a white doctor's coat. Consider, for example, the following case reported by the *New York Times* on March 27, 1989:

> Until recently, few people outside of law enforcement had ever heard of the New York City Hospital Police, the tiny, unarmed security force deployed in the often chaotic wards and hallways of the city's municipal hospitals. All that changed Jan. 7, when a young doctor was raped and strangled in her office at Bellevue Hospital Center. The suspect in the murder of Dr. Kathyrn Hinnant, a 23-year-old homeless man with a history of psychiatric problems, told astonished New York City police detectives that he had been living for weeks in a storage closet, from which he had been making regular forays around the hospital wearing a stolen lab coat and stethoscope.[3]

The absence of a photo ID badge may present a key opportunity to spot an unauthorized person on hospital facility property. Security protocol should mandate that an employee who forgets to bring his or her ID badge to work will be issued a temporary badge. Likewise, an employee who loses an ID badge should report the loss immediately.

The purpose of photo identification is defeated if miscellaneous buttons, stickers, and other items are placed on the badge, obscuring the photograph of the employee's face. All personnel should be instructed not to place any foreign items on an ID badge (Scott, 1994). Badges in plastic sleeves should not be used to carry other objects or as money holders.

The next case example focuses on the need for sophisticated security measures regarding the screening of visitors. "Bill" was a corrections officer and a former Marine marksmanship instructor. When he acted violently toward his wife, "Sarah,"[4] she told him she wanted to end the relationship, and she moved out. Bill refused to accept this fact. Days later, he broke into the home where his estranged wife was staying and kidnapped her at gunpoint. When she subsequently attempted to escape, he shot her in the back, one inch above her heart.

Bill attempted to treat his wife's through-and-through gunshot wound by pushing her insides back into her body, pouring rubbing alcohol over the wounds, and stitching her up with a common sewing kit. He ultimately agreed to take her to a hospital, but only after she swore she would lie and tell the doctors that the shooting had been an accident.

Bill took his wife to the hospital. Once at the hospital, Sarah finally felt safe. No one questioned her false explanation of an accidental shooting. Staff hooked her up to two IVs, one in each arm. Bill remained in the waiting area. A police officer present at the hospital on unrelated business became suspicious regarding the claim of an accidental shooting because there had been no calls to the police for shots fired in the locale where Sarah claimed the gun had discharged. The officer confronted Bill and asked him whether he was armed. Bill pulled his coat back on his right side to show that he was not. The officer did not frisk Bill; rather, he turned and diverted his attention away from him.

Suddenly, Bill pulled out a handgun he had concealed in his pants waistband, in the small of his back. He put the gun to the officer's head and took the officer's service revolver. Bill proceeded to the treatment area, where Sarah lay on a stretcher, and demanded that she go with him. Forcing her to comply with his demands at gunpoint, he made her tear the IVs from her arms. Meanwhile, another police officer arrived at the hospital. Bill got into a shootout with the second officer in the crowded emergency room as he fled the hospital. Bill forced Sarah into his car and sped away. He was subsequently apprehended. Miraculously, Sarah survived, and no one in the hospital was injured.

These facts demonstrate how volatile a situation can become in a matter of minutes. Any number of persons inside the hospital could have been killed or injured. This potential is not unique. Workplace homicide is not uncommon among those in health care. A 1994 study of workplace-related homicides of health care workers found that the second most common cause of death was homicide. On the basis of an analysis of data from the National Traumatic Occupational Fatalities Surveillance System, of 106 work-related homicides of health care workers between 1980 and 1990, firearms were used in 74% (Goodman, Jenkins, & Mercy, 1994). A frightening reality is that these statistics reflect only shootings that resulted in death. They do not include cases in which health care workers were shot but survived, firearms were discharged without effect, or firearms were brandished.

A metal-detection device would have discovered the gun Bill carried into the hospital. The absence of such a security measure enabled him to walk into the facility armed. In addition, there were other opportunities to find out that Bill was armed. Although the hospital staff was treating a gunshot victim, no one asked the patient where the gun was that had been discharged. Finally, once Sarah was separated from her husband and staff began to treat her, no one asked her whether the claim of accidental shooting was true and whether her husband was responsible for her injuries.

All emergency department entrances should have walk-through magnetometers for detection of weapons hidden on one's person and x-ray metal detectors for scanning of carried belongings. Alternatively, security guards can scan visitors with hand-held detection devices. A sign should be posted at the entrance informing the public that scanning will be conducted (Simonowitz, 1993). This is important inasmuch as the mere presence of such equipment may deter an armed individual from even attempting to enter the facility. The sign should be in languages other than English, as appropriate to the community. Anyone who refuses to go through the detector should be denied admittance to the facility.

The use of metal detectors in hospitals has been viewed as somewhat controversial. The American College of Emergency Physicians (ACEP; 1988) has noted that a metal detector in an emergency department not generally perceived as dangerous could be met with public resistance or could create an image of dangerousness. Alternatively, however, public perception regarding a metal detector may be a heightened feeling of security due to the facility's precautions.

Even if security precautions to detect traditional weapons, such as guns and knives, are in place, a perpetrator may pose a danger without such weapons. For example, if a perpetrator becomes violent, his weapons may include fists, feet, teeth, furniture, or available medical equipment. According to a 1992 hospital survey, items commonly used in assaults in hospital facilities included IV poles, food trays, syringes, and wheelchairs (Stultz, 1993). Because a single piece of furniture can be used as a weapon, furniture should be affixed to the floor or to other pieces of furniture if this is practical. Staff should be trained to recognize that certain equipment could be used as weapons. With this heightened awareness, staff members would know, for example, to try to avoid confrontational situations when standing near objects that could easily be used as weapons.

Hospitals should employ or contract to have well-trained security guards at the facility with a 24-hour presence in the emergency department. Off-duty police officers are an excellent source of security. If 24-hour emergency department presence is not feasible, guards should make regular rounds and be able to respond immediately if summoned. According to a 1988 survey of 127 U.S. emergency department medical directors of emergency medicine residency programs, facilities with 24-hour security personnel had less frequent assaults and threats than facilities without such security (Lavoie, Carter, Danzl, & Berg, 1988).

Some may fear that the display of uniformed security guards, as opposed to plainclothes security guards, will cause a person to escalate to violence. However, there are no studies to support this position. If that were the case, the police would not send uniformed officers on patrol in high-crime areas as a deterrent to criminal activity. In fact, the absence of a uniform raises certain issues. For instance, putting a security guard in street clothing or a colored blazer may create the perception that he or she is not a "real" security guard and therefore need not be obeyed.

A first step in treating the victim/patient should be to separate her from a companion who may have battered her. Knowing how to speak to a potentially violent individual so as not to incite this person is important. Staff should never make demands of someone accompanying the victim, saying such things as "If you don't leave now, we'll call the police." Making demands may cause the person to escalate to violence and force a confrontation that staff cannot handle. Rather, staff should be trained to use a sympathetic style and a simple explanation, such as "I can see that you are concerned about your girlfriend. We know that you want her to get the medical attention she needs. I'm sorry, but we do not allow visitors in the treatment area. Please have a seat in the waiting room, and we'll be back with you as soon as we can." If the patient's companion refuses to leave her side, security should be discreetly alerted.

As soon as the victim/patient and companion are separated, voluntarily or otherwise, staff should inquire of the patient whether her companion committed the injury. If so, and if hospital security has not been alerted, they should be discreetly alerted at this point. If the victim discloses that her companion is or may still be armed with the weapon used in the attack, security staff should also be advised of this fact.

Note that many states require that injuries caused by the discharge of a firearm or by other dangerous weapons be reported to the police. If reporting is mandated by law, the law must be complied with regardless of the wishes of the victim/patient (see Chapter 5 of this volume).

A staff member, such as an admissions clerk, should regularly monitor the behavior of waiting visitors with a view toward watching for persons who are becoming violent. Signs to look for in evaluating potentially violent behavior include pacing, yelling, and making angry gestures such as shaking one's fists (Federal Protective Service, n.d.). The staff member should also be on the alert for visitors who may be under the influence of drugs or alcohol. These individuals may exhibit signs of intoxication such as the smell of alcohol, slurred speech, staggered walking, and belligerent or erratic behavior. Such persons may have a warped sense of reality and may not be easy to reason with.

If a visitor seems to become angered or is acting inappropriately, the staff member should alert security staff. Security assistance needed at this point may be nothing more than having a security presence in the emergency department with no particular focus on the visitor. Such presence may defuse some potentially violent individuals.

One way to notify security is through the use of concealed silent alarm systems, also called "panic buttons." Such alarms should be installed at key locations, including the reception area, the nurses' stations, the triage and treatment areas, the hallways, and the staff lounges. The system must be operational 24 hours per day and should provide direct relay to hospital security and to local law enforcement (Simonowitz, 1993). ACEP (1988) suggested the additional use of direct or dedicated telephones that connect directly to a central security station or to police headquarters when the telephone receiver is lifted. With well-established policies concerning use, ACEP strongly endorsed concurrent system usage. All alarm systems and security equipment should be regularly tested and maintained in good working order. A system that is in a state of disrepair is of no value.

As a supplement to panic buttons, emergency code signals transmitted over the loudspeaker can be effective in alerting security personnel quickly and discreetly. For example, "Dr. Grey to the ED" could be designated as the code for security to respond to the ED.

Emergency telephone numbers, including 911 and contact numbers for facility security, should be posted on all nonpublic telephones. In unexpected emergency situations that pose danger to the staff, even the most highly trained professionals may panic and forget critical telephone numbers.

Another way to monitor critical areas of the hospital is by closed-circuit television. This equipment may be particularly useful in monitoring the visitor waiting areas and entrances of the emergency department. Should violence erupt, security personnel watching the monitors can immediately dispatch guards. Ideally, the system should be equipped with video-recording equipment. The additional feature of videotape recording allows for documentation of violent outbursts and can provide powerful evidence in a subsequent prosecution of the perpetrator. Facilities should post signs that indicate that the area is being monitored and video recorded via closed-circuit television. The signs should be posted in languages other than English as appropriate to the community.

According to Colling (1992), the presence of a camera may provide a psychological deterrent to violence. This would also hold true for signs that state that monitoring and recording is taking place, as indicated above. Even a facility that cannot afford such an elaborate monitoring system with personnel to monitor it may benefit from posting such a sign and installing "dummy" cameras (cameras that appear functional but in fact are not).

In addition to the security precautions detailed above, hospitals may wish to consider other measures to enhance safety:

1. Install bulletproof glass at all admission/reception areas, triage, or other areas where staff interact with the public (Simonowitz, 1993).
2. Install good lighting in the facility and on the grounds. Increase existing lighting as needed.
3. Install security direct-access telephones in isolated areas such as the parking lots and the grounds.
4. Provide diversions in the waiting areas for visitors, such as television and magazines (AMA, 1995b).
5. Make waiting areas more environmentally pleasant for visitors by designing or redesigning such areas to be as spacious as possible. Equip waiting areas with items such as vending machines, pay telephones, comfortable furniture, and sufficient seating to accommodate the volume (AMA, 1995b).

Regardless of the security measures chosen, all facilities should have regular staff training, staff meetings, and incident-reporting and incident-debriefing sessions.

Employee training should include security issues, how to use security equipment, personal safety/self-defense, and recognition and management of aggression and violence. Training should also be provided in the dynamics of domestic violence. Such training enables employees to understand the unique issues involved in an abusive relationship. Staff may not be able to prevent violence. However, all staff can be trained in how to respond when violence does occur. Training should be provided to all members of the facility, including administrators, doctors, nurses, residents, interns, security, clergy, housekeeping, reception/information, switchboard operators, and volunteers.

Staff meetings should be conducted on a regular basis to alert the staff to security issues and procedures. Feedback on the procedures in place and staff concerns about safety should be elicited and addressed as appropriate.

A system for in-house reporting of violent incidents against staff should be implemented. All reports should be standardized. Keep the reporting forms easy to complete. Encourage reporting, and allow staff sufficient time to complete the reports. A proposed model standard incident report is shown in Figure 6.2.

After any violent episode, a debriefing session should be conducted with the staff. Employee assistance and counseling should be offered (Wasserberger, Ordog, Kolodny, & Allen, 1989).

[Facility Name, Facility Address]

Please print.

Date of Report: _____

Reporting Person: _____

Title: _____

Telephone (w): (___)_____-_____

Name of Victim: _____

Job Title: _____

Telephone (w): (___)_____-_____

Date of Incident: _____

Time of Incident: _____ a.m./p.m.

Location of Incident: _____

(ED, workstation, etc.)

Incident is best characterized as:

_____ an assault

_____ a threat to do bodily injury

_____ destruction of property

_____ a weapon-related offense

_____ theft

_____ other: _____

Was the victim injured? *yes/no*

If the victim was injured, the injuries are best described as:

_____ nonurgent   _____ urgent   _____ critical

If victim was injured, describe the injuries:

_____

_____

_____

Did the victim require medical treatment? *yes/no*

Was the victim hospitalized as a result of the injuries? *yes/no*

Figure 6.2. Model Standard Incident Report

If property was destroyed, describe the property:

_____

_____

_____

Approximate value:

_____

If a weapon was used, specify type:

_____ firearm, description: _____

_____ knife, description: _____

_____ furniture/equipment, description: _____

_____ other: _____

Narrative of the Incident: (attach additional pages, if needed)

_____

_____

_____

Description of Perpetrator:

_____

_____

_____

Name, if known: _____

(last, first, middle initial)

Address, if known: _____, _____, _____

(street)   (city)   (state)

Sex: *Male/Female* Approximate age: _____Approximate weight: _____

Approximate height: _____

Description of Perpetrator's Clothing:

_____

Race: _____ Caucasian

_____ African American

_____ Asian

_____ Hispanic

_____ Other: _____

Figure 6.2. *Continued*

continued

Perpetrator's status at the facility was:

_____ a patient

_____ a visitor

_____ an employee

_____ other: _____

Witnesses to the offense (for facility employees, provide work telephone number; for nonemployees, provide home address):

Name: _____

Address: _____, _____, _____
                    (street)   (city)   (state)

Telephone numbers: W: (__)_____-_____

                            H: (__)_____-_____

Name: _____

Address: _____, _____, _____
                    (street)   (city)   (state)

Telephone numbers: W: (__)_____-_____

                            H: (__)_____-_____

(Attach additional pages, as needed).

Have the police been notified? *Yes/No*

Was a telephone call placed to 911? *Yes/No*

Did the police respond to the 911 call? *Yes/No*

If the police were *not* notified, the reason for nonreport is best described as:

_____ Victim does not want the incident reported to the police.

_____ Victim was not physically injured or suffered minimal injury.

_____ Other: _____

Police notification was made to:

Law Enforcement Agency: _____

Officer Notified: _____

Badge No.: _____

Telephone (__)_____-_____

Figure 6.2. *Continued*

◙ RECOMMENDED SECURITY MEASURES
FOR CLINICS AND PRIVATE OFFICES

Security options for clinics and private doctors' offices are obviously more limited due to the size of the facilities and available resources. Security options may also be limited when the clinic or doctor's office leases only part of the building and the building is owned and managed by others. These facilities may nonetheless implement many of the security measures discussed in connection with hospitals. Some basic, cost-efficient measures include creating a facility safety protocol, conducting staff training, debriefing staff following incidents, posting emergency telephone numbers, and securing furniture. In addition, if funding or resources allow, panic buttons and closed-circuit television are options. If a panic button is used, it should be linked directly to local law enforcement. If the clinic or doctor's office is in a large building that already has a security staff, the panic button should also be linked directly to the security staff's office. It should be noted that such a system is effective only if someone is continuously present in the security office to monitor the alarm.

Some office buildings with multiple tenants may already have central intercom systems that allow building-wide paging. Generally, in such circumstances, the management alone can access the building-wide system. It may be possible to work out an agreement with the building management company whereby the medical facility staff can directly access the building-wide paging system to call security in emergency situations. If such equipment exists and an arrangement can be reached with management, facility management should consider use of a code system, as discussed in connection with hospital security measures.

Security at private doctors' offices in small buildings may present special challenges. However, a physician in private practice is probably much less likely to see a patient immediately after serious trauma. Private physicians may be more likely to be presented with the aftermath of repeated abusive trauma, such as illness or vague or somatic complaints.

◙ NOTES

1. Not their true names.

2. From "Knife Assailant, Healthcare Provider," by W. Kosova, December 1991, *Washington City Paper,* p. 8. Copyright 1991 by Washington City Paper. Adapted with permission.

3. From "Hospital Police: No Guns, No Respect, Lots of Trouble," by D. Pitt, March 27, 1989, *The New York Times,* p. B-1. Copyright © 1989 by The New York Times Company. Reprinted by permission.

4. Not their true names.

7

PROSECUTION OF DOMESTIC VIOLENCE CRIMES

This chapter provides basic information about criminal proceedings, giving testimony, and the use of medical evidence at a trial. Health care providers may find it helpful when working with patients who might become involved in the criminal justice system to have an understanding of how the system operates. In addition, because medical professionals may become witnesses in criminal cases, this chapter is intended to answer common questions about the judicial process.

◆ CRIMINAL PROCEEDINGS

A criminal case that is prosecuted for a violation of state law is ordinarily handled by the District Attorney's Office. In that event, the prosecutor is called a deputy district attorney. If the case involves a violation of Federal law, the prosecution may be handled by a U.S. Attorney's Office. The prosecutor there is called an assistant U.S. attorney. The prosecutor does not represent the victim in the case. Rather, the prosecutor represents the government, and it is his or her role to see that justice is done. Although the prosecutor does not represent the victim, the prosecutor is an advocate for the victim.

136

A criminal case usually begins with the arrest of the batterer. Between the date of a batterer's arrest and his trial, there may be several court proceedings scheduled in the case. Ordinarily, witnesses do not have to appear at such proceedings but may attend if they wish to do so. These proceedings can include an arraignment on the charge(s) for which the batterer has been arrested, a preliminary hearing, a second arraignment following the return of an indictment by a grand jury, and one or more status conferences.

Arraignment

An arraignment is a court proceeding during which the accused is formally advised of the charge(s) against him and at which he enters a plea of guilty or not guilty. The defendant is represented by counsel, either retained or, if the defendant is indigent, court appointed.

At the arraignment, the judge will set conditions of release. Victims of crime, particularly domestic violence victims, often want to know whether, if charges are filed, the defendant will be held in jail. The answer is that it depends. The general purpose of conditions of release is to ensure that the defendant will return to court for future court proceedings. Conditions of release are normally not designed to protect the victim or the community because the law presumes that the defendant is innocent until proven guilty.

Bail laws vary from state to state. But generally, a judge evaluates two primary factors in determining whether a defendant should be held in jail pending trial or whether some other less severe conditions should be imposed on his liberty: dangerousness and risk of flight.

The dangerousness factor usually arises in certain crimes such as murder or violent armed offenses. In such cases, the judge may consider the potential danger the accused presents to the victim or to other members of the community in setting conditions of release. In assessing dangerousness, the judge will consider the circumstances and character of the offense with which the defendant is charged, including the severity of the victim's injuries; whether the crime involved the use of a weapon; the defendant's criminal record; and the strength of the government's case.

In all criminal cases, a judge may consider a defendant's risk of flight in setting conditions of release. Risk of flight is the likelihood that a defendant will fail to return to court for future proceedings. Factors the judge may weigh include whether the defendant is employed; whether the defendant has ties to the community, such as family, property ownership, and affiliations; whether he has a criminal record of arrests or convictions and the nature of the previous offenses; whether there is a history of alcohol abuse or drug use; whether the defendant has ever failed to appear for court proceedings in previous cases; whether the defendant has a history of violating court orders; the strength of the case against the defendant; and the maximum possible jail sentence the defendant could receive if convicted of the crime(s) with which he is charged.

If a decision is made not to incarcerate the defendant pending trial, the arraignment judge has a number of bail options and will look at various factors in fashioning appropriate conditions of release. These options are discussed below.

1. *Release on personal recognizance.* The defendant is released on his promise to return to court for future court proceedings. The defendant signs a written notice to that effect. If the defendant fails to return to court as promised, the judge can issue a warrant for his arrest, and the defendant may face additional charges for failing to appear for the scheduled court proceeding.

2. *Release to third-party custody.* The defendant is released into the custody of a third party who agrees to ensure that the defendant will return to court. The third party can be a friend or family member or a third-party custodial program. If the defendant fails to return to court, the judge can issue a warrant for the defendant's arrest, and the defendant may face additional charges for failing to appear.

3. *Cash or surety bond.* The defendant must post an amount of money with the court or find a surety, usually a bondsman, to post the bond on his behalf. Bond can also be posted by a friend or relative of the accused. If the defendant fails to return to court, the bond is ordered forfeited, and whoever posted the bond loses that amount of money. Just as with the previous conditions, if the defendant fails to return to court, the judge may issue a warrant for his arrest, and he may face additional charges for failing to return to court. A bondsman will go out looking for a defendant who has absconded. If the bondsman brings the defendant back to court, the bond is returned, and the court may order the defendant to be held in jail pending trial.

4. *Other provisions.* The judge also has the option of imposing numerous conditions in connection with bail, largely determined by the circumstances of the case and the particular defendant. It is the responsibility of the prosecutor to request that the judge impose these conditions. Such orders may include conditions that the defendant maintain his employment, stay in school, report for drug testing, attend drug or alcohol counseling, refrain from using drugs or alcohol, refrain from committing any new violations of the law, surrender his passport, stay within a certain geographical location, and stay away from and refrain from all contact with the victim and/or other potential witnesses in the case. This last condition is commonly referred to as a *Stay-Away/No-Contact Order.*

The Stay-Away/No-Contact order has particular significance for victims of domestic violence. Such an order can usually cover the victim's residence, place of employment, school, and place of worship. The order can bar all personal contact and contact by mail, by telephone, or through third parties. In stranger-committed crime, the defendant has every reason to stay as far away from the victim as possible in the hope that she will not be able to identify him in the future. In contrast, defendants charged with domestic violence crimes frequently seek out their victim after release to harass her, threaten her, or commit additional crimes against her. The defendant may also attempt to obtain a "reconciliation" with the victim in the hope that she will not follow through with the criminal prosecution. Even if the defendant is detained pending trial, the Stay-Away/No-Contact Order is important. Defendants who are held in jail have been known to write to the victim and ring her telephone off the hook if not ordered to refrain from all contact.

The violation of a condition of release can be prosecuted as a contempt of court, which is a crime that carries a separate penalty from the originally charged offense. Further, if the violation of the condition of release is also a crime in and of itself, as when the batterer assaults the victim again, additional criminal charges can be filed against him. Finally, in some jurisdictions, once the defendant has violated the conditions of release and a hearing has been held to prove that he has done so, the defendant may be ordered held in jail pending trial on the theory that there are no conditions of release that will reasonably ensure that the defendant will not flee the jurisdiction or pose a danger to the victim or to other members of the community.

Usually in misdemeanor cases, the defendant is released on his own recognizance pending trial with a number of conditions imposed, which can include a Stay-Away/No-Contact Order. In felony cases, depending on the law in the jurisdiction, the circumstances of the case, and the defendant's background, he may be ordered to post bond, placed in third-party custody, or detained pending trial.

Preliminary Hearing

After the arraignment is held, there may be a preliminary hearing. The preliminary hearing is a "probable cause" hearing, held before the case is presented to the grand jury. At this hearing, the judge listens to testimony, generally from law enforcement witnesses, and determines whether there is probable cause to believe that a crime was committed and that the person arrested committed the crime. If the judge finds probable cause, the case is continued pending action of the grand jury. If the judge does not find probable cause, the case is dismissed. When the case is dismissed, all conditions of release or orders of detention are vacated, as the court no longer has jurisdiction or power over the defendant. Even though the case is dismissed, the prosecution can still present the case to a grand jury if it chooses to do so. If a grand jury votes to return an indictment, which is the formal charging document, the defendant is arraigned on the new charges and the case is reinstated in court. A new bond determination is made at that time.

Plea Bargaining

The vast majority of criminal cases are resolved by guilty pleas. Ordinarily, early in the case, the government makes a plea offer to the defendant that he has a certain period of time to accept. The offer usually includes some concession by the government, such as allowing the defendant to plead guilty to a reduced charge or promising that the government will not ask the judge to incarcerate the defendant pending the sentencing date. Plea bargaining or the process of plea negotiations is a fact of life in all jurisdictions in almost all criminal cases. Resources and other issues dictate that the prosecutor simply cannot take every single criminal case to trial.

There are several advantages to a guilty plea. First, there is the guarantee of an adjudication of guilt. When a case proceeds to trial, no matter how strong the evidence, there is always the chance that a jury will acquit the defendant. Second, a guilty plea means that the case will be resolved quickly. The time between the arrest and sentencing is normally much shorter than in cases where there is a trial. Third, when a defendant pleads guilty, he must admit his involvement in the offense(s) to which he enters a plea of guilt. A defendant who goes to trial may protest his innocence even after he is convicted and sentenced. Finally, when a case is resolved by guilty plea, there is no need for the victim or any other witness to testify. At a trial, the government must present the testimony of all witnesses needed to prove its case beyond a reasonable doubt.

In a very serious case, the government may decide not to extend a plea offer or, if it does, to require a plea to a very serious offense. In this regard, it is critical that the prosecutor be fully informed as to the true extent of the victim's injuries and the history of violence, if any. Otherwise, the prosecutor may underestimate the seriousness of the offense and make an inappropriately lenient plea offer.

If a defendant accepts the government's plea offer, he will plead guilty, and there will not be a trial. Following entry of the guilty plea, the proceedings move directly to the sentencing. If a defendant rejects the plea offer, the case is scheduled for trial.

Alternatives to Prosecution

In some jurisdictions, as an alternative method of case disposition, the prosecutor's office will offer the defendant the option of a pretrial diversion program, a deferred-sentencing program, or a deferred-prosecution program. Some jurisdictions may have only one of these options; some may have more.

Pretrial diversion is an option usually extended to first-time offenders charged with nonviolent crimes who have no disqualifying background factors. Such disqualifying factors might include a criminal record or present drug use. Under the terms of such a program, the defendant is not required to admit guilt but must "assume responsibility" for the offense with which he is charged. A defendant who agrees to enter a diversion program may be directed to perform community service; participate in a batterer's treatment program, if one is available in the jurisdiction; abide by all conditions of pretrial release, including any Stay-Away/No-Contact Order; and make restitution for the victim's medical expenses. Other conditions may be available and imposed as appropriate to the case. Usually, a defendant has several months to complete the terms of diversion. The case is essentially in a state of suspension for the term of the diversion period. If the defendant successfully completes all conditions of the diversion program, the criminal case is dismissed. The defendant will have no record of conviction, but he will have an arrest record. If the defendant fails to complete or violates the terms of diversion, the government will request that the court schedule the case for trial.

In a deferred-sentencing program, the defendant must admit guilt for the offense and enter a plea of guilty. Sentencing is deferred until after a period of time appropriate for the defendant to complete the conditions imposed by the court. These conditions may include all of those referenced in connection with pretrial diversion. In addition, the court generally may impose any other condition it deems appropriate. As in the case of diversion, the defendant is given several months to complete the conditions of the program. If he successfully completes the program, the case is dismissed. The defendant will have no record of conviction, but he will have an arrest record. If a defendant fails to accomplish successfully or abide by the conditions imposed, the court schedules the case for sentencing.

A deferred-prosecution program is merely a method of suspending action on a case for a specified period of time. The defendant neither admits guilt nor assumes responsibility for the offense. The prosecutor requests that the court, in effect, put the case "on hold" for several months or up to 1 year. During this time, the defendant is generally under no obligation other than to remain arrest free. At the end of the period, if the defendant has not committed any new crimes, the case is dismissed. Generally, his arrest record for this offense will not be affected.

Of the three options, the deferred-prosecution program is the most unsatisfactory in domestic violence cases. A defendant in such a program is not required to admit guilt and suffers no consequence at all for his crime. If the defendant commits another crime while the case is pending, such as threatening the victim, his only consequence is the possibility that now he will finally be prosecuted with what is surely a "stale" case. Criminal cases are not like fine wine; they do not improve with age. It is most doubtful that the victim will be cooperative with the prosecution after such a protracted period of time. Such a victim may conclude that the system offered her no protection and failed to hold the batterer accountable for his criminal actions.

A pretrial diversion program is not a preferred prosecution response to domestic violence either (National Council of Juvenile and Family Court Judges, 1994). Diversion programs are intended for nonviolent, first-time offenders. Most domestic violence crimes are, by nature, violent. In addition, by the time a victim is willing to call the police and report a domestic violence crime, there have usually been numerous prior battering incidents. Therefore, by definition alone, domestic violence is not appropriate for pretrial diversion. Furthermore, the first step in changing a batterer's behavior, if that is indeed possible, is for him to admit guilt. Diversion allows him to avoid an admission of guilt by merely "assuming responsibility" for the offense. If the offender fails to complete diversion successfully, no new penalty will be attached; the worst that will happen to him is that he will be prosecuted with what by then will be a stale case.

Of the options, the deferred-sentencing program is the most favored for domestic violence cases (National Council of Juvenile and Family Court Judges, 1994). The program requires that the defendant admit guilt. He also remains under the supervision of the court while completing the terms of the program. Finally, if the defendant does not successfully complete the program, the case proceeds directly to sentencing. There is no trial, and the victim is not required to testify.

Grand Jury

If the case involves potential felony charges, a witness, such as a health care provider, may be subpoenaed to testify before a grand jury. A grand jury listens to testimony, views evidence, and decides whether there is probable cause to believe that the defendant committed certain crimes. "Probable cause" means that there are reasonable grounds to believe that the crimes occurred and that the named defendant committed those crimes. If a grand jury finds probable cause, it votes to return an indictment. If the grand jury does not find probable cause, it declines charges by returning a "no true bill."

Those people present in a grand jury include the prosecutor, the court reporter, the witness, and the grand jurors. The number of grand jurors can range from 16 to 23 members. Neither the defendant nor the defense attorney is present in the grand jury room. Unlike court proceedings, which are open to the public, grand jury proceedings are secret. No one present in the grand jury room, except the witness, may ever repeat to others what happened during the proceedings (Fed. R. Crim. P. 6(e)(2)). However, at trial, testimony of a particular witness may become a matter of public record if this witness testifies at trial as he or she did in the grand jury proceedings.

Unlike a trial, grand jury proceedings admit hearsay, or statements made by others, as evidence. What this may mean to the health care provider is that a law enforcement witness can testify regarding the medical evidence as reflected in the victim's medical records. Therefore, the health care provider may not be required to testify during the grand jury proceedings.

Pretrial Hearings

Some courts hear all pretrial motions on a date in advance of the trial date. Other courts hear the motions on the first day of the trial. Depending on the issues raised by the motions, certain witnesses may be called to testify at the motion hearings. Such hearings take place in front of the judge only; the jury is not present.

Typical motions heard before the trial are those filed by the defense in an effort to challenge the government's evidence. For example, the government may intend to present at trial physical evidence, such as a gun or a knife, recovered from the defendant by the police. The defense may file a motion to suppress or exclude that evidence, arguing that the evidence has been tampered with or was obtained in violation of the defendant's constitutional rights. Similarly, the government may intend to introduce statements the defendant made to law enforcement officers. The defense may seek to challenge admission of the statements, claiming that the defendant was not advised of his constitutional rights (*Miranda v. Arizona,* 1966) or that a claimed waiver of the rights was invalid. If the defense is successful, the judge may rule that certain evidence may not be used at the trial.

Hearsay testimony is admissible at pretrial proceedings. Therefore, if medical evidence is required at such a proceeding, a law enforcement officer may be able to testify instead of a health care provider.

Jury Selection

After the motion hearings are conducted, a jury will be selected. The jury selection process is called *voir dire. Voir dire,* loosely translated, means "to speak the truth." The purpose of voir dire is to find 12 fair and impartial jurors who will listen to the evidence, follow the law as given to them by the judge, and render a verdict consistent with the evidence presented at trial. During this process, prospective jurors are asked a series of questions designed to elicit information establishing either that they have preconceived opinions, biases, or other impediments to jury service or that they can be fair and impartial jurors. Each side, the government and the defense, may strike potential jurors in an effort to seat a fair and impartial panel. A pool of prospective jurors from which the panel will be selected may consist of 40 or more people.

In some courts, witnesses are introduced to prospective jurors during jury selection. The purpose of this introduction is to find out, before jurors are selected to serve, whether anyone knows any of the witnesses. This is important because during trial the jurors must determine the credibility of the witnesses. They decide whom to believe and whom not to believe. A juror who knows a witness may have already formed an opinion about that person's character. This existing perception may affect the juror's assessment of the witness's credibility in this current matter. Ordinarily, a prospective juror who knows a proposed witness is excused from jury service.

Where the introduction process is used, prospective witnesses are introduced by name and actually walk in front of the jury panel while they are introduced. However, the prosecutor may request that the introduction of certain witnesses, including medical professionals, be accomplished by name and occupation only. Deviation from the normal procedure in the case of the health care provider witness is usually justified due to the witness's schedule and/or the hardship it would cause to the medical facility or to patients if the witness had to appear solely for the introduction. Normally, the court will allow such a deviation. When the witness is called to testify, the judge can inquire of the jury whether anyone recognizes the witness, now that he or she has had the opportunity to see him or her. If there is a juror who knows the witness and cannot be fair and impartial, an alternate juror may be substituted on the panel.

The Trial

Sometimes, in a criminal trial, there is no jury. Such a trial is called a "bench trial" because it is tried before the judge alone or "to the bench." In that event, the judge decides questions of law and of fact. Alternatively, a case may be tried before a jury. In that event, the judge rules on questions of law, and the jury decides the facts, including whether to believe or disbelieve the witnesses. For most crimes, including all felony offenses, a defendant has a right to a trial by jury. However, with court approval and the consent of the government, a defendant may waive his right to a jury trial (Fed. R. Crim. P. 23(a)).

At the start of the trial, the judge will make introductory comments to the jury. After the introduction, the parties may make opening statements. The government, because it has the burden of proof, must make an opening statement. The opening statement is the government's opportunity to explain to the jury what it intends to prove and how it will prove its case. At the conclusion of the government's opening statement, the defense may make an opening statement if it chooses to do so. Because the defendant is presumed innocent, the defense has no burden of proof in the trial and is not required to make an opening statement. Alternatively, the defense may "reserve opening." This means that the defense may give its opening statement after the government has presented all of its witnesses and evidence and has formally rested its case.

Following the opening statements, the government will present its "case-in-chief"—that is, present all of its witnesses and evidence. Then the defense, if it so chooses, may also present witnesses and evidence. If the defense presents a case, the government may present a rebuttal case to counter the defense evidence. After both parties have rested, the government must present a closing argument. The closing argument is the government's opportunity to explain to the jury how the testimony and evidence presented have proven each element of the crimes charged beyond a reasonable doubt. The prosecution attempts in its argument to persuade the jury to convict the defendant. If the defense wishes, it may also make a closing argument. The defense seeks to discredit the government's witnesses and evidence and asks the jury to acquit or to consider lesser included offenses than the crimes charged. If the defense makes a closing argument, the government is given a second opportunity to address the jury regarding any issues raised. This is called "rebuttal argument."

After both parties have argued the case, the judge will instruct the jury on the law through formal jury instructions. At this point, the jury will be asked to retire and deliberate. Jurors may deliberate for minutes or for days before reaching a verdict. If the defendant is acquitted or, in other words, found not guilty on all of the charges, the proceedings are over. If the defendant is convicted on all or some of the charges, the case will be scheduled for sentencing.

If the jury is unable to reach a verdict, the judge will declare a mistrial due to a "hung jury." In this event, the prosecution must decide whether to retry the case. If the government decides to proceed with the case, there will be a second trial.

Sentencing

If the defendant has been convicted at trial on any charge or has pleaded guilty, the next phase of the proceedings is the sentencing. Although witnesses may attend the sentencing if they wish to do so, it would be highly unlikely for any health care provider who was a witness to be requested to attend. Most domestic violence prosecutions occur at the state court level. At the sentencing, state court judges have a wide range of sentencing options. In Federal court, judges have much less discretion because they are bound by Federal sentencing guidelines, which mandate certain sentences for certain offenses. In state court, the maximum sentence available depends on the charge or charges of which the defendant has been convicted. Most crimes carry a period of incarceration and/or a fine as the maximum penalty. For misdemeanor offenses, the term of incarceration is less than 1 year. For noncapital felony offenses, the term of imprisonment may range from more than 1 year to life, depending on the crime. Capital offenses may carry a maximum sentence of life incarceration or the death penalty, depending on state law.

At the sentencing, the judge listens to the arguments and recommendations of the defense and the government attorneys. The defendant is given an opportunity to address the court. The probation department may also make a recommendation as to its view of the appropriate sentence.

A criminal sentence is supposed to serve a fourfold purpose: to punish the defendant, to incapacitate him so he cannot commit other crimes, to deter him and others similarly situated who might commit similar crimes, and to rehabilitate him. State court sentencing options include incarcerating the defendant; placing him on a term of probation; putting him in a halfway house and ordering work release during work hours; imposing a monetary fine; ordering him not to commit any new violations of the law; ordering the defendant to abide by a

Stay-Away/No-Contact Order relating to the victim of the offense; and/or ordering him to perform a number of hours of community service, to attend drug or alcohol counseling and surveillance, to attend a batterer's counseling program, to stay in school or maintain employment, and to make restitution for the victim's medical expenses, lost wages, or damaged property.

If a defendant is ordered by a state court to be incarcerated, he may be eligible for parole after serving a certain period of his sentence. For felony offenses, generally, such eligibility occurs after serving a third of the sentence or, if the sentence is a range, such as 3 to 5 years, a third of the bottom of the sentence. The state parole board determines parole eligibility. In Federal court, a defendant whose sentence includes a period of incarceration must serve that entire period of incarceration.

A defendant who is released on probation or parole must abide by a number of conditions. If he violates the conditions of his probation or parole, he may face revocation proceedings. If he is found in violation of probation or parole, the judge or the parole board, respectively, can order him to serve the remainder of his sentence in jail. Of course, if the violation is a new crime, he can also be prosecuted for that offense.

▣ THE HEALTH CARE PROVIDER AS A GOVERNMENT WITNESS

When a batterer is charged with a domestic violence crime, medical evidence can be a vital part of the criminal case against him. Three primary forms of medical evidence are commonly used in domestic violence cases: documentary, photographic, and testimonial. *Documentary* evidence includes the patient's medical records. *Photographic* evidence includes photographs of the victim's injuries. *Testimonial* evidence includes live, in-court testimony from the treating physician or other health care provider. Occasionally, there will also be physical evidence, such as a bullet fragment recovered from the victim by a health care provider.

Every doctor and other health care professional should recognize the important role he or she may be called on to play as a witness in a criminal trial. There are generally five instances in which doctors may be called to testify in a criminal case and three instances in which other health care personnel may be called to testify. First, and least common, would be if the doctor or other medical professional was an eyewitness and actually saw the crime being committed. Second, if the batterer accompanied the victim/patient into the medical facility for treatment, he may have made statements to the doctor or other medical personnel, incriminatory or otherwise, regarding the cause of the victim's injuries. Anyone to whom such statements were made, or who heard such statements, is a potential witness. Third, anyone who recovers, handles, or preserves physical evidence, such as a bullet recovered from the patient's body, may be called to testify. Fourth, the doctor could be sought as an expert witness. An expert is someone who by virtue of special education, training, skill, and experience is allowed to give an opinion regarding facts, usually offered in conjunction with a hypothetical question based on the evidence presented. Fifth, the doctor may be called to testify as to the examination, diagnosis, prognosis, and treatment of a victim. This would include testimony regarding the nature, location, and severity of the injuries treated; statements made by the victim/patient as to how the injuries were incurred; and any other relevant facts concerning diagnosis and treatment.

Because domestic violence crimes generally occur inside the home behind closed doors, the evidence at trial often boils down to the victim's word versus that of the batterer. The government's burden of proof to obtain a conviction is guilt beyond a reasonable doubt. This is a heavy burden, often difficult to achieve when left solely with one person's word against that of the other, the victim's versus the batterer's. Complete and accurate medical records can play an important part in establishing this proof. The testimony of a health care provider can also be an integral part of this proof. In fact, having a medical professional available to testify regarding the extent of the victim's injuries may tip the scales in the government's favor. In some instances, the prosecutor may view the doctor's testimony as crucial to convince the jury to reach a guilty verdict.

Frequently, however, the government can make its case through use of the medical records without testimony from health care providers if the documentation in the records is sufficient. This is true when there is nothing particularly significant about the injury or the course of treatment beyond the fact of documentation. For example, if a victim/patient presents for treatment for a punch to the eye, there should be little need to call the doctor or other staff member as a witness at the trial.

In a domestic violence crimes case, a diligent prosecutor will seek to obtain all medical records that document the current crime and any previous battering episodes. The records will be used at trial to corroborate the victim's testimony that the assault(s) in fact occurred, that the severity of the injuries inflicted necessitated medical treatment, and as proof of the magnitude of the injuries.

What constitutes sufficient documentation? Sufficient documentation includes:

1. the identity of the patient, including full name, date of birth, and social security number;
2. the date(s) and time(s) of treatment;
3. the full name of the attending physician(s);
4. the nature and location of all injuries;
5. the victim/patient's statements regarding who caused her injuries, how the injuries were caused, and the history of violence;
6. the diagnosis and treatment;
7. photographs of all injuries;
8. an injury location chart; and
9. documentation concerning all physical evidence recovered by health care providers and the disposition of the evidence.

Legible records are a must. If handwriting cannot be read, it has no value. If that is the case, a witness may be called to testify merely to decipher his or her handwriting. For an in-depth discussion concerning medical record documentation, refer to Chapter 4.

Specific legal rules govern the admission of evidence at trial in all courts, both state and federal. The U.S. District Courts follow procedures contained in the Federal Rules of Evidence. Some states have adopted or patterned their own rules of evidence after the Federal Rules. Other jurisdictions follow the common law, basing evidentiary rules on judge-made precedent. In jurisdictions that follow the common law, courts will nonetheless look to the Federal Rules of Evidence for guidance.

One of the rules that governs the admission of evidence in court is the rule against hearsay. This rule provides that a person may not testify about an out-of-court statement when offered to prove that what was said is true (Fed. R. Evid. 801(c)). In other words, the rule generally provides that a witness can only testify in court as to his or her personal knowledge of events, not to what someone else said about the events. For example, a witness would be permitted to testify, "I saw John Edwards punch Jennifer Durham in the face." However, a witness would generally not be permitted to testify, "Mike told me that he also saw John Edwards punch Jennifer Durham in the face."

Specific legal exceptions to the hearsay rule exist that allow the use of hearsay in court under certain circumstances. The laws concerning the hearsay rule and its exceptions are a complex area of the law that many lawyers do not fully understand. The information presented here is intended only to highlight hearsay and other common legal issues that may arise regarding information obtained in the medical setting.

Testimony Regarding Documentary Evidence

One exception to the hearsay rule concerns medical records. The Federal Rules of Evidence provide a business records exception formally referred to as "Records of Regularly Conducted Activity." This exception is contained in Federal Rule of Evidence 803(6). The legal issues regarding admission of medical records into evidence at trial are twofold. First, the records proffered must be an exact copy of the original records. This is a question of authentication—simply that the records are in fact what they purport to be. Second, the records must qualify as regularly kept business records of the medical facility.

The custodian of records or "other qualified witness" (Fed. R. Evid. 803(6)), who might be, for example, an office manager, can testify at trial to establish these two criteria. The treating physician is not an essential witness for admission of the records into evidence unless he or she also happens to be the only person in the medical facility who can testify to the following:

1. The medical records were made at or near the time of the events, conditions, or opinions reflected therein.
2. The medical records were made by a person with knowledge of the information contained in the records or from information transmitted by a person with such knowledge.
3. The medical records are kept in the course of a regularly conducted business activity.
4. It is the regular practice of the medical facility to make such records.

A sample testimonial examination follows. Assume that the witness is employed in the medical records office of a local hospital and is testifying during the government's case regarding medical records of a patient who was treated for an injury caused by an abusive partner.

Prosecutor: Please state your name and spell your last name for the record.

Witness: My name is Betty Green, that's G-R-E-E-N.

Prosecutor: Please tell the ladies and gentlemen of the jury where you are employed.

Witness: I work at Fairview Hospital on Main Street.

Prosecutor: What is your job title?

Witness: I am the hospital's records manager, and I work in the medical records office.

Prosecutor: What are your duties as the records manager?

Witness: I supervise the maintenance of the patient medical records system. I supervise the staff that files the records, and I ensure that the hospital complies with all patient medical record release requests and subpoenas for such records.

Prosecutor: Are you familiar with the procedures for maintaining the patient records of Fairview Hospital?

Witness: Yes, I am.

Prosecutor: Ms. Green, directing your attention to what has been marked as Government's Exhibit Number 1, are those the records of Fairview Hospital for patient Jennifer Durham for treatment on November 2, 1996?

Witness: Yes, they are.

Prosecutor: Are those records an exact copy of the original medical records?

Witness: Yes, they are.

Prosecutor: How do you know that?

Witness: Because this morning I compared that copy to the original records, and they were the same.

Prosecutor: Were those records made at or near the time of the events reflected in the records?

Witness: Yes.

Prosecutor: Were the records made by someone with personal knowledge of the events reflected in the records?

Witness: Yes.

Prosecutor: Are these records kept in the course of the regularly conducted business activity of the hospital?

Witness: Yes, they are.

Prosecutor: Is it the regular practice of Fairview Hospital to make such records?

Witness: Yes.

At this point the examination is concluded, and the prosecutor will request that the records, Government's Exhibit Number 1, be received into evidence. Once they are received into evidence, the jury may consider them in deciding the guilt or innocence of the accused.

Cross-examination of the custodian of records by the defense attorney is extremely rare. As the illustration demonstrates, the proffered testimony is straightforward, and the witness probably has no direct knowledge of the patient or the facts of the case. The sole purpose of the witness's testimony is to establish the requisite foundation for the business records exception to the hearsay rule.

In lieu of testimony by a custodian of records, the prosecution can sometimes obtain a stipulation as to authentication and hearsay admissibility. A stipulation means that both parties, the prosecution and the defense, agree that a particular matter is not at issue in the case. Generally, such a stipulation can be entered into in advance of the trial date.

Testimony Regarding Patient Statements

Even though medical records may be admissible as records of a regularly conducted activity, this exception to the hearsay rule does not cover a patient's statements reflected within the records. Such a situation presents hearsay (the patient's statement) within hearsay (the medical records). Under the Federal Rules of Evidence, such double hearsay is admissible in court, provided that each instance of hearsay falls within an exception to the hearsay rule (Fed. R. Evid. 805).

Federal Rule of Evidence 803(4) provides that "statements made [by patients or others] for the purposes of medical diagnosis or treatment and describing medical history, or past or present symptoms, pain, or sensations, or the inception or general character of the cause or external source thereof insofar as reasonably pertinent to diagnosis and treatment" are not excluded by the hearsay rule (Fed. R. Evid. 803(4)). Therefore, statements made by patients to their health care providers when seeking treatment for injuries are generally admissible at trial as evidence in support of the government's case. The patient's belief that accuracy is essential to effective treatment is seen as creating a special assurance of reliability to the truthfulness of the statements (see *Sullivan v. United States*, 1979).

There is no requirement that the statement be made to a doctor to be admissible—only that the statement was made for the stated purpose. Likewise, such statements made by patients to receptionists, nurses, ambulance drivers, and others may be admissible at trial.

Unfortunately, in domestic violence cases, patients do not always tell the truth about how they were injured. A victim may give a false explanation regarding the cause of her injuries. The reasons a victim might lie about her injuries are numerous and have been discussed throughout this book. False explanations can include that the injuries were self-inflicted "accidents," such as a fall down the stairs, bumping into a door, or the infamous "I bruise easily."

A well-meaning doctor might consider telling a patient that she should tell the truth because if she lies, her false statements may be used against her in court. However, one should never make such statements to a patient. Such comments could cause the victim/patient to focus on making statements to help her in her legal matters, not for the purpose of receiving medical diagnosis and treatment. If the patient's motivation for making the statements is for the purpose of litigation rather than for effective treatment, the statements will be inadmissible in court.

When patient statements, made for purposes of diagnosis and treatment, are held to be admissible, they may be introduced in the proceedings through the medical records, the testimony of the person to whom the statement was made, someone who heard the statement, or the patient.

Defense Use of Patient Statements Reflected in Medical Records to Discredit the Victim

The defense often uses the victim/patient's explanation regarding the cause of her injuries, as reflected in the medical records, to impeach or discredit her testimony at trial. Consider the following example. Assume that Jennifer Durham presented for treatment for a black eye. When asked by medical staff what happened, she responded that she was accidentally hit in the face with a book while attempting to get the book from a high shelf. The medical records reflect, "According to patient, she was struck on face by book which fell from shelf."

At trial, Ms. Durham testifies that during a jealous rage her boyfriend, John Edwards, punched her in the left eye with his right fist. She testifies further that she did not tell the doctors the truth about how she had been injured for two reasons: First, she was afraid John would hurt her again, and second, she did not think the doctors and nurses would believe her.

The defense will point out that the medical records contain a prior statement of the victim that is inconsistent with her trial testimony as to how the injuries were incurred. The defense will argue that Ms. Durham had a strong motivation to tell the doctors the truth about how she was injured. The defense will further argue that because she made those statements close in time to the actual event, her trial testimony, which is taking place long after the incident and which is different from the statements documented in her medical records, should not be believed.

Another method by which a victim's testimony is attacked is through impeachment by omission. Assume that Ms. Durham told medical professionals the truth about being assaulted by her boyfriend. However, the medical records state only that "patient reports having been hit in the eye." There is no mention whatsoever as to who or what caused her injuries. The records fail to state how, specifically, she was injured; that her boyfriend punched her in the eye with his fist; or that she identified her boyfriend by name when asked who had struck her.

The defense will seek to discredit the victim at trial by arguing that because the medical records do not contain a complete version of her statement as to the cause of injury, her current testimony, which is much more detailed, must be false or an exaggeration. The argument is, in essence, that if the victim had told her health care providers the truth about how she was injured, the medical professionals would certainly have accurately recorded that information in the records.

To make matters worse, Federal Rule of Evidence 803(7) provides an exception to the hearsay rule for the absence of an entry in records of a regularly conducted activity. The rule essentially provides that the failure of a record to mention a matter that would ordinarily be mentioned is sufficient proof of its nonexistence (Fed. R. Evid. 803(7), advisory committee's note).

The only challenge that can be raised by the government is that the source of the information or other circumstances indicate a lack of trustworthiness. However, it would be difficult for the government to overcome such an obstacle. Society in general, of which jurors and judges are a part, tends to presume that doctors, nurses, and medical facilities make accurate records. It is more likely that the victim/patient will not be believed. The failure to record accurately and completely a victim/patient's statements as to the cause of her injuries therefore can serve to revictimize her in later proceedings when that failure, through no fault of her own, is used against her. For a discussion concerning the documentation of patient statements, see Chapter 4.

Testimony Regarding Photographic Evidence

For a photograph to be admissible in evidence at trial, it must meet two basic requirements. First, it must be relevant to the case (Fed. R. Evid. 401). *Relevance* means simply that the subject matter depicted in the photograph tends to prove or disprove a fact in issue in the case. The fact of whether injury occurred and the extent of injury are always at issue in a domestic violence criminal prosecution. Therefore, photographs of injuries are always relevant. Second, the photograph must fairly and accurately depict whatever is represented (see generally Fed. R. Evid. 901; Mauet, 1980). Essentially, the photograph will not be considered a fair and accurate depiction if it distorts the subject matter in some meaningful way. Examples of distortions include photographs taken from such an angle as to make the injury appear much larger than it actually was or photographs that distort injury coloration such that the injury appears more severe than it was.

Assuming both of the above criteria are met, the judge in the case nonetheless can exclude a photograph deemed relevant if it is more prejudicial than probative (Fed. R. Evid. 403). For example, a photograph depicting victim injuries might be excluded from the trial if the judge believes that it is too gruesome and would tend to outrage the jury.

For a photograph to be introduced into evidence, all that is required is a witness who can testify that the photograph fairly and accurately depicts what is represented (see generally Fed. R. Evid. 901): that is, the victim's injuries on the date of the crime. Ordinarily, this is accomplished through the testimony of the victim.

Under normal circumstances, the party offering the photograph as evidence is not required to produce the photographer in court. However, the identity of the photographer must be known in case an issue arises that only the photographer can address.

Testimony Regarding Physical Evidence

The first evidentiary issue concerning physical evidence is one of authentication: How, for example, does the government prove that a bullet fragment marked as evidence in the courtroom is the same bullet fragment that was recovered from the patient at the hospital? One way to prove that the evidence is the same is to prove that there were no breaks in the "chain of custody." *Chain of custody* means the sequence of people through whose hands evidence passed from the time it was recovered until it was secured. Generally, this involves documenting the chain of recovery from the victim to receipt by the police officer. An officer who observes a health care provider recover a bullet fragment from a victim/patient can testify to the recovery and chain of custody of evidence. It may not be necessary for the health care provider also to testify in this scenario. The medical records should reflect the names of all staff who recovered evidence and the name, district, and badge number of the officer who took custody of the evidence. The second evidentiary issue concerning physical evidence is, how does the government prove that the evidence was not tampered with in any way? Again, being able to prove clearly through whose hands the evidence passed with no gaps in the chain of custody is essential.

◙ WHAT TO EXPECT WHEN YOU ARE
     NOTIFIED THAT YOU WILL BE CALLED
     AS A GOVERNMENT WITNESS AT TRIAL

Testifying in a criminal case can be a frightening experience, particularly if you do not know what to expect. However, once a prospective witness is given some basic information about the process, most fears are usually allayed.

Receiving a Subpoena or Summons

If a case is scheduled for trial, each of the witnesses will receive a subpoena or a summons directing him or her to appear as a witness for the government on a certain date at a specified time and location. A subpoena or summons is a formal directive issued on the authority of the court compelling the witness to appear at the trial. Failure to comply with a properly issued subpoena or summons may result in the issuance of a warrant for the witness's arrest.

If you, the health care provider, receive a subpoena to testify at a criminal trial as a government witness, you should review the patient's records and promptly telephone the prosecutor. This telephone call can often save you an unnecessary trip to the courthouse. You can discuss with the prosecutor whether your anticipated testimony is actually crucial to the case or whether the records alone will suffice. As for the medical records, ask about the possibility of a stipulation in the case or the use of an administrative person as the witness.

If you receive a subpoena and do not take affirmative action to contact the prosecutor, it is possible that you will not have any contact with the prosecutor until the day of trial. This is particularly true if the case is in a large metropolitan area, involves non-life-threatening injuries, and/or is assigned to an inexperienced prosecutor. Further, because the prosecutor may incorrectly assume that health care providers receive professional training with regard to testifying and have experience testifying, the prosecutor may view pretrial contact with you as unnecessary.

The Pretrial Conference

If you are in fact a necessary witness, you should insist on a pretrial conference with the prosecutor. The conference serves a threefold purpose: to streamline your testimony, to put you at ease with the criminal justice process, and to aid in the success of the prosecution. If this will be your first time testifying, be sure to alert the prosecutor to this fact. A prosecutor will probably spend more time preparing you to testify if he or she is aware that you have never testified before. However, even if you have testified many times before, you should still talk with the prosecutor.

During the pretrial conference, the prosecutor should provide you with certain basic information. This information may include a general description of the court proceedings, your anticipated role in the case, the location of the courthouse and the courtroom, when and where to report, and where to park. The prosecutor should also briefly review the case with you; explain the significance of your testimony to the success of the case; discuss your anticipated testimony, including any evidence that will be offered during your testimony; and explore anticipated areas of cross-examination.

Ordinarily, the conference can readily be accomplished telephonically. You should not be surprised or infer something negative if the prosecutor has a law enforcement officer listen in on the telephone conference call or has the officer sit in on the pretrial meeting. For reasons beyond the scope of this book, it would be exceptional for the prosecutor to interview any prospective witness, medical professional or otherwise, without a law enforcement officer or other witness to the conversation.

Requesting to Be Placed on Call

Note that the subpoena you receive will advise you to report to the courthouse on the date and time the trial is scheduled to begin. However, your testimony may come much later in the trial. For that reason, you should request that the prosecutor place you "on call," which means that you will not have to sit in the courthouse waiting for your turn to testify but will respond when notified. Generally, to be placed on call, you must be accessible by telephone during court hours and be able to arrive at the courthouse within 30 minutes to 1 hour of notice to appear. If you are a surgeon or other staff member who participates in surgery, explain to the prosecutor that you may only be available on certain days of the week and available by telephone during certain hours. Although your testimony may be needed, ordinarily the prosecutor should be able to accommodate your schedule so that your other patients do not suffer from your absence.

It is not unusual for trials to be continued: that is, not to take place on the day scheduled but to be rescheduled to a future date. This can occur when one of the attorneys is involved in another ongoing trial or the judge is not available because he or she is presiding over another case. Hence, this possibility is another good reason to be placed on call.

Commonly Asked Questions

During my career as a prosecutor, I have been routinely asked certain questions by countless prospective witnesses about the proceedings and what to expect when testifying in court. These commonly asked questions and answers to these questions follow:

1. Will there be a lot of people in the courtroom?

Certain people are always present in the courtroom. These people include the judge, who sits in the front of the room; the courtroom clerk, who is usually seated to one side of the judge and acts as the judge's secretary; a deputy marshall; and a court reporter who records everything that is said during the proceedings. If there is a jury trial, there will also be 12 jurors and perhaps two or more alternate jurors in the courtroom. The alternates generally sit through the trial and are excused only when jury deliberation is about to begin. Alternate jurors are chosen in the event that something happens to one of the regular jurors, such as illness, and a substitute is needed. All jurors sit in the jury box.

In addition to those participants, the prosecutor and the defense attorney will be present. The defendant is also present in the courtroom. A person charged with committing a crime is entitled to confront the witnesses against him (U.S. Const. Amend. VI). A defendant is entitled to have the witnesses against him testify under oath, in his presence and in the presence of the fact finder, and be subject to cross-examination (Fed. R. Evid., Article VIII, advisory committee's note).

Family members, friends, or associates of the victim or of the defendant may be present in the courtroom. Ordinarily, unless the case is sensational, no members of the press or community will attend the trial. A judge may have many other matters scheduled for the day or days of the trial in which you are participating. Therefore, it is likely that other attorneys and parties having business before the judge may wait in the courtroom for a break in the proceedings.

2. Can't you just use my deposition or the transcript of my grand jury testimony?

A deposition is a sworn statement ordinarily taken from a witness in a civil proceeding. During a deposition, the opposing party is given the same opportunity to cross-examine the witness as it would have at trial. In criminal cases, depositions are only taken in exceptional circumstances when the interests of justice require that the witness' testimony be preserved (Fed. R. Crim. P. 15). One such situation would include an essential witness suffering from a terminal illness who is physically unable to come to court or who is not expected to live long enough to testify.

A transcript of a witness's grand jury testimony is generally inadmissible at the trial as evidence of the accused's guilt. Such testimony is inadmissible because it is considered hearsay and because the defendant did not have the opportunity to confront and cross-examine witnesses in the grand jury. The use most often made at trial of the transcript of such grand jury testimony is to impeach the witness's credibility if the witness testifies inconsistently with that prior testimony. For these reasons, your live testimony will be required at the trial.

3. Can I watch the trial while I am waiting to testify?

Ordinarily, the court imposes what is referred to as the Rule on Witnesses (Fed. R. Evid. 615) and excludes from the courtroom all witnesses except the witness who is actually testifying. The rationale for prohibiting one witness from listening to the testimony of other witnesses is that you, the witness, may shape your testimony around what you hear, or you may learn information of which you had no personal knowledge. Ordinarily, the witnesses are permitted to listen to the closing arguments of counsel if they wish to do so, even when the court earlier invoked the Rule on Witnesses. However, counsel must seek the court's permission.

4. How can I best prepare myself to testify?

Before the day you are scheduled to testify, carefully review all medical records of the patient and any prior testimony or statements you may have given in connection with the case. This is the most effective method by which you can refresh your own recollection concerning treatment of the victim/patient.

5. Can I have notes and records with me on the witness stand while I testify?

A witness is supposed to testify on the basis of his or her personal knowledge and recollection of the facts. As indicated above, prior to testifying, you should refresh your recollection with any and every document, record, or statement you have that pertains to the case. However, unless you are directed otherwise by the prosecutor, you should not take such papers with you onto the witness stand.

If, while testifying, you forget certain details such as times, dates, or test results, do not panic. Simply state that you do not remember. The prosecutor is permitted to show you whatever would refresh your recollection, including records and notes. After your recollection is refreshed, you will testify on the basis of your revived memory of the event. Note that any document used to refresh your recollection, before or while you are testifying, may be turned over to the defense to inspect and may be used by the defense to cross-examine you (Fed. R. Evid. 612).

6. What should I wear to court?

A criminal trial is a serious matter, and you should dress accordingly. Normal business attire is appropriate. If you wear a pager, note that the sound of its alarm would disrupt the proceedings and greatly annoy the judge. Therefore, before you enter the courtroom, set your pager to the vibrate mode or turn it off. The same holds true for cellular telephones. Turn off your telephone before you enter the courtroom.

7. What should I take with me to court?

You should take identification, the subpoena you received, and anything requested of you in the subpoena. For example, the subpoena may direct that you bring with you the original medical records, including photographs, of the patient who is the victim in the case on trial. In addition to these items, because you may be kept waiting, it is a good idea to take something to read to occupy yourself during any downtime.

8. What should I know about testifying?

When you are called to testify, approach the witness stand, but do not take a seat until the oath is administered. The court clerk will administer the oath. You will be asked to swear or affirm that the testimony you are about to give is the truth, the whole truth, and nothing but the truth. After you take the oath, you will be asked to take a seat on the witness stand, and your testimony will begin.

When you are seated, there will ordinarily be a microphone in front of you. Position the microphone so that it is level with your mouth, several inches away. If you sit too far away from the microphone, no one will be able to hear you. If you sit too close to it, you will blast out your testimony. Note that some courts have sophisticated voice-activated microphones. For these microphones to function properly, the witness must position the microphone directly in front of, level with, and no more than 6 to 8 inches away from their mouth.

If the chair swivels or can be moved, turn your body slightly toward the jury so that if you look at the jury the movement is not unnatural. Refrain from rocking or swiveling during your testimony. Also avoid any other distracting mannerisms or movements. Be careful not to cross your arms over your chest; such a position may be viewed negatively.

Look at the attorney as you are asked questions. Some prosecutors may instruct you to look in the direction of the jury when you answer questions. However, in my opinion, if this is done routinely with each answer given, it can look artificial. Having observed such intentional unnatural movements, the jury may conclude that your testimony has been rehearsed and is insincere. Instead, I suggest that witnesses occasionally look at the jurors when they answer questions, as if they are engaged in a conversation with the jury and the attorney asking the questions.

Always speak in a loud, clear voice. Avoid having anything in your mouth, such as gum or breath mints. Always verbalize your response to each question. Gestures such as nodding one's head in the affirmative will not be reflected on the record of the proceedings. Further, if you fail to verbalize your answer, a juror whose attention is focused elsewhere may presume that you simply failed to answer the question.

Your testimony will begin with the prosecutor asking you a series of questions. This portion of your testimony is called direct examination. The questions asked during direct examination are generally open-ended and are called "nonleading questions." Nonleading questions begin with words such as *what, when, why, where,* and *who.* A nonleading question does not assume the answer you will give.

When you are asked a question, listen carefully, and answer only the question that you have been asked. Do not volunteer information. Keep your answers short and to the point. If you do not hear the question, ask that it be repeated. If you do not understand the question asked, say so. If a question is confusing, it is not your fault; it is the fault of the attorney who posed it.

Following the direct examination, the defense may cross-examine you. During cross-examination, the attorney is permitted to use leading questions. Leading questions assume the answer in their form. Such questions start with phrases such as "Isn't it true that . . . ?" "Isn't it fair to say that . . . ?" and "Wouldn't you agree that. . . ?" Listen carefully to the question asked. Do not delay your answer by trying to figure out what point the defense is trying to make. Do not look to the prosecutor for a reaction to the question. Just answer the question truthfully.

Often, leading questions can be answered with a simple "yes" or "no." If that is the case, you should answer in that manner. Sometimes, however, the answer would be misleading to the fact finder if you simply answered yes or no. For example, suppose you were working in the emergency department when a woman who had been stabbed in the chest was brought in for treatment. You were one of many staff members who attended the patient. You are thoroughly familiar with the case because it was complicated and required much effort. The hospital medical records do not mention you by name, and you are aware of this fact. At the trial on direct examination, you testify to the treatment provided. On cross-examination, the defense asks, "Isn't it true that your name is not mentioned in any of the medical records?" If you merely answer, "Yes," it may sound as if you were not actually present. For that reason, you could truthfully answer, "Yes, but I was there."

On television, one often sees the hapless witness abruptly cut off, while trying to give an answer on cross-examination, with outbursts of "Your Honor, please instruct the witness to answer just 'yes' or 'no.' " In real life, however, judges frequently allow witnesses to answer questions asked with more than just a "yes" or "no" response.

Watch out for compound questions. A compound question is a question that asks more than one thing at a time. For example, "Dr. Anderson, wouldn't it be fair to say that you were very tired by the end of your shift and you might not have heard correctly what the patient told you about the cause of her injuries?" This question is not only confusing but objectionable because it asks more than one question at the same time. Perhaps it was at the end of the doctor's shift, but the doctor was not tired. Perhaps the doctor was tired, but he or she heard everything the patient said very well. Maybe the patient repeatedly told the doctor what had happened.

The prosecutor should object to such a question. Whenever there is an objection, you, the witness, should stop talking immediately. If the prosecutor does object, the judge may ask for the grounds of the objection. The prosecutor will reply, "Compound question." The judge may then "sustain" or "overrule" the objection. If the judge sustains the objection, it means that the judge agrees that the question is not proper. You should not answer a question to which an objection has been sustained. If the judge overrules the objection, it means that he disagrees with the objection; the question was appropriate, and you may answer it. You need not worry about memorizing legal terms of art; the judge will ordinarily turn to you after a ruling and tell you that you may or may not answer the question.

If the prosecutor does not object to the compound question and you cannot truthfully answer the question "yes" or "no," say so. You might testify, "I cannot answer that question yes or no; part of it is true, part of it is false." Alternatively, you might ask that the attorney repeat the questions one at a time. At that point, the prosecutor may raise the objection he or she missed, the judge may direct you to answer the question as best you can, the judge may direct the defense to rephrase the question, or the defense may rephrase the question on its own.

Don't guess at answers. A common defense tactic is to ask the witness how much time something took to happen. Sometimes this gets quite dramatic, with a defense attorney using a stopwatch and telling the witness, "I will start the watch when I say 'now.' To show how long it took to happen, tell me when to stop." However, unless you timed the occurrence, the best you can give is an estimate. It is truthful and appropriate for you to respond to such a question by stating, "I don't know exactly how long it took. I wasn't timing it."

In a similar line of attack, a defense attorney may attempt to get a medical professional to "date" a patient's injuries. Such testimony might well then be used to attack the victim's credibility. For example, suppose the treating physician testifies on cross-examination that a fading bruise was 2 weeks old. The victim, however, testifies that she received that bruise during an attack 10 days prior to receiving the medical treatment at issue. The defense will use this inconsistency by arguing that the victim is not telling the truth because according to the doctor the injury was older. For this reason, medical professionals should not attempt to date injuries (Sheridan, 1995).

Do not answer questions about which you have no personal knowledge. For example, if you are asked questions about hospital policies and procedures and you do not know the answer, say so. I have found that educated individuals are often reluctant to say that they do not know something because they think they will look foolish. However, you cannot possibly know everything about everything. If you provide inaccurate or false information to save your pride, you may jeopardize the case.

Be courteous, and do not get angry when the defense attorney asks you questions. The defense has an absolute right to question you. Unfortunately, some defense attorneys employ the tactic of intentionally attempting to provoke you. If you become hostile, the jury may find that you are not credible. They may conclude that if you were telling the truth, you would not become upset when asked some questions by the defense.

After you have been cross-examined, the prosecutor has a second opportunity to ask you questions on redirect examination. During redirect examination, the prosecutor will try to clear up any inconsistencies or areas of confusion that arose during cross-examination.

9. *What should I say if I am asked whether I spoke to or had a meeting with the prosecutor, reviewed the patient's medical records, or read my statement or grand jury transcript before testifying?*

Always tell the truth. For some unknown reason, the average prospective witness thinks it is inappropriate to review his or her statement or transcript, to review the medical records, or to have spoken with or met with the prosecutor before testifying. It would be foolish not to refresh your recollection in advance of the trial by reviewing the medical records. Similarly, if you gave a statement to the police or testified before the grand jury, you should also read those statements to refresh your recollection. Finally, the prosecutor is calling you to testify as a witness for the government. How will the prosecutor know whether your testimony will be relevant to the case if he or she does not interview you? Speaking to or meeting with the prosecutor or other members of law enforcement before the trial is perfectly appropriate.

10. *What should I do when I am done testifying?*

Ordinarily, at the conclusion of your testimony, you will be excused by the judge from the proceedings. In this instance, your appearance is complete, and you will be free to leave the courthouse. Infrequently, under certain circumstances, one of the parties may want to recall you as a witness later in the case. If this occurs, before you leave the witness stand, the judge will conditionally excuse you on your promise to return to court when notified to do so.

11. *Can I tell other people what I testified about?*

When you have finished testifying, while the case is still ongoing, you should not discuss your testimony with anyone. In fact, the judge may give you a specific admonition to that effect before you are excused. In any event, you may not know that a prospective witness is within earshot of your conversation about the case. Discussing your testimony once you finish can defeat the Rule on

Witnesses if, even unintentionally, you disclose your testimony to another witness.

12. Is there anything else I should know about?

Often during the proceedings, there may be some downtime. If the court takes a recess, be aware that the jurors could be in the courthouse hallway where you are waiting. Maintain a professional demeanor at all times, and do not discuss the case in a public environment, such as the hallway, the cafeteria, an elevator, or a rest room.

13. How can I find out whether the defendant is convicted?

You can request that the prosecutor notify you as to the outcome of the case.

14. What will happen to the defendant if he is convicted?

If the defendant is found guilty, the judge will schedule the case for sentencing. As discussed previously, the judge's sentencing options depend on whether the case is in state or federal court.

15. Will I be compensated for my time?

Fact witnesses are entitled to statutory "witness fees" to compensate them for their attendance at grand jury and court proceedings and in witness conferences. The fees are unremarkable. For example, in the District of Columbia a witness is entitled to the fee of $20.00 for half a day and $40.00 for a full day (D.C. Code § 15-714; 28 U.S.C. § 1821 *et seq.*). Federal government employees are paid their salary and given administrative leave to comply with testimonial obligations. Likewise, some businesses grant leave to employees and compensate them for time in connection with the proceedings. When an individual is self-employed or has a job in which the work simply does not get done in his or her absence, there is a real hardship, not to mention a financial loss. Such is frequently the case with doctors who see patients. If you or the facility at which you work are in a hardship position, let the prosecutor know this fact. You may still be called to testify, but perhaps you can be accommodated at the first opportunity in the morning or at the end of the day so as to interfere least with your schedule.

Expert witnesses are generally compensated on a sliding scale according to their profession, area of specialty, educational background, and experience. The prosecutor will usually make arrangements with an expert witness well in advance of the trial date.

16. What should I do if a defense attorney or an investigator for a defense attorney tries to interview me?

It is up to you whether to speak to the defense attorney or to a defense investigator. You are not required to do so.

REFERENCES

Abbott, J., Johnson, R., Koziol-McLain, J., & Lowenstein, S. R. (1995). Domestic violence against women: Incidence and prevalence in an emergency department population. *Journal of the American Medical Association, 273,* 1763-1767.

Abramson, L. Y., Seligman, E. P., & Teasdale, J. D. (1978). Learned helplessness in humans: Critique and reformulation. *Journal of Abnormal Psychology, 87*(1), 49-74.

Adams, D. (1989, July/August). Identifying the assaultive husband in court: You be the judge. *Boston Bar Journal, 4,* 33.

American College of Emergency Physicians. (1988). *Emergency department violence prevention and management.* Dallas, TX: Author.

American College of Emergency Physicians. (1995). Emergency medicine and domestic violence. *Annals of Emergency Medicine, 25,* 442-443.

American College of Obstetricians and Gynecologists. (1995). *The abused woman* (ACOG Patient Education Pamphlet No. APO83). Washington, DC: Author.

American College of Physicians. (1986). *Domestic violence position paper.* Philadelphia: Author.

American Medical Association. (1992a). *Diagnostic and treatment guidelines on domestic violence* (Pamphlet No. AA 22:92-406 20M). Chicago: Author.

American Medical Association. (1994). *Violence toward men: Fact or fiction? Report of the Council on Scientific Affairs.* Chicago: Author.

American Medical Association. (1995a). *Diagnostic and treatment guidelines on mental health effects of family violence.* Chicago: Author.

American Medical Association. (1995b). *Violence in the medical workplace: Prevention strategies.* Chicago: Author.

American Medical Association, Council on Ethical and Judicial Affairs. (1992b). Physicians and domestic violence: Ethical considerations. *Journal of the American Medical Association, 267,* 3190-3193.

American Medical Association, Council on Scientific Affairs. (1992c). Violence against women: Relevance for medical practitioners. *Journal of the American Medical Association, 267,* 3184-3189.

American Psychiatric Association. (1994). *Diagnostic and statistical manual of mental disorders* (4th ed.). Washington, DC: Author.

American Psychological Association. (1996). *Violence and the family: Report of the American Psychological Association Presidential Task Force on Violence and the Family.* Washington, DC: Author.

Bachman, R. (1994). *Violence against women: A national crime victimization survey report* (NCJ Pub. No. 145325). Washington, DC: U.S. Dept. of Justice.

Blount, W. R., Silverman, I. J., Sellers, C. S., & Seese, R. A. (1994). Alcohol and drug use among abused women who kill, abused women who don't, and their abusers. *Journal of Drug Issues, 24,* 165-177.

Bokunewicz, B., & Copel, L. C. (1992). Attitudes of emergency nurses before and after a 60-minute educational presentation on partner abuse. *Journal of Emergency Nursing, 18*(1), 24-27.

Bowker, L. H., & Maurer, L. (1987). The medical treatment of battered wives. *Women and Health, 12*(1), 25-45.

Boyd, V. D., & Klingbeil, K. S. (1993). *Family violence: Behavioral characteristics in spouse/partner abuse* (Rev. ed.) [Chart]. Available from Vicki D. Boyd, Ph.D., 1836 Westlake N., Suite 302, Seattle, WA 98109-2755.

Bradley v. State, 1 Miss. (Walk. Miss. Rep. 156) 20 (1824).

Brown, J. (in press). Working toward freedom from violence: The process of change in battered women. In *Violence against women.* Thousand Oaks, CA: Sage.

Browne, A. (1987). *When battered women kill.* New York: Free Press.

Browne, A. (1992). Council on Scientific Affairs Report, American Medical Association, Violence against women: Relevance for medical practitioners. *Journal of the American Medical Association 267,* 3184-3189.

Browne, A. (1993). Violence against women by male partners: Prevalence, outcomes, and policy implications. *American Psychologist, 48,* 1077-1087.

Bullock, L. (1989). Characteristics of battered women in a primary care setting. *Nurse Practitioner, 14,* 47-55.

Burge, S. K. (1989). Violence against women as a health care issue. *Family Medicine, 21,* 368-373.

Campbell, J. C. (1986). Nursing assessment for risk of homicide with battered women. *Advances in Nursing Science, 8*(4), 36-51.

Campbell, J. C. (1995). Prediction of homicide by battered women. In J. C. Campbell (Ed.), *Assessing dangerousness* (pp. 96-113). Newbury Park, CA: Sage.

Caplan, P. J. (1985). *The myth of women's masochism.* Toronto: University of Toronto Press.

Cascardi, M., & O'Leary, K. D. (1992). Depressive symptomology, self-esteem and self-blame in battered women. *Journal of Family Violence, 7,* 249-259.

Charney, D. S., Deutch, A. Y., Krystal, J. H., Southwich, S. M., & Davis, M. (1993). Psychobiologic mechanisms of posttraumatic stress disorder. *Archives of General Psychiatry, 50,* 295-305.

Colburn, D. (1994, June 28). Domestic violence: AMA president decries "a major public health problem." *Washington Post,* Health section, pp. 10, 12.

Colling, R. L. (1992). *Hospital security* (3rd ed.). Stoneham, MA: Butterworth-Heinemann.

Colorado Dept. of Health and Colorado Domestic Violence Coalition. (1992). *Domestic violence: A guide for health care providers* (4th ed.). Denver: Author.

Commonwealth Fund, Commission on Women's Health. (1993). *Survey of women's health.* New York: Author.

Commonwealth Fund, Commission on Women's Health. (1995). *Violence against women in the United States: A comprehensive background paper.* New York: Author.

Confidentiality of Records, 42 U.S.C. § 290dd-2.

Congressional Caucus for Women's Issues. (1992, October). *Violence against women* [Fact sheet]. Available from the National Coalition Against Domestic Violence, P.O. Box 34103, Washington, DC 20043-4103.

Cosgrove, A. (1992). *Medical Power and Control Wheel* and *Advocacy Wheel*. Available from the Domestic Violence Project, Inc., 6308 8th Ave., Kenosha, WI 53143.

Dartmouth-Hitchcock Medical Center. (1994). *Domestic violence protocol: Identifying and treating adult victims in the emergency department.* Lebanon, NH: Author.

Davidson, T. (1977). Wife beating: A recurrent phenomenon throughout history. In M. Roy (Ed.), *Battered women: A psychological study of domestic violence* (p. 16). New York: Van Nostrand Reinhold.

Davidson, T. (1978). *Conjugal crime.* New York: Hawthorne.

Davis, P. (1994, February 9). Woman pleads guilty in death of son, 2. *Washington Post,* p. B-1.

de Beauvoir, S. (1974). *The second sex* (H. M. Parshley, Ed. & Trans.). New York: Vintage. (Original work published 1949)

Developments: Domestic violence. (1993). *Harvard Law Review, 106,* 1498.

District of Columbia Coalition Against Domestic Violence. (1994). *Safety/exit plan.* Available from the D.C. Coalition Against Domestic Violence, P.O. Box 76069, Washington, DC 20013.

Doctor shootings force hospitals to reconsider security. (1993, March 1). *American Medical News,* p. 3.

Donnelly, W. J., Hines, E., Jr., & Brauner, D. J. (1992). Why SOAP is bad for the medical record. *Archives of Internal Medicine, 152,* 481-484.

Dotterer, C. S. (1992, June 30). Breaking the cycle of domestic abuse. *Washington Post,* p. Z-9.

Dutton, D., & Painter, S. L. (1981). Traumatic bonding: The development of emotional attachments in battered women and other relationships of intermittent abuse. *Victimology: An International Journal, 6,* 139-155.

Dutton, M. A. (1992). *Empowering and healing the battered woman: A model for assessment and intervention.* New York: Springer.

Dutton, M. A., & Goodman, L. A. (1994). Posttraumatic stress disorder among battered women: Analysis of legal implications. *Behavioral Sciences and the Law, 12,* 215-234.

Duty to Report, N.M. Stat. Ann. § 27-7-30 (Michie 1992).

Federal Protective Service, U.S. General Services Administration. (n.d.). *What you should know about coping with threats and violence in the federal workplace.* Washington, DC: Author.

Feldman, M. K. (1992). Family violence intervention: Physicians find it's more than treating injuries. *Minnesota Medicine, 75,* 19-23.

Fellows, M. L. (1986). The slayer rule: Not solely a matter of equity. *Iowa Law Review, 71,* 489, 490-504.

Flitcraft, A. (1990). Battered women in your practice? *Patient Care, 24,* 107-108.

Flitcraft, A. (1992). Violence, values and gender [Editorial]. *Journal of the American Medical Association, 267,* 3194-3195.

Flitcraft, A. (1993). Physicians and domestic violence: Challenges for prevention. *Health Affairs, 1,* 154-161.

Fortune, M. (1987). *Keeping the faith: Questions and answers for abused women.* San Francisco: Harper & Row.

Frances, A., First, M. B., & Pincus, H. A. (1995). *DSM-IV guidebook.* Washington, DC: American Psychiatric Press.

Fulgram v. State, 46 Ala. 143 (1871).

Gaines, J. (1995, March 12). Domestic violence victims are routinely rejected by major insurers. *Boston Globe,* p. 1.

Geller, J. L., & Harris, M. (1994). *Women of the asylum: Voices from behind the walls, 1840-1945.* New York: Doubleday.

Gelles, R. J. (1975). Violence and pregnancy: A note on the extent of the problem and needed services. *Family Coordinator, 24,* 81-86.

Gelles, R. J., & Straus, M. A. (1989). *Intimate violence: The causes and consequence of abuse in the American family.* New York: Simon & Schuster.

Gentry, C. (1991, August 18). Women, abusers bond. *St. Petersburg Times,* p. 1-A.

Glazer, S. (1993). Violence against women: Is the problem more serious than statistics indicate? *CQ Researcher, 3*(8), 169-192.

Goodman, R. A., Jenkins, E. L., & Mercy, J. A. (1994). Workplace-related homicide among health care workers in the United States, 1980 through 1990. *Journal of the American Medical Association, 272,* 1686-1688.

Graham, D. L. R., Rawlings, E., & Rimini, N. (1988). Survivors of terror: Battered women, hostages, and the Stockholm syndrome. In K. Yllo & M. Bograd (Eds.), *Feminist perspectives on wife abuse* (pp. 217-233). Newbury Park, CA: Sage.

Haber, J. D., & Ross, C. (1985). Effects of spouse abuse and/or sexual abuse in the development and management of chronic pain in women. *Advances in Pain Research and Therapy, 9,* 889-895.

Hamberger, L. K., Saunders, D. G., & Hovey, M. (1992). Prevalence of domestic violence in community practice and rate of physician inquiry. *Family Medicine, 24,* 283-287.

Harris, M. (1992, January 6). The billion dollar epidemic. *American Medical News,* p. 7.

Hart, B. J., & Gondolf, E. W. (1994). Lethality and dangerousness assessments. *Violence UpDate, 4*(4), 7-8, 10.

Hart, B., & Stueling, B. (1992). Personalized safety plan. In C. J. Parker, B. Hart, & J. Stueling (Eds.), *Legal advocacy principles and practice* (pp. 16-22). Harrisburg, PA: Pennsylvania Coalition Against Domestic Violence.

Heise, L. L., Pitanguy, J., & Germain, A. (1994). *Violence against women: The hidden health burden* (World Bank Discussion Paper No. 25). Washington, DC: International Bank for Reconstruction and Development/World Bank.

Helton, A. (1986). Battering during pregnancy. *American Journal of Nursing, 86,* 910-913.

Helton, A. S. (1987). *A protocol of care for the battered woman.* White Plains, NY: March of Dimes Birth Defects Foundation.

Herman, J. L. (1992). *Trauma and recovery.* New York: HarperCollins.

Hilberman, E. (1980). Overview: The "wife beater's wife" reconsidered. *American Journal of Psychiatry, 137,* 1336-1347.

Hinds, D. L. (1993, July). Domestic violence documentation: Photographs improve prosecution success rates. *Law and Order, 41*(7), 86-89.

Houskamp, B. M., & Foy, D. W. (1991). The assessment of post traumatic stress disorder in battered women. *Journal of Interpersonal Violence, 6,* 367-375.

Howard-Martin, J., & Howard, D. (1994). How OSHA's response to workplace violence will affect healthcare facilities. *Healthspan, 11,* 21-24.

Injuries by Firearm; Assaultive or Abusive Conduct; Reporting Duties by Health Facilities, Clinics, Physician's Offices, or Local or State Public Health Department; Contents of Report, Cal. Penal Code § 11160(b)(3)(d)(18) (West Supp. 1995).

Injuries to Be Reported; Penalty for Failure to Report; Immunity From Liability, Colo. Rev. Stat. Ann. § 12-36-135 (West 1995).

Inter-University Consortium for Political and Social Research. (1981). *National Crime Surveys: National sample, 1973-1979.* Ann Arbor, MI: Author.

Isaac, E., Cochran, D., Brown, M. E., & Adams, S. L. (1994). Men who batter: Profile from a restraining order database. *Archives of Family Medicine, 3,* 50-54.

Island, D., & Letellier, P. (1991). *Men who beat the men who love them: Battered gay men and domestic violence.* New York: Hayworth.

Jecker, N. S. (1993). Privacy beliefs and the violent family: Extending the ethical argument for physician intervention. *Journal of the American Medical Association, 269,* 776-780.

Joint Commission on Accreditation of Healthcare Organizations. (1995). *1996 comprehensive accreditation manual for hospitals.* Oakbrook Terrace, IL: Author.

Keep, N., & Gilbert, P. (1992). California Emergency Nurses Association's informal survey of violence in California emergency departments. *Journal of Emergency Nursing, 18,* 433-439.

Kemp, A., Rawlings, E. I., & Green, B. L. (1991). Post-traumatic stress disorder (PTSD) in battered women: A shelter sample. *Journal of Traumatic Stress, 4*(1), 137-148.

Kiernan, L. A. (1993, June 5). Victim "stunned" by N.H. judge: Comments, sentence in domestic violence assault prompt outrage. *Boston Globe,* p. 1.

Klein, C. F. (1995). *Full faith and credit: Interstate enforcement of protection orders under the Violence Against Women Act of 1994.* Family Law Quarterly, 29, 253.

Klein, C. F., & Orloff, L. E. (1993). Providing legal protection for battered women: An analysis of state statutes and case law. *Hofstra Law Review, 21,* 801, 910-953.

Klingbeil, K. S., & Boyd, V. D. (1984). Emergency room intervention: Detection, assessment, and treatment. In A. R. Roberts (Ed.), *Battered women and their families* (pp. 7-32). New York: Springer.

Kosova, W. (1991, December). Knife assailant, healthcare provider. *Washington City Paper,* p. 8.

Koss, M. P., Goodman, L. A., Browne, A., Fitzgerald, L. F., Puryear Keita, G., & Felipe Russo, N. (1994). *No safe haven: Male violence against women at home, at work, and in the community.* Washington, DC: American Psychological Association.

Kurz, D. (1987). Emergency department responses to battered women: Resistance to medicalization. *Social Problems, 34*(1), 69-81.

Kurz, D. (1990). Interventions with battered women in health care settings. *Violence and Victims, 5,* 243-256.

Kurz, D., & Stark, E. (1988). Not-so-benign neglect: The medical response to battering. In K. Yllo & M. Bograd (Eds.), *Feminist perspectives on wife abuse* (pp. 249-266). Newbury Park, CA: Sage.

Langan, P. A., & Innes, C. A. (1986). *Preventing domestic violence against women* (NCJ Pub. No. 102037). Washington, DC: U.S. Dept. of Justice.

Lavoie, F. W., Carter, G. L., Danzl, D. F., & Berg, R. L. (1988). Emergency department violence in United States teaching hospitals. *Annals of Emergency Medicine, 17,* 1227-1233.

Lee, D., Letellier, P., McLoughlin, E., & Salber, P. (1993). California hospital emergency departments' response to domestic violence: Survey report. *Morbidity and Mortality Weekly Report, 42*(32).

Lerner, M. J. (1965). Evaluation of performance as a function of performer's reward and attractiveness. *Journal of Personality and Social Psychology, 1,* 355-360.

Lerner, M. J., & Simmons, C. H. (1966). The observer's reaction to the "innocent victim": Compassion or rejection? *Journal of Personality and Social Psychology, 4,* 203-210.

Levy, B. (Ed.). (1991). *Dating violence: Young women in danger.* Seattle: Seal.

Lobel, K. (Ed.). (1986). *Naming the violence: Speaking out about lesbian battering.* Seattle: Seal.

MacFarquhar, E. (1994, March 28). The war against women. *U.S. News and World Report,* pp. 42-48.

Mann, J. (1994). *The difference: Growing up female in America.* New York: Warner.

Martin, D. (1983). *Battered wives.* New York: Pocket.

Massachusetts Coalition of Battered Women Service Groups. (1990). *For shelter and beyond.* Boston: Author.

Mauet, T. A. (1980). *Fundamentals of trial techniques.* Boston: Little, Brown.

McDonald, K. A. (1990). Battered wives, religion, and law: An interdisciplinary approach. *Yale Journal of Law and Feminism, 2,* 251-298.

McFarlane, J., Parker, B., Soeken, K., & Bullock, L. (1992). Assessing for abuse during pregnancy: Severity and frequency of injuries and associated entry in prenatal care. *Journal of the American Medical Association, 267,* 3176-3178.

McKibben, L., Devos, E., & Newberger, E. (1989). Victimization of mothers of abused children: A controlled study. *Pediatrics, 84,* 531-535.

McLeer, S. V., & Anwar, R. A. H. (1987). The role of the emergency physician in the prevention of domestic violence. *Annals of Emergency Medicine, 16,* 1155-1161.

McLeer, S. V., & Anwar, R. A. H. (1989). A study of battered women presenting in an emergency department. *American Journal of Public Health, 79,* 65-66.

McLeer, S. V., Anwar, R. A. H., Herman, S., & Maquiling, K. (1989). Education is not enough: A systems failure in protecting battered women. *Annals of Emergency Medicine, 18,* 651-653.

Medical Data Collection Reports, R.I. Gen. Laws § 12-29-9 (Supp. 1993).

National Council of Juvenile and Family Court Judges. (1994). *Family violence: A model state code.* Reno, NV: Author.

Pacenti, J. (1995, March 15). Domestic violence victims testify they were denied insurance. *San Diego Union-Tribune,* p. A-26.

Parker, B., & McFarlane, J. (1991). Nursing assessment of battered women. *Maternal-Child Nursing Journal, 16,* 161-164.

Patton, D. (1994, January 30). He never hit me: The need for expert testimony in domestic violence cases. *Arizona Attorney,* pp. 10-15, 31.

Pence, E., & Paymar, M. (1986). *Power and control: Tactics of men who batter.* Duluth, MN: Domestic Abuse Intervention Project.

Pike, C. L. (1992). The use of medical protocols in identifying battered women. *Wayne Law Review, 38,* 1941.

Pitt, D. (1989, March 27). Hospital police: No guns, no respect, lots of trouble. *New York Times,* p. B-1.

Pleck, E. (1979). Wife beating in nineteenth-century America. *Victimology: An International Journal, 4*(1), 60-74.

Polaroid Corporation. (1992). *Domestic violence injury documentation.* Available from Polaroid Corporation, 575 Technology Square, Cambridge, MA 02139.

Pope-Lance, D. J., & Chamberlain-Engelsman, J. (1990). *A guide for the clergy on the problems of domestic violence.* Trenton: New Jersey Dept. of Community Affairs.

Powers, R. (1994, May 13). Insurers admit denying policies to battered women. *Patriot News,* p. A-5.

Protection From Abuse, 23 Pa. Cons. Stat. Ann. § 6101 *et seq.* (1991).

Protection From Domestic Abuse, Miss. Code Ann. § 93-21 (Supp. 1993).

Quinn, M. J., & Tomita, S. (1986). *Elder abuse and neglect.* New York: Springer.

Randall, T. (1991). Hospital-wide program identifies battered women; offers assistance. *Journal of the American Medical Association, 264,* 940-944.

Rath, G. D., & Jarratt, L. G. (1990, January). Battered wife syndrome: Overview and presentation in the office setting. *South Dakota Journal of Medicine, 43,* 19-25.

Reg v. Jackson, 1 Q.B. 671, 679 (1891).

Renzetti, C. (1992). *Violent betrayal: Partner abuse in lesbian relationships.* Newbury Park, CA: Sage.

Reporting Felony: Medical Personnel to Report Gunshot, Stabbing, and Burn Injuries and Suspected Domestic Violence, Ohio Rev. Code Ann. § 2421.24(F)(1) (Anderson 1993).

Rules and Regulations; Reports; Cabinet Actions, Ky. Rev. Stat. Ann. § 209.030 (Michie/Bobbs-Merrill 1991).

Ribe, J. K., Teggatz, J. R., & Harvey, C. M. (1993). Blows to the maternal abdomen causing fetal demise: Report of three cases and a review of the literature. *Journal of Forensic Sciences, 38,* 1092-1096.

Roan, S. (1991, August 20). Abused women may be "hostages." *Los Angeles Times,* p. E-1.

Robinson, L., & Epstein, J. (1994, April 4). Battered by the myth of machismo. *U.S. News and World Report,* pp. 40-41.

Rosenberg, D. A. (1994, March). *Prevention of family violence: The role of medicine.* Paper presented at the National Conference on Family Violence: Health and Justice, Washington, DC.

Rosenfeld, M. (1994, October 28). Mercy for a cuckolded killer: Women outraged over judge's light sentence. *Washington Post,* pp. C-1 to C-2.

Safety and Health Program Management Guidelines, 54 Fed. Reg. § 3904 (1989).

Saltzman, L. (1990). Battering during pregnancy: A role for physicians. *Atlanta Medicine, 64,* 45-48.

Saunders, D. G. (1988). Wife abuse, husband abuse, or mutual combat? A feminist perspective on the empirical findings. In K. Yllo & M. Bograd (Eds.), *Feminist perspectives on wife abuse* (pp. 90-113). Newbury Park, CA: Sage.

Saxton Mahoney, B. (1990). The extent, nature, and response to victimization of emergency nurses in Pennsylvania. *Journal of Emergency Nursing, 17,* 282-294.

Schulman, M. A. (1981). *A survey of spousal violence against women in Kentucky.* New York: Garland.

Scott, K. (1994, July). *Violence in health care institutions.* Presentation at the American Society for Industrial Security Seminar, Washington, DC.

Security and Safety Assessment; Development of Security Plan; Security Personnel; Assault and Battery Reports to Law Enforcement; Liability; Violation; Penalty, Cal. Health and Safety Code § 1257.7 (West 1993).

Security Training and Education; Emergency Department Employees and Medical Staff, Cal. Health and Safety Code § 1257.8 (West 1993).

Seelye, K. Q. (1994, June 1). In shift, State Farm will insure battered women. *New York Times,* p. A-19.

Seligman, M. E. P. (1975). *Helplessness: On depression, development, and death.* San Francisco: W. H. Freeman.

Seligman, M. E. P., & Meier, S. F. (1967). Failure to escape traumatic shock. *Journal of Experimental Psychology, 74,* 1-9.

Seligman, M. E. P., Maier, S. F., & Geer, J. H. (1968). Alleviation of learned helplessness in the dog. *Journal of Abnormal Psychology, 73,* 256-262.

Shalala, D. (1994, March). *Keynote address.* Paper presented at the American Medical Association National Conference on Family Violence, Washington, DC.

Sheridan, D. J. (1987). Advocacy with battered women: The role of the emergency room nurse. *Response, 10*(4), 14-16.

Sheridan, D. (1995, September). *Clinical interventions with battered women.* Paper presented at the Domestic Violence Assessment Training, Providence Hospital, Washington, DC.

Simonowitz, J. A. (1993). *Guidelines for security and safety of health care and community service workers.* Los Angeles: State of California, Dept. of Industrial Relations, Division of Occupational Safety and Health, Medical Unit.

Skodol, A. E. (1989). *Problems in differential diagnosis: From DSM-III to DSM-III-R in clinical practice.* Washington, DC: American Psychiatric Press.

Spatz-Widom, C. (1992). *The cycle of violence* (NJC Pub. No. 136607). Washington, DC: U.S. Dept. of Justice.

Spousal abuse earns slap on the wrist; Judge says real crime was the adulterous wife. (1996, January 18). *Detroit News,* p. A-1.

Stark, E., & Flitcraft, A. (1985). Spouse abuse. In *Surgeon General's Workshop on Violence and Public Health: Source book* (pp. SA1-SA43). Rockville, MD: U.S. Public Health Service.

Stark, E., Flitcraft, A., & Frazier, F. (1979). Medicine and patriarchal violence: The social construction of a "private" event. *International Journal of Health Services 9,* 461-493.

Stark, E., Flitcraft, A., Zuckerman, D., Grey, A., Robinson, J., & Frazier, W. (1981). *Wife abuse in the medical setting: An introduction for health personnel* (Monograph No. 7). Rockville, MD: National Clearinghouse on Domestic Violence.

State v. Black, 60 N.C. (Winst.) 162, 86 Am. Dec. 436 (1864).

State v. Oliver, 70 N.C. 60 (1874).

State v. Rhodes, 61 N.C. (Phil.Law) 445 (1868).

Stedman, B. (1917). Right of husband to chastise wife. *Virginia Law Register, 3,* 241.

Straus, M. A., & Gelles, R. J. (1986). Societal change and change in family violence from 1975 to 1985 as revealed by two national surveys. *Journal of Marriage and the Family, 48,* 465-479.

Straus, M. A., Gelles, R. J., & Steinmetz, S. K. (1980). *Behind closed doors: A survey of family violence in America.* Garden City, NY: Doubleday.

Strube, M. J. (1988). The decision to leave an abusive relationship: Empirical evidence and theoretical issues. *Psychological Bulletin, 104,* 236-250.

Stultz, M. S. (1993). Crime in hospitals 1992: The latest International Association for Healthcare Security and Safety survey. *Journal of Healthcare Protection Management, 10*(2), 1-40.

Sugg, N. K., & Inui, T. (1992). Primary care physicians' response to domestic violence: Opening Pandora's box. *Journal of the American Medical Association, 267,* 3157-3160.

Taliaferro, E. (1988). Violence in the emergency department: A very real concern. *Annals of Emergency Medicine, 17,* 1248.

Thomma, S. (1994, May 14). Some battered women denied health coverage. *Orange County Register,* p. C-5.

U.S. Commission on Civil Rights. (1982). *Under the Rule of Thumb: Battered women and the administration of justice.* Washington, DC: Author.

U.S. Dept. of Justice. (1992). *Crime in the U.S. 1991* (Uniform Crime Reports). Washington, DC: Author.

Violence against women: A week in the life of America. Report by the Senate Committee on the Judiciary, 102d Cong., 2d Sess. (1992).

Violence Against Women Act of 1994, 18 U.S.C.A. § 2261.

Walker, L. E. (1979). *The battered woman.* New York: Harper & Row.

Walker, L. E. (1984). *The battered woman syndrome.* New York: Springer.

Walker, L. E. (1987). *Terrifying love: Why battered women kill and how society responds.* New York: Harper & Row.

Warshaw, C. (1992). Domestic violence: Challenges to medical practice. *Journal of Women's Health, 2*(1), 73-80.

Wasserberger, J., Ordog, G. J., Kolodny, M., & Allen, K. (1989). Violence in a community emergency room. *Archives of Emergency Medicine, 6,* 266-269.

Weber, T. (1992, November 5). Spousal abuse a thorny issue for churches: Catholics' condemnation highlights approaches to dealing with problem. *Orange County Register,* p. A-1.

Williamson, P., Beitman, B. D., & Katon, W. (1981). Beliefs that foster physician avoidance of psychosocial aspects of health care. *Journal of Family Practice, 13,* 999-1003.

Willoughby, M. J. (1989). Rendering each woman her due: Can a battered woman claim self- defense when she kills her sleeping batterer? *University of Kansas Law Review, 38,* 169.

Wolfe, D. A., & Korsch, B. (1994). Witnessing domestic violence during childhood and adolescence: Implications for pediatric practice. *Pediatrics, 94,* 594-599.

Wolf-Harlow, C. (1991). *Female victims of violent crime* (NCJ Pub. No. 126826). Washington, DC: U.S. Dept. of Justice.

Women's Law Project and the Pennsylvania Coalition Against Domestic Violence. (1996). *Insurance discrimination against victims of domestic violence.* Harrisburg, PA: Author.

INDEX

Abbott, J., 3, 31
Abramson, L. Y., 60
Abuse assessment screen:
  questions, 74
Abusive behaviors, 1. *See also specific types*
  of abuse
Abusive relationship characteristics:
  coercive, 46
  denigrating, 48
  humiliating, 47
  manipulative, 47
  violent, 48
  See also Control; Power
Abusive relationships, theories for staying in:
  behavioral change transtheoretical model,
    61-62
  cycle of violence, 55-56, 58
  learned helplessness, 59-61
  problems related to, 55
  psychological entrapment, 61
  reasoned decision making, 61
  Stockholm syndrome, 58-59
  traumatic bonding/intermittent abuse, 56-58
Acute stress disorder:
  APA diagnostic criteria for, 66-67
  dissociative symptoms of, 66
  versus PTSD, 66
Adams, D., 2
Adams, S. L., 118
Advocacy Wheel, 70, 72

Alabama Supreme Court, 1871 ruling by, 19
Alcohol abuse:
  among battered women, 10, 68
  domestic violence and, 26-27
Allen, K., 131
American College of Emergency Physicians,
  6, 119, 128, 130
American College of Obstetricians and
  Gynecologists, viii, 10, 88
American College of Physicians, 6
American Medical Association, viii, 1, 4, 10,
  40, 60, 74, 75, 81, 88, 92, 95, 113, 131
  Council on Ethical and Judicial Affairs, 5,
    32, 39, 70-71, 80
  Council on Scientific Affairs, 28, 77
  1994 National Conference, 3
  past president of, 2
  physician's ethical duties, 39
American Psychiatric Association, 63, 64, 65,
  66, 67, 68, 69
American Psychological Association, 4, 28
Anwar, R. A. H., 5, 9, 35, 36, 39, 43, 74

Bad-faith reporting, 110-112
Battered women:
  chronic victimization of, 5
  common characteristics of, 50-52
  miscellaneous symptoms of, 11
  physical pain in, 10

pregnant, 10
psychosocial problems of, 10
somatic complaints of, 10-11
See also Alcohol abuse; Domestic violence
    victims; Drug abuse; Suicide
Battered women's movement, 21
Battered women's shelters:
finding victim advocates through, 88
first in London, 21
first in United States, 21
Batterers:
as child abusers, 4
as murderers, 3
common characteristics of, 53-54
creating own environment, 1
Batterer-victim relationships, 1
Battering syndrome, 30-31
Behavioral change, transtheoretical model of:
central constructs of, 61-62
decisional balance in, 62
processes of change in, 62
self-efficacy in, 62
stages of change in, 61
Beitman, B. D., 36
Berg, R. L., 128
Bible, domestic violence in, 14-15
Blackstone, William, 16, 17
Blount, W. R., 68
Bokunewicz, B., 33, 44
Bowker, L. H., 33, 35, 42
Boyd, V. D., 24, 26, 27, 34, 42, 43, 51, 52, 69,
    125
Bradley v. State, 17
Brauner, D. J., 36
Brown, J., 61, 62
Brown, M. E., 118
Browne, A., 5, 21, 26, 28, 43, 48, 60
Bullock, L., 11, 12, 75
Burge, S. K., 13

Cahill, Robert E., 23
California Emergency Nurses Association, 118
Campaign Against Family Violence, 28
Campbell, J. C., 93, 94, 95, 96
Caplan, P. J., 25, 26, 58
Carter, G. L., 128
Carter, Jr., Danny:
case of, 98-99

Cascardi, M., 68
Center for Disease Control, Injury Control
    Division, 22
Chamberlain-Engelsman, J., 61
Charney, D. S., 68
Cherubino, Friar, 15
Child abuse:
and future risk of battering, 4
cases, 99
long-term effects of, 4
Children's Center for Child Protection, San
    Diego:
child abuse intervention program, 99
Children's Hospital, Boston:
child abuse intervention program, 99
Children witnessing domestic violence,
    effects of, 4
Chiswick Center, 21
Civil protection order (CPO):
definition of, 89
petitioner in, 89
respondent in, 89
violations, 89, 91
Clinton Administration, 22
Cochran, D., 118
Colburn, D., 12, 13
Colling, R. L., 124, 125, 130
Colorado Dept. of Health and Colorado
    Domestic Violence Coalition, 4
Common law:
American, 16
English, 16
Commonwealth Fund, Commission on
    Women's Health, viii, 31
Confidentiality of Records, 104
Confidentiality violations, 73
Confusion, victim in state of, 1
Congressional Caucus for Women's Issues, 4,
    9
Control, 46, 47
tools of, 48
See also Power
Copel, L. C., 33, 44
Cosgrove, A., 70, 71, 72
Council of Toledo, 15
Coverture, 16
Cycle of violence, 55-56, 57
acute phase, 55-56
tension-building phase, 55, 56

tranquil phase, 55, 56

Danger assessments, 96-97
  cautions for use of, 93
  definition of, 93
  health care professional conducting, 93-95
Danzl, D. F., 128
Dartmouth-Hitchcock Medical Center, 75, 76
Davidson, T., 15, 20
Davis, M., 68
Davis, P., 116
de Beauvoir, S., 15
Declaration of Sentiments, 20
Depression, 67-68
  APA characteristics of, 67-68
  domestic violence victims with, 68
  PTSD and, 67
  suicide and, 67
Deprivation, victim in state of, 1
Deutch, A. Y., 68
Developments, 15
Devos, E., 99
District of Columbia Coalition Against
    Domestic Violence, 93, 94
Documentary evidence, 147
  testimony regarding, 150-152
Domestic Abuse Intervention Project of
    Duluth, MN, 48
Domestic violence:
  as public health problem, 2
  blaming in health care response to, vii
  costs associated with, 4-5
  disbelief in health care response to, vii
  dollar costs of, 4
  female motivation for, 28
  history of, 14-24
  impact of on health care community, 5-9
  inattentive health care response to, vii
  male motivation for, 28
  mental illness and, 29-30
  prevalence of, 2-3, 28
  religious sanctioning of, 15
  societal myths about, 24-30
  working definition of, 1
Domestic violence crimes, alternatives to
    prosecution of, 141-142
  deferred sentencing programs, 141-142
  pretrial diversion programs, 141, 142

Domestic violence crimes, prosecution of:
  arraignment, 137-139
  bail laws, 137
  bail options, 138
  conditions of release, 137, 139, 140
  criminal proceedings concerning domestic
    violence, 136-147
  defense use of patient statements in
    medical records, 153-154
  detainment of defendant, 139, 140
  District Attorney's Office and, 136
  grand jury, 139, 140, 142-143
  health care provider as government witness
    and, 147-155
  issuance of stay-away/no-contact order,
    138-139
  jury selection, 144-145
  plea bargaining, 140-141
  preliminary hearing, 139-140
  pretrial hearings, 143-144
  probable cause, 139, 143
  release of defendant on own recognizance,
    138, 139
  release of defendant pending cash/security
    bond, 138, 139
  release of defendant to third-party custody,
    138, 139
  risk of flight and, 137
  sentencing, 146-147
  state court sentencing options, 146-147
  trial, 145-146
  U.S. Attorney's Office and, 136
  voir dire, 144
  See also Federal Rules of Evidence;
    Hearsay rule; Testimonial evidence;
    Photographic evidence; Physical
    evidence
Domestic violence education:
  from health care professional, 87-88
Domestic violence episodes:
  as complex pattern of behavior, 1
  as continuing pattern of behavior, 1
Domestic violence injuries, common, 10, 29,
    75
  versus accidental injuries, 75
Domestic violence intervention:
  facilitating, 41-44
  justice and, 39
  obstacles to, 30-38

reasons for, 38-41
See also Health care domestic violence
    intervention
Domestic violence options/resources
    information, health care professional
    providing, 88-92
Domestic Violence Project, Inc., 70
Domestic violence trauma:
    acute stress disorder, 66-67
    alcohol/drug use, 68
    brain chemistry changes, 68
    depression, 67-68
    post-traumatic stress disorder, 62-66
    secondary outcomes of, 62-68
Domestic violence victims:
    isolation of, 1
    psychosocial problems of, 10
    receiving medical care, 5
    seeking medical help, 5, 9
    See also Battered women
Donnelly, W. J., 36
Dotterer, C. S., 79, 95
Drug abuse:
    among battered women, 10, 68
    domestic violence and, 26-27
Dutton, D., 5, 56, 57
Dutton, M. A., 54, 60, 62, 63, 66, 67
Duty to Report, 103

Egypt, domestic violence in ancient, 15
Emergency rooms, hospital:
    domestic violence victims in, 3
    nurses' attitudes toward domestic violence,
        33
    staff view of battered women, 33-34
    See also Violence in medical setting
Epstein, J., 2
Equality characteristics, 49. *See also* Equality
    Wheel
Equality Wheel, 48, 50, 70

Fear, victim in state of, 1
Federal Protective Service, 129
Federal Rules of Evidence, 149
    805, 152
    803(4), 152
    803(6), 150
    803(7), 154

401, 154
403, 155
615, 159
612, 160
901, 154, 155
Feldman, M. K., 39, 43
Felipe Russo, N., 21, 43
Fellows, M. L., 100
Feminist movement (U.S.), start of, 20
First, M. B., 63, 66
Fitzgerald, L. F., 21, 43
Flitcraft, A., 2, 5, 9, 30, 31, 34, 37, 38, 39, 42,
    73
Follow up, patient:
    by health care facility, 95
    through victim advocate, 95
Fortune, M., 61
Foy, D. W., 63, 64
Frances, A., 63, 66
Frazier, F., 37
Frazier, W., 5, 9, 30, 34, 38, 42
Fulgram v. State, 19

Gaines, J., 116
Geer, J. H., 59, 60
Gehrke, Joel, 23
Geller, J. L., 17, 20
Gelles, R. J., 6, 11, 25, 26, 27, 28, 40, 48
Gender discrimination, 14
Gentry, C., 58, 59, 69
Germain, A., 2
Gilbert, P., 118
Glazer, S., 73
Gondolf, E. W., 95
Goodman, L. A., 21, 43, 63, 66, 67
Goodman, R. A., 127
Government witnesses, health care providers
    as, 147-155
    pretrial conference, 156-157
    questions commonly asked by, 158-166
    receiving subpoena/summons, 156
    requesting to be placed on call, 157
Graham, D. L. R., 29, 58, 59
Green , B. L., 67
Grey, A., 5, 9, 30, 34, 38, 42

Haber, J. D., 10
Hamberger, L. K., 37

Harris, M., 4, 17, 20
Hart, B. J., 93, 94, 95
Harvey, C. M., 11
Health care community:
  being alert to domestic violence victims,
    9-12
  impact of domestic violence on, 5-9
  victims seeking help from, 5
  See also Health care domestic violence
    intervention; Health care professionals
Health care domestic violence intervention:
  addressing the violence, 74-75
  conducting danger assessments, 93-95
  developing safety plans, 92-93
  educating patient about domestic violence,
    87-88
  following up, 95
  interviewing strategies, 76
  power of, 70-71
  providing complete medical record
    documentation, 75
  providing options/resources information,
    88-92
  showing caring, nonjugmental support,
    72-73
Health care professionals:
  battered patient expectations of, 12-13
  beneficence and, 39
  civil lawsuits against by battered women,
    40
  domestic violence victims and, 9-10, 11-12
  empowering domestic violence victims, 13
  failure of recognizing domestic violence
    victims, 30-31
  failure to diagnose, 40
  nonmalfeasance and, 39
  See also Emergency room, hospital;
    Government witnesses, health care
    providers as; Health care community;
    Health care domestic violence
    intervention
Health insurance for battered women:
  companies denying coverage, 101
  companies providing coverage, 101
  preexisting conditions and, 100
  state legislation concerning, 101
Hearsay rule, 149
  and hearsay testimony, 144, 152
Heise, L. L., 2
Helton, A. S., 11, 12, 57, 85

Herman, J. L., 24, 68
Herman, S., 35, 36, 39
Hilberman, E., vii, 11, 26, 27, 34, 56, 63
Hinds, D. L., 82
Hines, E., Jr., 36
Houskamp, B. M., 63, 64
Hovey, M., 37
Howard, D., 122
Howard-Martin, J., 122

Injuries by Firearm, 103
Injuries to Be Reported, 103
Injury location chart, 85
  documenting injuries with, 84-85
Injury-reporting laws:
  bad-faith reporting and, 110-112
  California, 103
  Colorado, 103
  compliance with mandatory, 106-113
  consequences for noncompliance with, 103
  domestic violence and mandatory, 113
  exception to, 102
  Federal law affecting state, 104-106
  immunity laws and, 103
  Kentucky, 103
  mandatory, 100
  Mississippi, 104
  New Mexico, 103
  Ohio, 102-103
  patient consent to law enforcement
    notification and, 112-113
  Pennsylvania, 104
  physician-patient privilege and mandatory,
    107
  reason for, 102
  Rhode Island, 103
  state mandatory, 102-103, 105
  state voluntary, 104
  what to report and, 107, 110
International Association for Healthcare
  Security and Safety (IAHSS), 117
Inui, T., 31, 34, 37, 74
Isaac, E., 118
Island, D., 1
Isolation of victim, 1

Jarratt, L. G., 9, 13
Jecker, N. S., 33, 39

Jenkins, E. L., 127
Johnson, R., 3, 31
Joint Commission on the Accreditation of
    Healthcare Organizations (JCAHO),
    viii, 6, 13, 75, 91, 110, 119, 120
  description of, 6
  1996 security standards for medical
    facilities, 119, 120-121
  1996 standards, 6, 110
"Just world" hypothesis, 25

Katon, W., 36
Keep, N., 118
Kemp, A., 67
Kiernan, L. A., 45
Klein, C. F., 22, 89
Klingbeil, K. S., 24, 26, 27, 34, 42, 43, 51, 52,
    69, 125
Kolodny, M., 131
Koop, C. Everett, 2
Korsch, B., 26
Kosova, W., 135
Koss, M. P., 21, 43
Koziol-McLain, J., 3, 31
Krystal, J. H., 68
Kurz, D., 10, 32, 33, 35, 38, 44

Lavoie, F. W., 128
Law enforcement notification, patient consent
    to, 112-113
Laws:
  mandatory arrest laws, 21-22
  Maryland wife abuse, 20
  wife abuse, 19
  See also specific laws
Learned helplessness theory, 59-61
  reformulation of, 60
Lee, D., 88
Lerner, M. J., 25
Letellier, P., 1, 88
Levy, B., 2
Lobel, K., 1
Lowenstein, S. R., 3, 31

MacFarquhar, E., 2
Maier, S. F., 59, 60

Mann, J., 15
Maquiling, K., 35, 36, 39
March of Dimes Birth Defects Foundation, 56
Marital chastisement:
  abolition of in England, 20
Marshall, Stewart, 23, 24
Martin, D., 21
Massachusetts Coalition of Battered Women
    Service Groups, 2
Mauet, T. A., 154
Maurer, L., 33, 35, 42
McAfee, Robert, 2, 12
McDonald, K. A., 15
McFarlane, J., 11, 12, 74, 75
McKibben, L., 99
McLeer, S. V., 5, 9, 35, 36, 39, 43, 74
McLoughlin, E., 88
Medical Data Collection Reports, 103
Medical facility safety standards, 119-123
Medical facility security measures:
  for clinics/private offices, 135
  for hospitals, 123-131
Medical Power and Control Wheel, 70, 71
  goals represented in, 70-71
Medical records, providing complete
    documentation in, 75
  document entire patient exam, 75, 77-79
  document injuries with injury location
    chart, 84-85
  document injuries with photos, 79-84
  document physical evidence, 85-87
Meier, S. F., 60
Men:
  as victims of domestic violence, 2
  See also Batterers
Mercy, J. A., 127
Miranda rights, 143
Miranda v. Arizona, 143

National Association of Insurance
    Commissioners, 101
National Council of Churches, 21
National Council of Juvenile and Family
    Court Judges, 89, 90, 142
  Model Code on Domestic and Family
    Violence, 89, 90-91
National Crime Surveys:
  1981, 4

1973-1987, 5
National Crime Victimization Survey, 3
National Institute of Justice, 3, 4
National Traumatic Occupational Fatalities
    Surveillance System, 127
Newberger, E., 99
North Carolina Supreme Court:
    1864 ruling, 18
    1868 ruling, 18
    1874 ruling, 20

Occupational Safety and Health Act (OSHA)
    of 1970
    General Duty Clause, 119, 122
    Program Management Guidelines, 122, 123
Office on Violence Against Women, U.S.
    Justice Department, 22
O'Leary, K. D., 68
O'Neil, William J., 23
Ordog, G. J., 131
Orloff, L. E., 89

Pacenti, J., 116
Painter, S. L., 5, 56, 57
Parker, B., 11, 12, 74, 75
Patient examination, documentation of, 75,
    77-79
Patient follow up. *See* Follow up, patient
Patient information, obtaining truthful:
    factors in health care provider's ability in,
        99-101
    health insurance and, 100-101
    importance of, 98-99
    successful criminal prosecution and, 99
Patton, D., 15
Paymar, M., 49, 50, 70
Peacock, Kenneth, 23
Pence, E., 49, 50, 70
Pennsylvania Coalition Against Domestic
    Violence, Personalized Safety Plan of, 93
Pet killing, 1
Photographic evidence, 147
    accuracy of, 154-155
    relevance of, 154
    testimony regarding, 154-155
Photographs:
    as evidence, 79-80

documenting injuries with, 79-84
for coaxing reluctant victims to testify, 80
for contradicting defendant's testimony,
    80
for convincing jury of violence, 80
for refreshing witness's recollections, 80
for showing judge seriousness of injury, 80
importance of accuracy in, 84
instant versus standard, 82-83
obtaining informed consent for, 80-82
taking close up, 83
taking full-body, 83
taking midrange, 83
Physical abuse, 1
Physical evidence:
    authentication of, 155
    chain of custody and, 155
    documenting, 85-87
    testimony regarding, 155
Physician-patient privilege laws:
    purpose of, 107
    violation of, 113
Pike, C. L., 6
Pincus, H. A., 63, 66
Pitanguy, J., 2
Pitt, D., 135
Pleck, E., 15, 17, 19, 20
Polaroid Corporation, 83
Pope-Lance, D. J., 61
Post-traumatic stress disorder, 62
    APA diagnostic criteria for, 64-65
    APA noted symptoms of, 65-66
    avoidance symptoms of, 66
    diagnostic features of, 63-64
    distinguishing feature of, 63
    domestic violence victims and, 63
    stressors and, 63
Power, 46
    tools of, 48
    See also Power and Control Wheel
Power and Control Wheel, 48, 49, 70
Powers, R., 100, 116
Pregnancy, battering during
    reasons for, 11
    results of, 11
Property destruction, 1
Psychological abuse, 1
Psychological entrapment theory, 61
Puryear Keita, G., 21, 43

Quinn, M. J., 2

Randall, T., 5
Rath, G. D., 9, 13
Rawlings, E., 29, 58
Rawlings, E. I., 67
Reasoned decision making theory, 61
Reg v. Jackson, 20
Renzetti, C., 1
Reporting Felony, 102
Ribe, J. K., 11
Rimini, N., 29, 58
Roan, S., 69
Robinson, J., 5, 9, 30, 34, 38, 42
Robinson, L., 2
Roman Catholic bishops, U.S., 21
Rosenberg, D. A., 34, 74
Rosenfeld, M., 23, 45
Ross, C., 10
"Rule of Thumb," 17-18, 19-20
Rule on Witnesses, 159
Rules and Regulations, 103

Safety and Health Program Management
     Guidelines, 123
Safety plans:
     health care professional developing, 92-93
     information card, 94
     issues to be discussed in, 92-93
Salber, P., 88
Saltzman, L., 11
Sarno, Susan, 23
Saunders, D. G., 28, 37
Saxton Mahoney, B., 117, 118
Schulman, M. A., 26
Schumer, Charles E., 100, 101
Scott, K., 125, 126
Security and Safety Assessment, 123
Security Training and Education, 123
Seelye, K. Q., 116
Seese, R. A., 68
Seligman, E. P., 60
Seligman, M. E. P., 59, 60
Sellers, C. S., 68
Seneca Falls Convention, 20
Sexual abuse, 1
Shalala, D., 3
Sheridan, D., 163

Sheridan, D. J., 32
Silverman, I. J., 68
Simmons, C. H., 25
Simonowitz, J. A., 126, 128, 130, 131
Skodol, A. E., 66
SOAP progress-note formula, 36
Soeken, K., 12, 75
Southwich, S. M., 68
Stark, E., 2, 5, 9, 30, 34, 35, 37, 38, 39, 42
State v. Black, 18
State v. Oliver, 20
State v. Rhodes, 18
Statutory laws, 16
Stay-Away/No-Contact order, 147
     issuance of to defendant, 138-139
     significance of to domestic violence victim,
        139
     violation of, 141
Steinmetz, S. K., 6, 27, 28, 40, 48
Stockholm syndrome, 58-59
     characteristics of, 59
Straus, M. A., 6, 11, 25, 26, 27, 28, 40, 48
Strube, M. J., 55, 61
Stueling, B., 93
Stultz, M. S., 117, 128
Sugg, N. K., 31, 34, 37, 74
Suicide:
     attempts by battered women, 10
Sullivan v. United States, 152
Support, emotional:
     health care professionals showing, 72-73

Taliaferro, E., 119
Teasdale, J. D., 60
Teggatz, J. R., 11
Testimonial evidence, 147, 152-154
Thomma, S., 116
Tomita, S., 2
Traumatic bonding, 56-57

U.S. Code (Confidentiality of Records), Title
     42 of, 104-105
U.S. Commission on Civil Rights, 21, 28
U.S. Dept. of Justice, vii, 2, 3, 4, 5, 28, 29,
     39
Uniform Crime Reports of the FBI (1992), 3
Uniform Healthcare Information Act,
     105-106

University of Alabama-Birmingham Pain Center, 10

Verbal abuse (threats), 1
Victim advocate, 88-89
Victim blaming, 24-25
Victim-blaming questions, 32
Victimization pattern, 48
Victims, domestic violence. *See* Battered women; Domestic violence victims
Violence:
  as learned behavior, 5
  gender-based, 14
  generation-to-generation, 5
  health care professional addressing, 74-75
  See also Domestic violence; Violence in medical setting
Violence Against Women Act of 1994, 22
Violence in medical setting:
  as growing problem, 117
  California legislation concerning, 123
  homicide, 127
  in hospital emergency rooms, 117-118
  medical center liability and, 119
  potentials for, 117
  types of, 118

Violent Crime Control and Law Enforcement Act of 1994, 22
  provisions of, 22

Walker, L. E., vii, 25, 26, 29, 40, 50, 52, 55, 56, 58, 60, 69
Warshaw, C., 35
Wasserberger, J., 131
Weber, T., 45
Wellstone, Paul, 101
Williamson, P., 36
Willoughby, M. J., 19
Wolfe, D. A., 26
Women:
  as victims of domestic violence, 2, 28
  viewed as chattel, 16, 23
  See also Battered women; Domestic violence victims
Women's Law Project and the Pennsylvania Coalition Against Domestic Violence, 101
Women's rights, 14
  voting, 20
Wyden, Ron, 101

Zuckerman, S., 5, 9, 30, 34, 38, 42

ABOUT THE AUTHOR

Sherri L. Schornstein, J.D., is a 1979 graduate of the University of Iowa and a 1983 graduate of California Western School of Law. She is an Assistant U.S. Attorney for the District of Columbia who has worked for the U.S. Department of Justice since 1983. She is a trainer for law enforcement agencies and a frequent guest lecturer at colleges, universities, and hospitals. She consults nationally and internationally on domestic violence interventions.

The author welcomes your comments. Please write to her at:
P.O. Box 11833
Alexandria, VA 22312